ATLANTIS MAGIC

This book may well arouse curiosity regarding the community in which the psychic work reported here takes place.

The following books by the same authoress, all published by Caliban Books, should satisfy that curiosity:

ROOM TO BREATHE
THEY CALL US THE SCREAMERS
ATLANTIS IS...
ATLANTIS ALIVE

And soon to be published:

MALE SEXUALITY - THE ATLANTIS POSITION

ATLANTIS MAGIC

by

Jenny James

CALIBAN BOOKS

© Jenny James

Published by Caliban Books
c/o Biblios Ltd, Glenside Industrial Estate,
Star Road, Partridge Green, Horsham, Sussex
1982

ISBN 0 904573 58 3 Hardback
0 904573 61 3 Paperback

Printed and bound by
Redwood Burn Limited, Trowbridge, Wiltshire

This book is dedicated to:

> My baby daughter, Louise
> and my grown-up daughter, Rebecca

With thanks to:

> Simon and Fred
for looking after the baby, cooking, and shopping
while I typed this book ready for litho-printing.

<u>A Note</u> about my daughter Rebecca who did most of the psychic readings in this book:

Becky has had no formal education whatever, either in schools or at home. She knows no history, has never read a book (not even mine!), her spelling is entirely individual; she knows nothing of the Christian or any other religion, except what she gleans through her everyday contacts.

This has been deliberate policy, and we are delighted with how she has turned out. At completion of this book, she is nineteen, not married and expecting her first baby.

CONTENTS

PART ONE

PART TWO

READINGS ON:

INTRODUCTION

One morning in a stale and sterile University library many years ago, a most sensible and conventional friend of mine came in rather excited, sat down beside me and said, "Something very strange has just happened to me."

She told me that she had been lying in bed asleep in a back-room of her lodging-house, slumbering uneasily, sensing that it was time to get up. Just before waking, she had a dream involving a double-decker bus which broke down outside the house, and all the people had to be transferred to another bus.

Her alarm clock rang, she got up, washed, dressed, and went to breakfast. Then she got her books together and left the house. As she stepped outside on to the busy London street, a double-decker bus proceeded to break down in front of her house. The people had to get out to await transfer to a second bus. Detail for detail, she watched her dream unfold before her eyes.

I listened to this staid, usually unflustered woman and my natural respect for her caused me to believe without question what she was telling me. Then I told her a story my mother had told me: how one morning she had woken bothered from sleep, knowing that the baker had been knocking at the door and that he would be annoyed at being kept waiting. She hurriedly donned her dressing-gown and rushed downstairs, pulling open the front door just as the baker was about to knock again. She began to apologize to him for keeping him waiting, but the surprised baker looked at her strangely and said, "Madam, I haven't knocked once yet."

Little stories. Everyone has them. Usually forgotten until someone brings out their anecdote. Then you remember yours. Little coincidences, unexplained happenings that slip unbidden from life's normal rails. Pushed away quickly. Recalled as party pieces on special intimate occasions.

What if you could tap this twilight land, this time-and-distance warp, this fertile source of clairvoyant knowledge, just whenever you wanted to? You can. We do.

What if you lived without buses and trains and telly and schedules and stereos and offices and noise and city dirt, and left room in your life for grass and wind and water and rocks, left space for the psychic and the mystical to become the Everyday? A dream? We do it.

Have you ever been in love and wanted so much to know your lover from inside, just for a moment? Have you ever said, "I wish I were in so-and-so's shoes." How often do you say, "If I were you..."? Well, you can be me; I can be you. Just for a while. For long enough anyway to know what it's like to view the world through another person's eyes.

PSYCHOMETRY is the method we started with at Atlantis. It's simple, it's always available, and it always works. (Thelma Moss in her book The Probability of the Impossible says that true psychics never claim that 'it always works'. Well, we know what she means, but we're not working under the stress of laboratory conditions and never do psychic work unless we 'feel like it' - perhaps this is why 'it always works' for us.)

Psychometry is the name given to holding an object belonging to someone in order to 'pick up' information about them, speaking out

anything that passes through the mind. It sounds
pretty mysterious and vague. Mysterious it
certainly is, but often amazingly un-vague.
You can do it too. You need time, trust, courage
and good company. That's all.

*****

This is the story of the psychic happenings
at ATLANTIS, a self-sufficiency commune and
enlightenment centre situated in the village
of Burtonport and on the island of Inishfree,
on the north-west coast of County Donegal,
Eire. It is the tale of how a group of completely down-to-earth, no-patience-with-spiritual-
nonsense type people, came quite suddenly into
contact with what is around us all the time
- that Other Dimension which co-exists with
the narrow strip of reality we usually choose
to live in, that Wide River of alternative
consciousness that just flows along there beside
us, waiting to be stepped into, sampled, tasted,
used to enrich and change our lives.
Did we look for it? No, we didn't. Were we
hoping to find it? Weren't interested. What
did we think of 'magic'? All very nice, but
we were too busy with <u>real</u> things. What happened
then? Well, I'll tell you ...

CHAPTER ONE: PAVING THE WAY

My parents were in the Communist Party. I was brought up a complete atheist. We were middle-class and abhorred superstition. Like religion, it emanated entirely from ignorance and could be cured by Education and Right Thinking. Everything in the world had a reasonable, tangible explanation. Any belief in a continued existence after death was the tragic inability to face one's own mortal end (though my mother couldn't help wishing that 'the scientists would discover something to make people live forever' before it was her time to go).

With this busy, political, sensible background, imagine my discomfort when two working-class male friends, visiting me in my caravan in the woods when I was a young mother, came out with comments like: "Jenny, are you a witch?" or "Jenny, have you ever thought that you might have psychic powers?" I did not appreciate their knowing twinkle, thank you very much. I was a rational woman, engaged like them in Campaign for Nuclear Disarmament work, and there was no call for them to be unnerving me with their frivolous talk. I answered them defensively and changed the subject, recalling uneasily however, a certain strange little incident that had occurred when I was about thirteen in Grammar School. I had written a story for English homework, pinched I think from something read to me by my stepfather out of 'Readers' Digest.' It was a pretty gripping tale, about a young brother and sister who used to lie holding tightly to one another at night for comfort, knowing that their mother was a witch out sailing gaily across the skies on her broomstick.

The punch line came when the little boy reached out for reassurance one night from his now adolescent sister and he finds the bed empty. She has flown away too, to learn the delights of conjuring up storms and feeling the new-found power surging through her young body as she joins her cackling mother. But the punch-line for me, reading the story out loud in class at the request of my English teacher, came as I described this 'new-found power to conjure up storms.' At that very moment, a perfectly clear summer's day suddenly darkened over with a clap of thunder, and torrential rains bucketed out of the skies. The whole class of girls went silent, staring at me. I stared back. Then I burst into tears. My teacher completed the reading of the story.

I suppose I should have known then.

A couple of years later, at the same school during a rainy indoor dinner hour, I walked into my classroom to find a group of the other girls clustered together, talking excitedly. "Let's try it with her!" they said. I was sent outside the room again, then called in, and I had to stand, eyes closed, in the middle of their circle. They too closed their eyes and leaned on one another's shoulders, concentrating their thoughts on one of the girls present. In no time at all, a cry went up from all of them, and I opened my eyes in surprise, unaware that anything had happened. I found that I had sway-ed, leaned, then fallen right on to the girl they were thinking of, almost as soon as I'd relaxed in the circle.

This was a pleasurable and interesting ex-perience, but it was isolated and so I thought no more of it, and managed to reach the age of twenty-six without anything too weird happening

as far as I remember. Then I went with a group
of pacifists to South East Asia on a Vietnam
peace mission. This campaign involved at one
point hitching up the Malaysian peninsula with a
new male friend. We were picked up by a man who
claimed to be a Yogi of twenty years standing –
whatever that meant – and who drove us slowly
through his country over a period of three days,
accommodating us in all the best hotels, and
providing us with food, entertainment, outings –
and a special branch of knowledge which he
seemed determined to plug into us.

First of all, he confidentially opened
the boot of his car and showed us a huge collection of boring-looking books on all kinds of
weird things I'd never heard of, like Numerolo-
gy. He insisted on dumping several of these
heavy tomes on me (I lost them on a bus as soon
as I could). My new boyfriend sat in the front
of the car as we drove our long dreamy way
through this country, and I took as little
notice as possible of the conversation passing
between them, which was about all kinds of
'spiritual' things that made me feel uneasy.
However, I was called upon at one point to
give my birth day – not the month, or the year,
just the day. "The eleventh," I answered guard-
edly. I was then delivered information which did
indeed give me a jolt, considering that this
odd character had only just met me and I hadn't
exactly been forthcoming. He told me, not facts
about my brittle abrupt Aries exterior which
anyone could pick up, but gentler, more hidden,
domestic, female aspects of myself that no-
one had any business knowing about, and that I
didn't recognize anyway.... He told me eleven
was a "moon" number, what nonsense. My guy,
on the other hand, was born on the ninth. This

was a 'Mars' number, we were told, full of
war and strife. Huh!

It got worse. 'Charlie,' as the incongruous
name of our yogi turned out to be, took me
aside on a ferry-boat going to Penang Island
(he was determined to show us a zoo as well
as the secrets of the cosmos), and kept warning
me about my companion – he had a red 'aura'
I was told, and was violent and dangerous.
I should get away from him quickly. I felt
embarrassed and intruded upon. The only person I
wanted to get away quickly from was this damn
Yogi.

'Charlie' also kept warning us against
crossing the border into Thailand. Bad things
were going to happen to us there. War and danger. We shouldn't go; we must definitely not
enter Thailand. This was more worrying – and
more impressive. Charlie could hardly know that
his two English hitchhikers were not in fact
holidaymakers, but dedicated anti-war campaign-
ers on their way to possible death by walking
on to an American airbase 'to stop the bombers
taking off for Vietnam.'

The night before we were to cross the
border, our yogi spent the evening with us
at the latest hotel he had booked for us. He
was showing my boyfriend all kinds of tricks,
and as usual I was taking as little notice
as possible. The whole episode with Charlie
made me thoroughly uncomfortable from beginning
to end, from his right-wing politics to his
haphazard driving, from his extravagant hospit-
ality to his claiming that his money came from
winning lotteries whenever he fancied to!
Now of all things, he was messing around with a
pendulum on a string, showing it move in different directions. What a con, I thought, surely

the poor fellow doesn't think we'll believe this
stuff? Next he was chatting on about being
able to stop his heart-beat and blood flow -
what rubbish. But then I did get a shock because
he said as he turned his back to me, "I won't
let her see this, she's so squeamish." Evidently
he was sticking a pin into his arm up to the
head, leaving no trace of blood, nor betraying
any sign of pain. But that wasn't what impressed
me. How the hell did he know I was squeamish? It
was one of my all-pervading characteristics -
and secrets. He hardly knew me! How the devil
did he know that?

        I was still nursing my thoughts when he
told me he was going to show me that I was
psychic. Oh no, not trying to involve me again.
I was so polite and well-brought-up though, that
I grunted and blushed and sat uncomfortably as
if about to go into the dentist. He got a hotel-
boy to bring in a brand-new pack of cards,
unbroken seal shown with great flourish, which
naturally made me even more suspicious. Charlie
made a 'fan' of the cards, face down so that
neither he nor I could see them. Then he told me
to pick out a card. "Do you want to look at
it?" he asked. "No, I don't need to," I replied,
thinking that I meant, "I don't have any curiosity about this silly game." He told me to put
the card on the floor beside me, still face down.
Then he said, simple as can be, "What card is
it?"

        Silly so-and-so, what does he mean, what
card is it? "How do I know, I don't know," I
sweated. "Just say the first card that comes
into your mind," he answered, unruffled. I
hated him. I was hot and red. I wanted to get
out of the situation as soon as possible. I felt
a bit sorry for him, too, for obviously I was

going to make him look a fool, fifty-two cards
in a pack and all that.

"Eight of diamonds," I thought to myself.

"Ten of diamonds," I said to him.

"Not bad," said he - he who had never
seen the damned card - "It's actually the eight
of diamonds."

I picked it up. I don't need to tell you
what the card was.

"How did you do that?" I asked him.

"How did you do that?" he asked me.

*****

CHAPTER TWO: MOVING CLOSER

In 1962, at the age of twenty, as I breast-
fed my first baby, I was reading a then rare
book by a then practically unknown author:
The Sexual Revolution by Wilhelm Reich. I was
transfixed, fascinated. I loved Reich's talk of
'orgone energy' - of the body streamings we feel
when we are fully alive and in tune with ourselves. A year later, I was thrilled again, this
time to be introduced to reading Freud - in
German! - with all his talk of the power of unconscious motivation, and his magnificent book
on the interpretation of dreams. Such psychological concepts were allowable in my system of
thought, couched as they were in such heavy
scientific intellectual terms. Reich and Freud
passed my own censors easily and entered into my
stream of understanding.

By 1968, my patching-up, mending and alter-
ation of the external world in my political
activities was proving inadequate to cope with
the swelling flood of internal difficulties
threatening to engulf me, and I landed myself
at a point of personal crisis in the arms of a
Reichian therapist, where my already long-estab-
lished acceptance of theories of body energy now
became rooted in direct experience. I used
to leave my once-a-fortnightly sessions suffused
with energy, immensely excited with life and
with my new journey of self-discovery. No mental
leap at all was required for me to accept completely that our personal past can be relived
through deep breathing, sensing out of body
blocks, and through allowing crying and anger
and fear to surge up from the darkness of childhood. I could quite well see that even birth

could be re-experienced: it was all there, mapped out in the body. Reliving too of intra-uterine sensations did not seem far-fetched as the years of my therapy went by. Deep crying, deep 'going into' body sensations, led me syst-ematically into feeling what it was like to be a tiny curled-up foetus, with arms and legs no more than buds, yet with all the exuberant pushing life-force of a seedling. LSD too, with its extraordinary therapeutic stripping-away of everyday blocks to perception, led me ever deeper into the amazing potential that each one of us has to experience ourselves and the world around us.

I had also meanwhile been entirely convert-ed to Astrology, originally by what I thought was a trick played on me by a political friend. He asked me my birthday. "11th April." "Oh, Aries." He then proceeded to read out to me all kinds of embarrassing details about my charact-er. I snatched the book away from him, thinking he'd typed up some intimate knowledge he had of me and inserted the page in a book, pretending it was all written down. But it <u>was</u> all written down: it was there in black and white. Printed, not typed. I could hardly get angry at the woman who'd written the book and never met me. Good lord, so astrology works. I could hardly ignore such a direct impact on me as that.

*****

At the beginning of 1969, my rather young father died suddenly of cancer. He was only known to have the disease three months prior to his death. It would take me nearly a decade to get over the loss. Meanwhile, despite my sorrow,

I remembered something. I rummaged through my papers till I found a dream I had written down two years previous to my father's death. It ran something like this:

My father is visiting me in my caravan. I notice him tugging surreptitiously at his shirt sleeves, trying to pull them down to cover his arms and hide them from me. "What is it? What's wrong?" I say. Then gently, but very insistently, I take hold of one of his arms and push back his sleeve, in spite of his protest. I stare shocked and horrified at what I see: his arms are rotting away. They are blackened and dead. He is rotting away from inside. I can see right inside him. He is dying. He will die if he doesn't do something about himself immediately. I say this to him urgently, half-crying, trying to get him to listen and to care about himself. In the dream, he finally gives in to me and agrees to do something about the state he is in.

In real life, I pushed the dream from my consciousness after writing it down, gave it no more thought, and didn't mention it to him. And so the cancer I had sensed took over and killed him.

*****

CHAPTER THREE: UNCOMFORTABLY CLOSE

As the years of my therapy went by, the borderline between 'sensible, explicable, material' things and telepathic or psychic phenomena continued to blur. I explained it all to myself in terms of 'energy,' but wouldn't be able to elaborate very 'scientifically' on what I meant by that!

A woman patient of mine would make a breakthrough in a session about her mother. Next day, she would report to me that her mother, who hadn't contacted her for a year or so, had telephoned her. On another occasion, I was helping a young friend to deal with feelings about his elder sister who lived in Australia. His session was taking place in his own flat. The phone rang and he had to interrupt his angry yelling to answer - his sister, phoning from Australia.

I myself had a very painful session early on at Atlantis about my long-lost half-brother, whom I hadn't seen since he was a child. I was wanting him to seek and find me once he grew up and left his mother's influence. A phone call during that group session - from one Nick James. "I'm afraid I don't know you," I said. "I have an awful lot of people writing here - are you someone wanting to come for therapy?" "No, I'm NICK JAMES - you know, Ted's son." "I'm afraid I can't think of anyone I know called Ted," said I. Exasperated noises at the other end of the phone. "Ted JAMES." "I'm afraid I don't ... OH! My own father! OH! - You're my brother!" It was happening to me, and I wouldn't believe it.

Then a young primal therapist from the United States started writing to me. He was having trouble. Things were happening to him that he was finding it hard to accept, and even harder to get others to accept. He was having what he termed, 'pre-conception experiences' - deep sessions which led him to feelings which he could only interpret as the sensations a tiny sperm would have - the one that won on its way to fertilize the female egg. He was naturally scared of getting laughed at. He was also scared he was going barmy. But his long detailed accounts of such sessions were anything but mad. They were sober and self-questioning.

He came to stay with us in Atlantis for a while. During his visit, my young daughter, about twelve then, was getting deeply into her own therapy for the first time. In his presence, she had one of the most physically painful sessions I have ever seen, screaming with the agony of what she described as "water around her brain." Her own twin sister had died aged three weeks, hydrocephalic.

In a session of my own at another time, I felt the hot piercing pain of 'forceps in my temples.' My elder sister, born one year before me, had been killed at birth by forceps. In another session involving this same pain, I felt the forceps become teeth as a giant mouth - a lion's mouth? - closed over my head, and I, a smaller, helpless creature in a jungle giving out my last life-cry. Fantasy? Delusion? I hoped so.

*****

Giving therapy to so many hundreds of people over the years, I got used to many things that would cause a newcomer to eye me strangely. Like always knowing what a person needed to say - what would crack them to their core. Like knowing what they needed to do, knowing always the right suggestion to help them lead a richer life. Paranoid onlookers would say I was 'putting ideas into people's heads,' 'taking people over,' 'trying to lead people's lives' for them, and all the etceteras. But the person getting guidance or help from me would experience me differently: my suggestions would feel like a relief, like a key slipping easily into the right lock, like a nail being hit on the head. I know, because so many people have helped me in my hours of struggle. I know what it feels like to have someone 'see' you completely - the relief, the softening, the gratitude. I never thought of any of this 'feeling each other from the inside' as psychic; I wouldn't have bothered to give it a name. It was just us helping one another.

We did start calling Anne a witch though, jokingly and lovingly, out of our appreciation of her talents. She was a dark Irish girl who had a knack - horrible for the person on the receiving end - of knowing exactly what mean thoughts and evil impulses were being held back hidden by a scowl, a sulk, or a long-standing silence; or by unreal niceness. When such 'bad vibes' from someone threatened to darken a whole group session at Atlantis, Anne would clear the air by getting up and acting out exactly what was going on inside the brooding culprit. This has since become a bread-and-butter everyday activity at Atlantis, but again, to a new observer, Anne's powers would seem

like 'witchcraft,' for what she spoke out was
so precise and so obviously accurate judging by
the squirming and face-changes of the 'viber'
when Anne brought out their dreaded secrets.

*****

In my first years at Atlantis, I had a love
and hate affair with a young Irishman that
bit deep into my soul.* After the final final
breakup, when he was gone from me, I woke up
with a jolt one morning very early. My head felt
concussed with the pain of his going. I stared
wildly at the space by my bed. He was squatting
there, scowling at me, his face a mixture of
violence and twisted pain. But I knew he wasn't
there, because I could see right through him
to the fireplace on the other side of the room.
I squeezed my eyes tight, looked again, and
this time there were several of him there,
like after-images of a light-bulb when you've
looked at it too long.

I yelled out his name and mercifully he
disappeared. I was exhausted with the emotional
upheaval of our relationship and assumed these
apparitions were simply projections of my own
pain. But with all I know now, I wonder what was
he thinking about at the time he was sitting on
my carpet by my bed?

_____

*The full story is told in 'Atlantis Alive' published by
Caliban Books.

CHAPTER FOUR: OH DEAR! IT WORKS

I needed a new path. For years I had been pouring myself out into people, helping them through therapy. The catastrophic relationship with my first Irishman left me drained and needing to take in rather than give out. So I left Atlantis in the capable hands of friends and went on the next stage in my search. We had long since known that such methods of divination as the I Ching and Tarot cards worked amazingly, poetically. It was time now to go on what we came to call our 'witch-hunt.' First we travelled round Ireland, visiting anyone we heard of who might introduce us to this new realm. Then I went to London - we had a branch of our commune there - and visited my first ever clairvoyant. His name was Peter Lee.

I sat in blissful anonymity across the table from him. At last, someone who didn't know my name, wouldn't have heard of me if he did, didn't know who I was or who I was supposed to be, or what I did; someone who wouldn't look up to me or down on me or indeed look to me for anything. Stripped of all but the clothes on my body, I sat pale and washed-out in front of him, naked inside myself, not having the faintest idea what to expect. So I expected nothing; I was simply intrigued and quiet. "Have you some personal possession of yours that I could hold? A ring or watch maybe?" he said. I had only my address book. "Will this do?"

He sat holding the booklet, his eyes closed. "You've just left some job, as a waitress maybe, where you felt unappreciated. You just

downed tools and walked out saying, 'Damn them,
I'm off.'"

I felt a bit uncomfortable. This was way
off. I'd never done a serving job in my life.
I hadn't walked out of anywhere, and I wasn't
telling anyone to get lost.

Then a little jolt went through me and
I didn't have time to question the validity,
however poetic, of the rest of his reading.
"I get the word author - authority - you have
authority over people. Oh, I know, you've written a book!"

Oh dear, it works! I gulped deeply, sat
back, relaxed and absorbed all that he said.
Later on, trembling at a bus-stop, I would
also see how accurate the first 'metaphor'
of his reading had been - me, the serving-maid
of Atlantis, taking a well-earned leave of
absence.

During the reading, he told me my life-
history, with dates: "At the age of two, your
troubles began, and you lost trust in your
mother" (my sister was born, which proved traumatic for me in our tense, unhappy family where
every bit of attention I could get meant the
world to me). "At the age of six, there is
a tremendous break, and things take a decided
turn for the worse." (My parents divorced and
all my feelings went underground.) And so on,
through my life.

He told me of the hopelessness of the
affair I was just dragging myself out of, that
it had been a 'tragic mistake.' (I hadn't mentioned any affair that I was 'dragging myself
out of'!) He picked up two little semi-circular
magnets from his desk and said my fellow and
I had been 'like this' together - placing the
magnets back-to-back so that they repelled one

another; "whereas a relationship should be like this" - placing the magnets together so that they formed a circle of attraction.

He told me he could see a man standing behind me and that I would eventually meet him and that he would stay by me; he told me that more and more people would look to me as an authority in my chosen field of work as the years went by; he told me Atlantis (he didn't call it that) would acquire a more con-servative image and that although I didn't seek this, I would see the need for it to furth-er my work. (My commune in Ireland has had the most outrageous dose of publicity, but this has quietened down over the years - to the point where the Health Board sent us pat-ients, the local police give us every support, and I get invited by the villagers to judge a festival week dog-show: surely the height of social acceptance!)

He ended up by telling me that if I was in my ideal situation, the one in which I'd be happiest and most fulfilled, I'd be setting up a colony on the Moon, and teaching people to build grass huts there. The fact that there isn't any grass on the moon is precisely what makes this image so accurate! (As I write, plans are well under way to transfer the whole commune to a mountain-top in South America!)

Then Peter asked me if I wanted to put any questions to him. I said, "No," faintly as I staggered out to use his loo. My mind was reeling. Out there, I thought of my Caesar-ean-scarred stomach and wanted to know whether I'd ever be able to have another child. As I walked back into him, before I could speak, he indicated his lower abdomen and said, "You've had some trouble down here, haven't you? Womb

trouble. It will be healed by you having another
child. Having this new baby will be like com-
pleting a circle for you." (As you will see
from the dedication of this book, his word
became flesh and materialized five years later
in my new baby daughter.)

I shivered my way home, and told all my
friends. A few days later, I got Peter to spend
three whole days at our squat, giving readings
to about forty Atlanteans. The first to go
in was my daughter Rebecca. He told me afterwards that she was so powerfully psychic that
if she'd known how to direct her powers, she
could have given him a reading; that she was
already as powerful as most grown-up psychics
and would continue to develop into adulthood. He
said he was worried that "her powers would
disturb her if not channelled properly," and
he offered to train her himself, free of charge.
Needless to say, I jumped at the offer, and
a few days later, she went along to him for
the first time.

We all sat round her eagerly when she
returned home, wanting to know what had happened. "Nothing much," she said. She had been
handed various objects and told to say whatever
came into her head. Peter had asked her questions and said her answers contained a high
degree of accuracy. At another training session,
Peter brought a young teenage girl into the
room and Becky was able to say what part of
the world she came from (Canada) and various
details about the girl's family situation,
which turned out to be right.

Not long after this, our own personal
needs took us back to Ireland, and so that
was the end of Becky's 'training.' She had

had just a few sessions. Following this, we thought no more of Becky's powers for many months as other events commanded our attention.

Then one day a letter came to Atlantis that we knew was not to be trusted. The words were sweet and innocent. And empty. We wanted to know what lay behind them. The writer of the letter was intimately connected to us and his letter affected his daughter, who was living with us, in the extreme. She needed to know the reality of what was coming towards her.

I wondered if Becky could help. I wasn't sure how to guide her. She didn't know anything about the arrival of the letter, so I simply told her we wanted a reading done and that if she was willing to try it, I'd give her all the support and encouragement I could. She was nervous. I told her it didn't matter at all if nothing happened, or if she 'got it all wrong,' no-one would have lost anything.

I went into a room alone with her, not at all confident myself. But the issue at stake was so important to me, that I thought I'd just plunge in and give her the kind of help and guidance I'd give anyone having their first therapy session.

Becky sat on a chair, with the letter sealed in a blank envelope in her hand. I told her to relax, breathe deeply, and to notice whether she got any sensations in her hand 'coming from' the letter. I told her to go with any impulses that came to her, and to speak out everything she felt. I had no idea whether anything would happen at all, and was quite prepared for us both to end up feeling rather silly having meddled with something that was quite out of our depth.

"I feel like squeezing you, holding tightly

on to you," she said, her face tensing up.
I grabbed a lined writing-pad and a biro and
started scribbling down rapid shorthand which,
luckily, I had learnt years ago. I was sweating
and it was hard both to write and to contain
my reactions to what was coming out of her,
so as not to interfere with or influence her
in any way. What I couldn't take down in shorthand was the fact that not only was Becky speaking just like the writer of the letter (if
he let himself go), but that she was beginning
to <u>look</u> like him as well - the hunched shoulders
and necklessness, the tight mouth; his mannerisms of movement as she got up and walked around
the room.

By the time the reading was over, I had
written pages and pages of shorthand. I told
Becky who the letter was from, and we stared at
each other, stunned. Then I rushed to my typewriter and typed the whole thing up.

Meanwhile, in a room just above us, the
man's daughter was screaming her head off.
Both Becky and I knew instinctively that she
was going through feelings occasioned by the
letter that had come that day.

I went up to the room where my sister was
giving the session we had heard. I handed her
the written-up reading, but I had to wait for
the praise and wonderment I expected, because my
sister was even more excited than me. She just
<u>had</u> to tell me details of the session that
had just occurred.

It coincided perfectly with what I had just
typed.

The first time, it's a bit like taking a
deep breath and not daring to breathe out again
in case 'it' goes away. But 'it' didn't go
away. It got stronger. We gave other readings to

Becky. And the miracle repeated itself.

I must explain at this point that my own daughter had recently been away from Atlantis for a very long time, months on end in fact – hence the gap in her psychic activities. She had cut off emotionally from myself and the rest of the commune, having come face-to-face with blocks inside herself that she felt unwilling and unready to work through. So she'd gone off into the Big Wide World to experience life outside the commune. Now she was back, but still very walled-off against us all. Doing this reading was her emotional re-entry into the community. And doing the next reading I gave her was her re-entry into herself. For I gave her the letter of another man, also intimately known to us, who was an extremely emotional person, but someone in whom these emotions were tied up in knots, coming out only in brutal and twisted ways. For a young girl to do a reading on a calcified older man was a traumatic experience, but the kind of trauma that is therapeutic. Becky had reached a stage of pride and isolation inside herself that was preventing her from getting warmth from anyone. Doing this second reading started to break down her walls once again: with the 'ticket' that she was 'only doing a reading,' she could let go, cry and rant and rage, just as the man the reading was of would need to do to regain himself. The result was a brilliantly accurate reading, but also a new and extraordinarily effective therapeutic 'trick' which Becky could play on herself to bring herself through to full communication and contact once again.

And use it she did. We gave her reading after reading. They were always deep, perceptive

- and eventually, when the major backlog of
trauma was over - increasingly funny, then
funnier, then utterly hilarious. Becky found her
new mode of self-expression. My dark brooding
Scorpionic little daughter stepped into her
Sagittarian Ascendant and became a fully-fledged
clown. Here was indeed an aspect of the psychic
that we had never expected.

"My goodness!" we said as we rolled around
hurting from laughing so much, "It's a good
thing our livelihood doesn't depend on her
doing these readings commercially, we'd send
every client running, seeing themselves depicted
like that!" Accents became Becky's speciality -
not necessarily the actual accent of the person
whose reading she was doing (and whose identity
was never revealed to her until after the reading, though unfortunately she would often guess
who it was quite early on) - but an accent
which humorously brought out the character
of the person, such as a drawling Deep South
American accent for a lethargic spoilt girl,
or a Cockney accent for a working-class Irishman's mother, or a terribly posh British accent
for someone snooty and puffed-up. Soon the
accents became whole acts, plays, stories.
No scientist would be in the least impressed
with the concreteness of the information delivered - I mean, I came across in one reading as
James Bond, leading a fizzing, quick-fire life
of adventure and intrigue, with a dozen absurd
details taken from films she had seen - but we,
the audience, knowing our friends and enemies so
well, knew exactly what she meant and spent some
superb evenings of entertainment that TV stars
would be paid thousands to deliver.

What had we tapped? Was it telepathy? Was
it 'vibes' from a person's handwriting? Would

Becky pick up a person as they were at the time of their writing a letter, or as they were at the time of her doing the reading? This was easily ascertainable: we gave her a letter written months beforehand by a girl who had lived at Atlantis for years and who had now departed from us in a great huff and was still sulking. At the time of writing her letter, she had been feeling friendly and longing to be with us. Becky's reading picked her up as rancorous, stiff, quarrelsome, defensive and hostile towards us. So it seems readings provide a direct link with a person as they are now.

Whenever any of us were away in London or elsewhere, we got into the habit of going to other clairvoyants. Each one had his or her own style, but basically commercial clairvoyants lean towards predicting the future, which is something we don't do so much, being oriented strongly towards revelation and expression of a person's character; though this in itself involves prognosis for the future - "if this person carries on the way they are going, they will seize up completely with arthritis."

Each time I went to a clairvoyant, the excitement was tremendous. I usually went when I was in a bad state, cracked up about someone or other; and inevitably, as I left, I'd be walking on air, renewed and healed, with strength and optimism to carry on.

At a time when I had written just one book, and considered it all I'd ever write, an Egyptian clairvoyant mentioned "all your future books and articles." I protested, but he looked at me steadily, and carried on the reading. Sometimes, of course, predictions did not come true at all - but the power and optimism engend-

ered even by an 'inaccurate' forecast was pheno-
menal. 'Stealing energy from the future' I
came to call it. Sometimes too, a clairvoyant
would pick up a strange mix of the Very Important and the Highly Insignificant - as when
Aleph told me "I see you in a room full of
mirrors," which was quite simply a "reflection"
of the fact that I had covered the walls of
my room with mirrors from junk shops!

The cosmic, the funny, the trivial, the
tragic. Just like life. But always, always, a
reading was a nourishment, a deepening and
widening of awareness and sensitivity to life.
Anne went to a gypsy in Cork who told her amongst other things: "You live in a house where
it's alright to shout and scream and say what
you like. There's a woman there with an English
accent. She keeps in the background, but she's
keeping an eye on everything and taking care of
you all." And another of our women was told by
a London clairvoyant, "There's enough energy
being generated by your community on Inishfree
Island to light up a whole city."

*****

CHAPTER FIVE: HELP! I'M PSYCHIC

One afternoon in the autumn of 1978, I was staring at my boyfriend, Jim. I was amused. I could see what his father was like. Everyone wants to think they are so different from their parents, but of course they're not; an outsider can always see similarities. Jim in particular hated to think he had anything in common with his father, whom he despised. But I could see all the little mannerisms, the way he stood or slouched or walked, the way he wore his clothes, his attitudes and ways of being.

I had never met Jim's parents, nor had he told me much about them. But I had such a strong intuition about his father that I said, "Jim, I can see your father in you, shall I tell you what he's like?" Jim went into such a huff at the very idea of being anything like his father, that he stopped talking to me and soon left Atlantis. Two weeks later, he was back, and I still kept getting the feeling about his father. "Jim ... er, would you be ready now for me to tell you what I see?" I asked. He was.

I lay beside him and stared at him. I did not connect what I was doing in the slightest with 'readings' or 'the psychic' or anything that Becky had been up to. As far as I knew, I was just messing around with my boyfriend, teasing him.

I was in a good mood and very relaxed. I started joking around about newspapers stuffed under the armchair cushions, and Dad insisting on the TV always being on the channel he wanted, and his general morose air, and the way he always crossed the road at the exact same point,

and the way he related to the dog (I didn't know
they had a dog) more than he related to his
wife or offspring, and the way the reddened
flesh at the back of his neck stuck out over his
stiff collar (I could actually feel it at the
back of my neck), and the way he'd gone to seed
round the middle so that his trousers looked
baggy and scruffy and not quite done-up; and I
mentioned the dog-bowl under the kitchen table,
and the concrete path down the garden with
the shed on the right-hand side and about his
father's ritual surrounding taking the dog for
a walk. And then I had to stop, because Jim was
looking awfully ill and sweaty and pale. "What's
up?" says I, a bit apprehensive myself. "You're
going round my house as if you had a TV camera
in your hand," says he. And then I felt a bit
ill too. Oh, so it's not just Becky; oh, so I
can do it too. Oh.

I continued the reading then. I gave Jim
more and more details about his father, his
character, habits and attitudes. But now I
was very sober. Then we called in my sister
and daughter and told them what had happened.
And then I 'did' Jim's mother. And it worked
again. Detail for detail. Jim told me I sounded
like her, was moving like her, that I was using
phrases when I spoke that she would use, that
I had brought her right into that room.

Becky looked glum. Huh! So the grown-ups
are taking over. So mum can do it too. And
better - so she thought - using all them educated words and concepts. Damn.

We tried it then using someone's writing. I
came into the room and was handed a blank envelope. Immediately I started to feel awfully
shy and giggly and silly and bouncy and full of
energy. I thought it must just be the strange-

ness of my new situation. I wanted to leap
and hop all over the place, but I didn't quite
like to in front of the - grownups? So I started
staring blankly and fixedly at the pictures on
the wall, containing myself, and going all
'spacey', losing my good feeling and getting
stuck. I wasn't clear what was happening to
me at all, but I just kept speaking out what was
going on in me like I've taught other people
to do when they're in trouble. I had no idea
whether what I was saying had any meaning or
not. I just knew I hated that 'spaced-out'
feeling.

Eventually, I stopped the reading, turned
round and said, "Is this anything like the
person you've given me?" My sister was sitting
sewing with her sensible, knowing, amused face
on, and she spoke to me like a school-mistress,
"Yes, Jenny, I'm afraid it is. You can do it.
It's Sara." Sara was her ten-year-old daughter.
Point by point, they went over with me what
I had said so that I could see how it related to
my niece. It was certainly very accurate, and
also helped us to understand an aspect of Sara
that we all found difficult to deal with, namely
what we used to call her 'glassiness.'

Well, that was that. I could do readings.
Good lord.

"Huh!" said my sister. "Well, if two members of the James clan can do them, I know
a third who damn well can as well."

So out of the room she went, while the
rest of us chose someone's writing.

She was brilliant. Much better than me
- so I thought. We all always think we're not as
good as the others. I reckon that's because
when you're doing a reading, you're so absorbed
feeling, speaking, moving, sometimes crying,

laughing or being defensive and difficult, that
you don't feel you're specially 'doing' anything. You become the person; you're living
their way for a while. And you don't know 'who
you are.' Meanwhile, the others sitting watching
you are devastated with your brilliance. You are
using the exact mannerisms and phrases of the
person whose identity has not been revealed to
you; you're showing their inner motives and
machinations and moods. But you standing there,
all you think you're doing is leaning on a
mantelpiece wiping a speck of dust away, or
stretching an aching limb. You don't feel brilliant at all!

We launched into an orgy of readings.
At first, I had been in the habit of religiously
scribbling down all Becky's readings in shorthand and spending laborious hours typing them up
and filing them. It seemed so precious. It
was The Psychic. It was Cosmic. You couldn't
just let things like that happen and go into
thin air, it must all be recorded. Then one
day, she was doing a reading that affected
me so much - it was of my own father - that
I could write no longer. I sank back on the
bed and give in to the experience of the reading. And having let the most significant reading
of them all go by unrecorded, I realized how
silly I was being, and hardly ever bothered to
write one down again, though we eventually
started taping a few of them from time to time.
Now we just enjoy them. They are as much a part
of our lives as our home-baked bread.

We did hundreds of them. We did everyone of
any significance that any of us had ever known.
This is considered awfully 'unethical' is some
circles, but at Atlantis we are not renowned for
giving a damn about ethics invented to stunt and

constipate fun and knowledge. We loved every
minute of it - the deliciousness of opening
up a person who had closed up on us, former
friends and lovers, 'stealing our energy' as
we call it. Now we could pinch it back! We
did relatives. We did ourselves, over and over
again. We tricked the 'reader' into doing a
reading on themselves. We tested, we checked,
we double-checked. All three of us would, at
different times, do a reading of the same person
to see what would come out. What happened was
of course, that we each had our individual
mode or style of delivering the portrait of
a person, but the readings would always contain
certain basic elements in common. Becky would in
general pick up the most hidden, devious or
ill-wishing aspects of a person - a true Scorpio
she loves everything Black and Suspicious.
I would in general pick up any pain or unhappiness or discomfort in a person, and would focus
very much on how they felt in their body. My
sister, benign Taurus that she is, would inevitably pick up anything rich, sunny or benevolent
in the person.
    Yes, hundreds and hundreds of them we
did. But did we ever discover how it worked?
No, we did not! How to explain that when Becky
was doing a - blind - reading of someone called
"Wilf" that she kept interrupting herself to
say, "I keep wanting to go 'Woof!'" What do
you make of the fact that one summer, doing
readings in our crowded centre cottage on the
island, I could not for the life of me think of
the English word for 'Anstrengung' (tension).
In our large summer group, there was a German
visitor. It just had to be a reading of him.
Suddenly, he confirmed it by bursting into
tears at something I'd touched in him.

What about picking up a piece of folded paper and immediately getting bad eyesight? Everything I looked at was slightly blurred. I kept blinking my eyes. "Goodness, this person must have slightly double vision, perhaps their eyes are slightly crossed." Rob, a new friend, was very annoyed with me afterwards, being sensitive about his eye which no-one would have noticed was slightly out of alignment. "You must have noticed," he said acidly. But I hadn't. Not until I picked up that bit of paper he'd written on.

On another occasion, there were just me and Sean from Cork in the room. He gave me a letter in a blank envelope. When I started the reading, I found I was meticulously picking my way round words, as if scared that I would stutter or stumble. I was speaking extra-specially perfectly. "Sean, is this a foreign person, someone for whom English is not their first language?" "No," said Sean. Oh, I thought, I wonder what this feeling is then. It persisted. I didn't dare just let my speech hang loose, as I had the sensation that I would start speaking strangely if I did. "I'm sure this isn't an English-speaking person," I insisted. Sean shook his head. When the reading was over and he told me who it was, I spluttered indignantly, "But he's POLISH." Sean, an Irishman with a strong local accent himself, could only hear the man's perfect upper-class educated English accent. Myself, coming from near London, I could hear quite clearly the over-posh, over-perfect, careful pronunciation of a highly educated foreigner.

*****

Meanwhile, alongside all this readings business, the everyday ordinary extraordinary phenomena continued. The kind that are happening to you every day, brushed aside like out-of-place cobwebs annoyingly strung across your path.

We got very used to picking up the unexpressed tensions and feelings of people we slept with. Met at first with amazement and the need to seek confirmation from one another, eventually these happenings came to be accepted by us as readily as the snores of a partner - that is, to be complained about, but not to be treated as 'something we were imagining.' An example? One night I slept in friendship alongside a self-effacing, terribly nice, awfully accommodating, do-anything-for-you, wouldn't-harm-a-fly young Irish boy, you know the sort who still gets his shirts washed by his mother when he is in his mid-twenties and who has, for some mysterious reason, never had a girlfriend. We were both asleep, he lying peacefully with his back to me. Suddenly, I felt his arm stretch out slowly towards me, and the fingers of his surprisingly strong hand start to close on my throat, choking me so that I couldn't breathe.

I struggled in desperate silent panic. I felt the life going from me, but somehow managed to gasp out his name. That woke me. I lay stiff with terror. Gradually recovering myself, I carefully investigated to see if any clothing of mine, or any of the blankets, had touched or wound around my neck, causing this extraordinary 'dream.' Nothing. "Oho!" thought I, "I know where this is at." Had I not come across this kind of thing before, I would have dismissed the happening as a 'nightmare.' But the next day, I jokingly confronted the Irishman in question as to whether he might have one or two teeny weeny hostile feelings towards me, perhaps for arousing rather violent sexual desires to interrupt his chaste existence? He immediately 'fell in a pit' as we call it at Atlantis - that is, he cut off, not able to bear what I was saying, and left soon after. Psychics and spiritual groups throughout the ages have talked of an 'etheric' body that usually sticks fairly closely to our own physical body, but which can on unusual occasions take leave and 'do its own thing.' It seems my young friend's arm had gone off on a spree of its own that night, and I felt the effects in no uncertain terms.

Each person's psychic sensitivities take different forms - you will have your own talent. My own take the form mostly of mental knowledge and direct physical effects from a person's 'vibrations.' My sister also gets visual effects - one day we were all sitting amicably round the carpet in my room, when she said, "Good lord! Did you see Fred spit on the floor?" None of us had, because it hadn't happened. But what had happened was that the gentleman in question, being of a crochety and disgusted frame of mind, whilst sitting meekly and silently in our midst, had felt like doing just that. And some part of him had done it, because my sister spotted him!

A visiting acquaintance, Les, got auditory impressions. At first I didn't take much notice, thinking he was 'just trying to be psychic.' He was telling me that he was getting a high-pitched whistling sound in his ears whenever he was in my room, and that he always got that in place of 'high energy.' I thought he was just

handing me a clumsy compliment and boosting himself - but then I was completely convinced,
because he told me that 'the only other place in
the house he got it even stronger was in the
Craft Shop.' Now there was no way he could
have known that that front room, now our shop,
had been the scene for years and years of Atlantis life of huge non-stop, sometimes all-night
primal therapy groups, where hundreds of people
had cried and yelled out at peak energy level
all the pains of their past. There had been
countless emotional births and deaths and murd-
ers and reunions and love affairs in that room;
there was certainly no place to compare with it
for the amount of energy that had gone into
those walls!

*****

CHAPTER SIX: WHATEVER NEXT?

Well, you'd think it was enough, the whole
family going psychic and all that. You'd think
it was enough, being able to pick up a person's
mood and character structure and tensions and
motivations from some bit of paper they'd sent
you through the post - without even looking
at it or knowing who it was from, just through
holding it, wrapped in a blank envelope. I
often say to people before I do a reading,
"I don't believe in this you know." How else
can I mend the chasm in my brain between my
life-long training and belief in the nice solid
material world, and this strange new facility
that had been dumped so unexpectedly on our
doorstep?

But no, it wasn't enough for my crazy
sister. She came home from a trip to England one
day and announced she had discovered you don't
even need a person's writing to do a reading.
She said all you have to do is write down their
name yourself, and hand it to someone to sense
out. That did it. I was really annoyed. How
could she be so haphazard with these cosmic
matters? How could she be so flippant? How
could it possibly work to write 'Aunt Maud' on
a piece of paper, put it in an evelope, hand it
to someone and get a reading on Aunt Maud?
Wasn't the whole business ridiculous enough
already, without this new and absurd leap into
... what? I wouldn't let in what she was saying,
and stubbornly insisted on going to the bother
of seeking out some writing of a person we
wanted to do a reading on.

But then they tricked me anyway of course.
Becky wanted to know about her new boyfriend.

She hadn't anything written by him, so unbeknown to me, she wrote his name down herself and handed it to me. For all I knew, I had someone's letter in my hand, so I proceeded to do a perfectly accurate reading on - no, not Becky, whose writing it was, but her boyfriend. Afterwards, I opened the paper to see who I had 'done.' And then I eyed her accusingly, and gave up yet another chunk of my poor rational mind.

We had already discovered that having a photograph in an envelope worked. So then we tried newspaper cutting photographs. Yes, they worked. (Why didn't we get readings on the printers?) OK, let's see, said I, branching out a bit myself. What would happen if we put two people - their writing that is - into an envelope? Would we get a 'relationship' reading, like superimposing two astrological charts to get a compatibility analysis? It turned out we could, though it is a bit of a strain on the medium, getting the jumbled vibrations of two people.

One day, I gave Becky an envelope containing a photo of myself and one of my one-time husband, Becky's father. I told her only that it was a relationship reading, and that she should count anything she felt as the dynamic between two people, rather than as the vibrations of an individual, and we'd see what happened.

What happened was she told me simply yet intricately of all the difficulties, stubbornness, lack of communication, and pride that had been my relationship with her father. "What would any child of this union come out like?" I asked. Becky felt awful. She could feel the tensions and conflict of the marriage. She told me, "The child would be in a dreadful

state; it would be deformed; there would be
something wrong with its legs." "Strange," I
thought to myself, "She's not that bad, and
there's nothing wrong with her legs."

When she had finished the reading, and
I told her who the couple were, and we were
going over all the amazing details she had
come up with, suddenly she said, "Oh – and
Nicole! I picked up how Nicole was."

I felt an electric shock go through me.
Such is the trickery of the mind that I, the
mother, had managed to blot out of my consciousness temporarily the fact that Becky had had a
twin sister, badly deformed, who died aged
three weeks. Had she lived, she would never have
walked, as she had paralysed, unequal legs.

*****

On another occasion, my sister and daughter
gave me a relationship reading to do. Although I
didn't know it, it was of Becky and her father.
As I was doing the reading, I kept saying,
"I can only feel one person; they must be much
bigger and stronger than the other, so much
so that one of the two is almost completely
obscured." And just for good measure, I delivered a couple of sentences in Spanish (Becky's
father is Spanish), and didn't even bother
to think why, I was so absorbed in the feelings
of the reading.

At another time, wanting to give my sister
a reading to do that would be of personal interest to her, I searched through our family photo
album and assembled a collection of relevant
photos. Then I put two of them into an envelope,
thinking I was handing her a reading of herself
and her ex-husband. My poor sister got into a

terrible pickle. She was making very strange faces - quite normal for her as she's always a clown. But there was something extra-specially queer about her today. She was also making strange noises. She told me that this was an 'impossible relationship,' it just couldn't exist. Oh dear, I thought, I knew it hadn't been the most passionate of marriages, but was it as bad as this? My sister was writhing around on the floor and soon had to give up the reading. I opened the envelope to show her who she had been 'picking up.' Then I turned very red, apologized profusely, assured her I hadn't meant to trick her, and we both fell about laughing and couldn't speak for ages. In the envelope was, sure enough, a photo of my sister's ex-husband. But stuck to the back of him accidentally was none other than Snowy's subsequent lover. An impossible relationship indeed.

My frequent feeling that 'my sister is more psychic than me' often seems verified by fact. That same day, I gave her in an envelope the photos of two young men, Colm and Jim, with whom I had been intimately involved, but who also had a lot of connections with one another. They had a kind of love-hate relationship that I was intrigued to know more about. But when my sister came to do the reading, the very first thing she picked up was that "there is a third person in this relationship who is more important to each of these people than they are to one another, and a great deal of their connection is due to this third person." She then proceeded to give a great deal of detail about how each of them related to me!

I didn't dare to tell you earlier in this
book, but actually the first reading my sister
ever did was a reincarnation reading on just
these same two fellows. You don't believe in
reincarnation? No, of course not. And nor did
we. But then my sister did this reading.

You see, my sister is younger than me, and
she's never got over the fact, so of course she
has to try and do everything better than me. And
she often manages to. Not content with confidently standing up that first day and announcing,
"Well, I can do readings too," she then proceeded to do the most extraordinary reading any of
us had ever seen. It lasted for several hours.
At first, it was just 'normal' - normally magical that is. She picked up Jim, whose writing we
handed her (and who was not in the room) just
as he actually is, striding around the place
pretty confident. She stood like him, put her
hands in her pockets like him, knew immediately
she was a man, and was generally Jim-ish. Then
she moved to the next layer. This is quite
'normal' too. We don't deal in superficialities
and there's hardly any point in simply reproduc-
ing a person's top layer and showing things
we already know. So she started picking up
other, deeper aspects of him, more and more
hidden parts. Perfectly normal psychic activity.
Then we moved on to question time. This is
something we often do, as it adds a delicious
dimension to a reading - finding out how a
person would relate to the people in the room if
they were to be completely real with us. Colm
wanted to know what Jim felt about him. Colm was
sitting on my bed, happily enjoying a relationship with me, who had once been Jim's woman.
Jim was away, brooding, cut off from us all.
Snowy, as 'Jim', scowled at him in answer and

started tapping her front teeth. "The answer's here," she said, and she adopted one of her perfectly horrible faces. We were used to aggression and ill-feeling at Atlantis, but this was really monstrous. We felt jolted as Snowy's expressions got more and more like something out of the underground caverns in Lord of the Rings. My sister is a very uninhibited person when it comes to making faces and noises and expressing rather disgusting impulses. And express them she did.

She turned into a snorting, distorted monster, for all the world like a prehistoric cave-man. And then she started slowly and deliberately raising her right hand and leaning ominously towards Colm. We could almost hallucinate the club in her hand. Suddenly, I realized we had all gone daft. There we were, sitting transfixed, as if watching a horror movie, and there was a murder about to take place. I jabbed Colm firmly in the ribs. "Stop her!" I yelled. "Warn her off!" Colm alerted himself, stopped shrinking, and threatened her firmly. Snowy - or whoever she was - subsided, lost some of her crazy power and sat there scowling and snuffling, her right hand now lowered on to her own head, with the fingers pulling back her mouth in a fashion which did not improve her good looks. Whatever next?

Next, we had a scene which I can only describe as witnessing the re-enactment of a murder, only this time it wasn't Colm's. It was largely non-verbal, with my sister - who did not look very much like a sister - being dragged, in fact by her own hand, but in 'feel' by other people, on to the ground and into a dark tunnel where she was evidently robbed and generally pummelled to death.

Not having sat in my room that night watching this scene, you will quite understandably
mutter 'hysterical nonsense' to yourself at
this point. I don't blame you. You will also
probably think my sister is a pretty good act-
ress with a vivid imagination. You are right on
both points. You could also be forgiven for
thinking she was having us on, putting on a
good show, having fun at our gullible expense,
or maybe just 'trying to be cosmic' as we sometimes scathingly say of others.

I would think those things too if the
story had been told to me, and if I hadn't sat
in that room, in that very intimate company of
people who all knew each other extremely well
and did not need to be putting on any shows and
who would know from experience that it was
pointless trying to fool one another. And the
difference between a mood where there is general
hilarity and theatrics, and the tense, reverent,
abated-breath atmosphere of my room that evening
had to be felt to be believed.

And anyway, I haven't told you the half
of it yet. My 'sister' was finally thoroughly
battered and lying groaning, exhausted and
dying on the floor. She had evidently been
mugged rather a lot of centuries ago, and what
is more, to our discomfort, Colm and myself had
had rather a lot to do with it. Meanwhile,
my sister was lying peaceful now, as if in deep
sleep. And here I have to explain that this
'primal therapy' that we're into at Atlantis, or
indeed Reichian therapy, or any deep body therapy at all, involves learning to breathe really
deeply, naturally, and to 'go with' any body
feelings, impulses or movements. My sister,
having years and years of self-exploration
behind her, was well-equipped to 'go with'

the feelings of this reading.

So she did. She lay there curled up and resting after her long death struggle, and then after some time, she began to stir slightly. She was lying on her side in a foetus position.

'Birth primals' are a fairly well-known phenomenon in therapy circles. They're not invented, acted out or suggested, not if they're genuine. The body simply has these movements and impulses deep inside it, recorded in the cells: the stretching and pushing, contracting and resting, grunting and straining, twisting and slithering, the urgency, the relaxation, the fear, the relief and delight, of a baby getting itself born out of one element and into the next.

'Death primals' are a new invention as far as I know! At least I'd never heard of them until I saw my sister go through one on my floor that evening. [Years later, I came across a fascinating book - though written in dreadful academic language - called The Human Encounter With Death by Stanislav Grof and Joan Halifax, where it says: "Sequences of agony, death and rebirth belong to the most frequent experiences in psychedelic sessions. They occur quite spontaneously, without any specific programming, and sometimes even to the great surprise of an unexperienced and uninformed subject."]

And then what more natural in the world to slip into, when the time is right, than a birth primal? Birth following death. That evening, it seemed completely organic. Never mind all my previous anti-religious prejudice, never mind my distaste for all 'Eastern mystical nonsense,' never mind all the straitjackets of my mind. My body felt and saw; and there's one thing I've

learnt for sure in ten years of primal therapy,
and that's to trust my body sensations.

My body felt the completely organic shift
from death to life; I saw my sister's body
start once more to suck in air, to gurgle and
grunt. We watched then as she became another
person - or rather the same person, but in
a new time, with a new character structure,
which carried scars and lessons and talents
from the life she had previously been through.
We saw her develop into a mighty lord, proud
and stiff and unbending. We saw her suffering
from her own rigidity. We saw her finally brought to her knees. And then we saw her hung.
Yes, we saw her death once again. Some ancient
lesson, still not learnt by my equally proud,
stiff friend, Jim, of this day and age, repeatedly brought home, lifetime after lifetime,
until learnt. Unbelievable? Well, that evening
finally consolidated the shift in my belief
system. We saw and experienced so much that
evening, that of all the many colourful, dramatic and magical Atlantean evenings, it still
stands out as a breakwater, a turning-point.
That evening made us humble, made us proud,
made us doubt, made us believe. That evening
made us relax - forced us to relax into our new
discoveries. That evening blew our minds, and
our prejudices, clean away. There was no sense
in fighting any more. There was no point in
being careful or timid or trying hard to retain
some vestige of 'scientific' explanation. There
wasn't even any point in wondering, "Are we
inventing it? Are we fooling ourselves?" because
whatever was happening, was happening, and
sooner or later we would find out what 'it'
was. There was no hurry. Of some things in
any case there was no doubt: there was no doubt

that it was totally absorbing, electrifying,
and sobering. It was an experience which changed
us all, or rather consolidated and confirmed
so many little strands that had been intertwin-
ing in our lives. Everything started to click
and fit in, once we stopped struggling and
dismissing and 'trying to work things out.'

OK, so reincarnation is real. Or at least,
it is a poetic metaphor for something that
we experience as very real. And groups reincarnate. We have known some of the people we know
now in previous lifetimes. We're back together
again to carry on our unresolved or our enjoyable relating. I'm hardly the first person
to notice this, but when you notice it for
the first time, it is a revelation, and it
takes a lot of getting used to when you're
a 20th century Western atheist (this time around
that is).

"OK, we give in" became our attitude.
We've gone and opened this door, and the winds
are rushing through, and there's no point in
trying to shut it again, so we might as well
enjoy the wind, see what it brings, and what it
blows away. The first thing it brought was a
kind of humorous adoption of 'mystical' terms:
everything is 'meant.' "Why have I met you and
why are you meeting me, and what are we supposed
to learn from one another?" OK, that stone
just dropped on my foot, now what was it trying
to tell me, and what did I do to deserve it
- for most surely I did something very specific
to deserve everything that happens to me. Blame
is abolished. It is always my 'fault' and my
responsibility. Suddenly, conventional spiritual
theories fitted strangely well with our new
attitudes: everything that happens to me is
up to me to deal with, and blaming is a childish

cul-de-sac. Well, what beauty am I going to extract from this present set of dreadful circumstances that has befallen me and what did I do to bring the cosmos down so heavily on top of me?

Death - personal death, the death of an animal or of a civilization or of a planet - became more acceptable; and I have always, like most people, had terrible difficulty facing death. Death becomes part of life, and there is no longer any such thing as accidental death; there's no such thing as a 'victim.' Oh, this is a difficult one to get across, isn't it? Especially to all those lefties and samaritans out there - and I've been both, and would have been thoroughly disgusted and enraged by all this primitive 'reward and punishment' talk fifteen years ago. Why, doesn't that mean accepting the status quo? It certainly means letting yourself know that however horrible what you're looking at is, it still is: you've got to accept that much. But it does not mean going limp, giving up and not fighting; it doesn't mean not talking back, not getting angry, not doing something about it. But it does mean that there aren't loads of poor innocent people being 'done to' and another set of evil grasping people doing all the dirties.

And it means there's no such thing as coincidence. The universe isn't accidental, isn't chaotic - and isn't particularly organized either, not by some benevolent bearded fellow anyway; it is finely tuned and structured though and we are a completely responsible part of that tuning and structure. This planet wasn't just dumped here because someone else didn't want it for us to mess up and muck up at will. If we play Bonfire Night with Planet Earth in

the ultimate firework display, all our surrounding planets will be affected. Likewise, if
the inhabitants of some of those UFOs choose to
start messing around with things down here,
we'll soon find out we're not the omnipotent
universe-owners we fondly imagine we are, and
we'll have to start taking account of our neigh-
bours before they decide we've done enough
damage to ourselves and take charge of us.
Whether life is pre-programmed by a superior
force, or has evolved from inside according to
a natural law of survival, the result is the
same: an interdependent universe inhabited by
interdependent beings. We were taught in god-
lessons at school that not a sparrow can drop
from the sky without the Lord taking note of
it - and it's true, metaphorically, as today's
wild life conservationists are painfully aware:
·unbalance things as they are, and in the end you
unbalance yourself. If we don't straighten up
and pay our dues to Mother Earth, we'll get
ourselves tipped right off this particular
space-globule. We are tenants of a beautifully
furnished cosmos, and gross misbehaviour can
only lead to us being kicked out on our necks,
without any comfy liberal Rent Act to protect
us.

   Our new insights into 'what's going on in
the cosmos,' accepted with a sigh, a grin and
a twinkle, gave us a fuller and richer angle on
life, a deeper peep into what it's all about.
"Oh dear, she's gone all religious" you might
well say. No, she hasn't actually, though a
young friend of mine did say recently in a
different context, "This woman is the most
religious person I ever met." If it's religious
to take responsibility for everything that
happens around us and to us, and to tell others

to do likewise, then I am. But I know it's
no use looking to any god to do it for me.

I've got a 'splitting' headache writing
about all this stuff. The split is in me, but
it's represented at this moment by you, unknown
reader. You represent for me my cynicism, my
disbelief, my fear of ridicule. It's not a
sensible fear, for I know there are thousands of
people all over the planet who have come to
the same conclusions as we have at Atlantis.
But it's still a shock when it first happens.
It's still a shock when you have to trust only
your own senses, when you can no longer look to
precedent or authority around you, nor to mum
or dad, or leaders, experts, teachers or gurus;
when there's no longer anyone above you, because
you've reached the limit of what anyone can
teach you; you're pioneering and cutting new
pathways and making your own experience and
leading and teaching and showing others the way.
And this has to happen to anyone who wants
to truly grow up and step fully into their
own power.

Well, at Atlantis we say, "If you've got a
headache, it's because you're tensing against
something. And if you're tensing against something, it's because you're frightened of the
consequences of letting go. And if you're frightened of something, there's only one cure for
that, and that's to face the fear. And a really
good way of facing fear is to walk straight
into it." In other words, do more fully the
thing that makes you tense, till you burst
your own bubble.

So, I'll tell you more and more strange
tales, make more and more outrageous statements,
claim more and more outstanding knowledge,
and leave you to dismiss or enjoy me.

We decided to let it all flow, we decided
to dive in and swim in it, or not even to swim,
just to let ourselves be taken by the current.
I got the idea of 'doubling' our powers by
doing readings on clairvoyants, not to find out
about the clairvoyant, but in order to use
the 'open channel' for others in the group
to ask questions, 'cosmic' questions, spiritual
questions, questions about the future of the
world. I lay holding something written by a
London clairvoyant. I relaxed completely and
with the 'excuse' that I wasn't 'just Jenny'
but this magical, far-distant psychic, I allowed
wisdom to pour forth from me without embarrassment or censorship. One of the questions I
was asked was, "What happens to suicides when
they die?" Without hesitation, I felt and 'saw'
the answer, feeling somewhat spooked out, remembering a good friend of mine who had killed
herself. "Oh, they're immediately, instantane-
ously, faced with themselves in a mirror. They
have to look and look and look at the face
staring at them, they have to see the horror
in that face, they have to see what they have
done to themselves. They have to experience
and re-experience and go on experiencing, for
ages and aeons and eternity, the face they
tried to obliterate. They have to go on and
on suffering the absolute lesson of existence:
that YOU CAN'T GET OFF THE BUS WHEN IT'S MOVING,
JUST BECAUSE YOU DON'T LIKE YOUR FELLOW PASSENG-
ERS. And this bus never stops moving. You can't
stop the cosmos, you can't opt out of the flow.
Because if you could, it would make life meaningless, a joke, an option. And life is none
of those. Life just is, and it carries on being,
and no little upstart molecule of existence
has the right or the power to say, "STOP!"

How strange it was to see the Christian concept of 'Hell' from a new angle. How weird that what I was coming out with tied in with religious attitudes against suicide. How ironic that when I was a child, before I'd come to recognize the longing to die, to get off the bus, in myself, I once said, "People who commit suicide ought to be killed." I realize now that I must already have been finding life such a struggle that the thought of anyone being able to opt out, find an easy way, infuriated me. How many times my philosophy would change! Later, I would maintain that "suicides were the bravest people on earth" because I wanted so much that my torment would stop, but was never resolved enough to kill myself.

Nowadays if someone threatens suicide, I say, "The sharpest knife is in the second drawer on the right," and carry on weeding the beans. It makes people so furious, we've never had a suicide at Atlantis. And if we ever did, I'd only be annoyed at the mess. Because I know so well now how you can't get off the bus. And if you try, there'll be another identical one there waiting to pick you up.

*****

CHAPTER SEVEN: RELAX, IT'S ONLY MAGIC

Once, on a second visit to the clairvoyant Peter Lee, he told me: "Your parents made a lot of mistakes, but they're still learning. They see things differently now. They understand more about what they did with you." Both my parents were dead, and he knew this.

I had swallowed this little snippet, along with so many others, and packed it away in the 'pending' file in my brain, musing upon it from time to time when other little snippets came my way.

One evening I sat in my bedroom with my daughter opposite me, my sister to one side of me, and several other friends dotted around the room. Becky, without knowing it, was doing a reading of my father. And in the course of the reading, she was relating directly to me. At one point, she cracked up crying and told me that she (he) needed my help. I sat upright in my chair. "How can I help you?" I asked softly. "I feel you are helping me, just by bringing me here tonight. I need you to keep calling me, keep calling on me." Then I started to cry gently. The very thing I most needed to do, call on my father from time to time, was the thing Becky was saying he needed too. "I feel you are older and wiser than me; you have been around longer than me," she was saying - thus confirming what many of us have often sensed: that children are sometimes more evolved beings than their parents. That your parents are not your parents, to rephrase Khalil Gibran.

Becky felt she was floating around, homeless. She felt airy and gassy and ungrounded. "Oh, so he's not found a new place yet," I thought, according to our new attitude of simply accepting all these weird theories.

We experimented with other readings of dead people, not that the medium would know beforehand that they were dead. Becky was handed the letter of a man who had died alcoholic, the father of one of the girls in our commune.

This became one of her 'hilarious' readings in spite of the sombre content. She sat on a chair throughout, in a droopy posture, talking with the slurred accent and self-pitying tone of a chronic drunk. She said she was sitting on a toilet seat in a tiny concrete loo, and that she was stuck to it, too sick and drunk to move. She said the door was locked, and although the handle was only inches away, because of her condition, she couldn't reach it to let herself out. She could sense light and movement through the crack in the door, people moving about and living their lives, unaware of her presence or the dreadful state she was in. Their talk and laughter came through to her. Her body felt dead and dreadful, full of alcohol poisoning. She would have liked to call out to the people outside her concrete cell, but she couldn't, she was too drunk and couldn't articulate the words sufficiently well to be heard. She was getting cold and stiff.

Stuck there, she was forced to meditate upon the wastage of her life, her emptiness, degradation and lack of self-respect. She had to sit there endlessly, unable to reach out, unable to get help.

When our laughter at Becky's brilliant portrayal of the drunk had subsided, the hairs started standing up on our backs as the significance of the words she was using filtered

through to us. Hilarity gave way to horror
as it dawned on us that what she was actually
showing us was a man in his grave. Conscious, on
some level. Stuck there, endlessly having to go
over all that he had done and been, all that
he had let slip by. Is this what is meant by
karma, by 'hell', by paying for our sins? This
man had thrown away the gift of life, tried
to drown it in alcohol. Now he had to experience
this same state forever. Until forever ends,
and he's permitted to move on and learn his
next lesson.

*****

In 1979, four of us women from Atlantis
went to London to run a stall at the 'Aquarian
Festival.' On the next stall to us was a homeo-
path who invited us home to dinner with him
and his wife. He talked about his work, we
told him of ours, mentioning of course that we
could do readings. He said he had a patient
that he needed help with. It was decided that
each of us would do a reading, and see what
combined information we came up with. The patient turned out to be a five-year-old child
who had been born normal, but who had had a
series of fits, nearly dying several times,
but always being caught just in time on the
verge of death by someone who knew how to give
heart-massage or whatever else was needed.
And so he was constantly hauled back 'by chance'
to continue his pain. He was now completely
seized up, his face fixed in an expression
of terror, his fists clenched and unreleasable,
autistic, unable to speak or communicate in
any way, his eyes constantly wide open, staring
at his parents and the nurses and doctors atten-

ding him. Every conventional medical method had
been given up.

I felt a surge of anger and disgust when I
heard the story. "Why don't you let the child
die! He obviously needs to die, why do you
want to keep him alive?" I said hotly.

The homeopathic doctor was quiet and pens-
ive. He said, Yes, he would normally agree,
but the circumstances of the repeated last-
minute rescues of the child had impressed him.
"It seems something very strong is wanting to
keep this child alive," he said.

So I agreed to do a reading on the boy,
to see what I would see.

When I picked up the boy's photograph,
I was in for a shock. I held it in my hand,
with my eyes closed, waiting for any change
in sensation. I didn't know what to expect –
indeed one never expects anything in particular
when starting a reading. But I was certainly
basically sympathetically predisposed towards
the child.

I found it hard to accept the stark images
which immediately assailed my mind. I felt
myself as a cold bespectacled professor, a
scientist in a laboratory. I was 'tending'
voiceless, helpless, alive, awake, semi-dissect-
ed animals that could not move. I was a vivisectionist. Oh my god. A very heavy penny dropped.
Could it be true? That this child, forced to
silent, conscious misery, prevented from dying
by 'kindly' last-minute interventions, was
simply having to feel, endlessly feel, what
he had inflicted in his last life as a vivisectionist? Was I just making it up? Where did
the images come from? Had these fantasies simply
popped into my mind through some unconscious
false-equation-making mechanism? I can't answer
you.

                            *****

     We started passing on our newfound skills
to others. Chris was next. She had been so
long associated with us and was so talented
and bright, it seemed obvious she would be
able to do readings. Nervous and excited as
she started, she nonetheless produced straight
away boppy, bright, energetic readings, readings
like herself. She wasn't at all lacking in
self-confidence once she started and moved
into them as easily as she had done into making
bread. Four of us now, all women. I wonder if
the men can do them? Well, we weren't going
to teach them!
     Huh! They taught themselves. And if we
thought we were confident! They just did them,
no nerves.
     I was sitting in my hand-made velvet tent
at the Festival of Mind and Body in 1979. Liam
slipped in to join me, an Atlantean exile living
in London. While I was attending to my stand at
the Festival, I was delivered a poisonous anonymous letter - 'anonymous' because signed by
one of those silly new Indian names it has
become the fashion to adopt. I didn't know
the name, and I didn't recognize the handwriting. The letter affected my system for twenty-
four hours; my stomach seized up, I couldn't
eat, I felt stagnant and dreadful. These things
aren't called 'poison pen' for nothing! "Do you
want me to do a reading on that letter, to
see if it helps to clear things up?" said Liam.
"What here?" I asked aghast, looking at the
thousands of people milling around Olympia.
I was so used to doing readings in the seclusion
and privacy of my home, where us women would
always move around a lot and be very flamboyant

in our delivery. Doing a reading in this atmosphere seemed about as comfortable as having
sex in a football crowd.

   But it didn't bother Liam. He sat there
mumbling quietly for my benefit what he picked
up from the letter. Within half a minute, I
realized who it was from, what the grudge was,
why he had written it - and my bloated stomach
and sick feeling vanished.

   [I've just realized the reader may find the
idea of feelings suddenly manifesting themselves
physically and just as suddenly being cleared
up at least as 'magical' as doing psychic readings. All I can say is, it's completely 'normal'
to me after spending years focussed on such
sensitivities. This suggests once again that
'magic' is simply any phenomenon we don't understand or aren't used to experiencing. For this
reason, I refuse to go in aeroplanes as no
matter how many I see flying overhead, as far
as I'm concerned that heavy metal can't get
up in the air, and it's the kind of 'magic'
I'm not prepared to trust.]

   Later in the week, I agreed to do a whole
evening of readings for the people who were putting me up during my stay in London. It was
a community of a dozen or more people. One
couple handed me a reading. It was one of the
most enjoyable I have ever done. My skin felt so
magnificently soft and sensitive, running with
life, open to everything. My body felt light and
springy; I just wanted to bounce up and down.
I noticed with delight some oranges in a bowl,
and spent the rest of the reading sucking on
one. Everything was a pleasure. I loved being
the centre of attention. "This is a very healthy
independent attractive human being," I said.
The couple were delighted. I was their six-

month-old baby, born under the sign of Leo.

More people arrived, including a musician friend of mine, Pete Cooper, a brilliant violinist. The readings were shuffled so that I never knew whose reading I was doing. In one of them, I kept hearing a buzzing, humming noise in my ears. I asked if the radiators were about to explode. I couldn't get away from the noise. But no-one else could hear it. When I had finished the reading and asked who it was, Pete said astonished: "It's me, and I've been hearing that sound all evening. I often hear sounds that other people don't. I think that's why I have to make music, to translate them into music. Else I'd go mad!"

A couple of evenings later, I was asked to do an encore, for yet another group of people in that community. The 'Poet Laureate' of Atlantis, our friend and annual visitor, Jeremy Ward, attended this group. After sitting through several readings, he said, "I'd like to do one now." He'd never done one before and was in company made up mainly of total strangers. Where was his hesitation, his nervousness, the reticence which I'd experienced helping my daughter through hundreds of readings and never presuming I could do them too?! None such shyness. Jeremy performed. Perfectly. He's now up to a hundred different psychic capers in London like he was born into it.

You can all do it. We know that for sure now. We never met anyone who couldn't. Sean, who won't normally speak, he did readings. Henry, a top computer businessman from England, he came for a one-week visit to Atlantis and was so amazed by our readings, he put them on tape. Then one evening before he was due to

leave, I said, "I'm going to give you a going-
away present. Sit in that chair." I put a piece
of paper in his hand. "Now just say whatever
comes into your head - or body." I had given
him the reading of the most extremely different
person from him I could think of, just to make
sure that if there was anything in it, he'd
feel it.

He felt it. Our smooth cool well-ordered
English businessman turned into a shivering
shaking wreck. I had given him the reading
of an extremely neurotic chaotic tense Irishman,
paranoid and crazy. Henry had a terrible time,
but he found out that he could do readings.

Steve came to Atlantis. Another smooth
cool Englishman. Never a ruffle, never a wrink-
le, never a quiver. Damnably annoying. Especially when all hell is let loose around him and
he still smiles benignly through the lot saying
he's 'not affected.' I got him to do readings.
He did them brilliantly. Damn him. Walked into
them like he'd been doing them all his life.
So I plotted. I put on the tape-recorder and
three times during his stay of four months,
I gave him himself to do a reading on. And
then afterwards I played him back the tapes.
Oh, I had such a delicious time, listening
to Mr. Cool himself say how 'this person' was
a violent maniac and that if he ever let himself
go, he'd be a danger to Atlantis. Steve said
he wouldn't like to be around if the fellow
came here. I don't know how I kept a straight
face. I was busting, dying to tell him he was
talking about himself. At the end of one reading
I asked him, "So if I wanted to deal with this
fellow therapeutically, get him to express
himself, drop his front and show who he really
is, what kind of advice could you give me?"

"Oh, get him to do all kinds of unusual things, get him to stand in the centre of the room where he can't hide.." "Like getting him to do readings for example?" I said, with a wicked twinkle in my eye. Steve squinted at me side- ways. "You bitch," he said.

Readings are fun. Readings are informative. Readings are therapeutic. Readings are fascina- ting. And readings are within the reach of everyone. One of our Atlantis sayings is: EVERY- ONE KNOWS EVERYTHING ALL OF THE TIME. It's true. But we narrow our consciousness down to a tiny sliver of reality in our daily lives. You only have to breathe deeply and decide to let a bit more in.

I wondered how I'd fare doing readings commercially - not for the sake of the money, but from the point of view of being able to couch my expression in terms that would be presentable to a complete stranger, a man in a suit or a lady with a handbag walking diffid- ently into Atlantis for the afternoon.

I found that I could. And I loved doing them, loved the challenge. I was really pleased to bridge the gap between our wild magical Atlantean happenings and the 'Outside World.' I found my way to talking about body energy and blocks and the need for personal growth and what path to take if one wanted to move forward, and inhibitions and pressures and deep-seated feelings, in a way that reached out simply to my visiting clients. I found it was quite instinctual to settle for whatever level was right and meaningful for each individ- ual stranger. And I recognized the special air about these occasional callers after having a reading done. It was the air I had about

me when I left the offices of clairvoyants
in London. An air of wonder and of opening
and of thoughtfulness; a new sense of self;
a feeling of fresh doors magically appearing and
a light shining through.

Doing readings made me a more tolerant
person - and an Aries is not generally noted for
her tolerance. They showed me that people really
are different, that there really are a million
different ways of seeing the world, and of
being and moving in it. I had never really
believed this before. I used to think other
people were just being silly! I had been awfully
restricted in my vision.

And other people's tolerance astounded
me too. I would have expected a blanket cynicism
or hostility from most people towards 'things
psychic.' But no. Practically every person
to whom the subject is mentioned expresses at
least an openness to being 'converted.' And
conversion is rather a simple affair once they
have a reading done.

*****

When I was sixteen, I went to the local
cinema with my boyfriend and saw a delightful
film called <u>Bell, Book and Candle</u>. It was a
witchy comedy. One scene always stuck in my
mind. In it, a beautiful young witch-woman was
in love with an ordinary mortal man. He was
trying to get away from her because her powers
scared him. He was raging at her and breaking
off from her. He stormed out of the shop they
were in where she was serving behind the counter. As he strode out, she just purringly looked
at him with her cat-like eyes. He swung in
high dudgeon through one of those circular-

door contraptions on to the street, glad to
be away from her. But then there is a kind
of 'ping' in the atmosphere, and lo and behold,
he finds himself, not on the street, but back
in the shop face-to-face with his woman. That
scene always appealed to me.

A few years ago, I was giving a therapy
session to Anne. She was angry and upset because
her fellow had left her and gone off back to
Dublin. I said, "Anne, I'm bored with just
ordinary therapy sessions. It's all very well
you crying and ranting and raging about him, but
how about actually <u>affecting</u> him?" Anne perked
up greatly at the idea, and said she'd like
him to be walking along Grafton Street and
for a great big black hole to open up in front
of him and swallow him up. We had great fun and
giggles and thought no more of it.

Many weeks later, the young man in question
was back with us. He had a story to tell. He
said that he'd been walking along Grafton Street
one day when he suddenly stopped stock still
trembling all over and feeling that he didn't
dare to take another step forward in case a
big black hole opened up in front of him and
swallowed him up....

Some time ago, my sister and I were sitting
by the fire in my room. We felt a bit flat.
"I'd like someone interesting to turn up," I
said. "OK," says sister Snowy. "Who shall we
have? What about Colm?"

I backed off. I didn't like meddling with
such things. I didn't know which I feared most
- that it would work, or that it wouldn't.
My sister meanwhile, ignoring my nonsense,
simply stared with supreme confidence into
the fire and very quietly willed Colm to return.

He had been away from us for many months, had
left under very hostile circumstances, and
we hadn't heard a word from him since.

Two hours later, when my room was once
again buzzing with life, my door was suddenly
flung open and in walked - yes - Colm. My sister
and I stared at one another and were too stunned
for a while even to welcome him.

The guy I live with now has left and returned so many times I've lost count. One Sunday
morning, a couple of days after one of his
leavings, I was on my way out to feed the chickens when the thought came to me of simply turning him round in his tracks and bringing him
back. It was a clear, pure moment. But then
I stopped the thought and said to myself, "No,
he must come back in his own time." But I was
too late, the thought was out.

Next day, in he walked. He hadn't even
made it this time back to Cork, his home town,
because as he was hitching out of Dublin on
the Sunday morning, he got a lift in a lorry,
the lorry-driver asked him some simple question
about where he was going and where he had come
from, and Fred suddenly didn't know why he
was going away, asked the man to stop, and
got out. He then crossed the road and hitched
back up to Atlantis. I asked him what time
his turn-about had occurred. Unfortunately
it tallied with my accidental little thought
as I tripped along to feed the chickens.

More recently, Fred was away for several
weeks. When he finally returned, he told us
how during his first week of work away from
us, he had sprained his wrist and been off
work for a while. "I guessed someone was praying

for me up there," he said drily. I swallowed.
One evening, just after he had left, my sister
and I had been feeling extremely sore at some
nasty tricks he had played on us and had planned
detail for detail a little accident for him
just to let him know that his dismissing
us didn't stop us existing. The specifics of
the accident didn't come off, but it seems
that the general intention did.

I believe they call this black magic.
It is also said that it backfires on the user.
This is not our experience. Maybe it's something
to do with the humour and sense of amusement
we always have when engaging in these matters,
and the fact that the objects of our attentions
are usually quite close to our hearts!

Several mornings before Fred's return to
me that time, I half woke up one night in my
cottage on the island, feeling his hand on
my neck. "Is that you, Fred?" I said, placing
my hand on his. It wasn't, but it turned out
that he was very close to me in thought at
that time.

A few mornings later, I woke suddenly
with a jolt and sat bolt upright in my bed.
I looked at the clock: 5 a.m. Whatever could
have made me wake like that? There were no
unusual noises on the island, just the animals
and the wind. I felt terrible. I had pictures
of Fred in my mind, and I didn't like him.
He was being cut-off and unfriendly. He had
been away five weeks.

Later that day, I got a phone-call from
my daughter on the mainland. "Fred's here,"
she announced. "He wasn't even going to call
in, but we found him in Glenties [about eighteen
miles away] and brought him home." I nearly

fainted. And then it turned out he had in fact been on the island that very morning extremely early, but had left again without attempting to see me.

Because of his very strong emotional bond with us and high degree of repressed energy, psychic experiences with Fred abound. While he was away that same time, my sister had a very strong psychic contact with him. Here is a letter she wrote to him telling him about it:

"Well, Fred, where were you last night? Prowling around my bedroom, waking me from my sleep, muttering my name!

At 3 a.m. last night, I was woken by my bedroom door seeming to softly open and the vibrations of Fred Moloney entering. I lay frozen with terror with my back to the room - not terrified of Fred, but of the powerful supernatural event that was taking place. Then I felt my name being spoken twice urgently in a deep rich Cork accent - Fred had returned to Atlantis and he needed my help. He spoke my name but didn't say anything else. He just stared vacantly out of the window, wanting everything, saying nothing.

After a while, I dared to move one finger to make sure I was awake. And then I dared to open my eyes and look straight ahead of me at the wall. I wanted to call out "Is anyone there?" but I was too terrified. Suddenly, there was a bright flash of light behind me.

I lay completely frozen, very aware that my spine was exposed and vulnerable towards the room and its occupant.

Then I felt 'Fred' enter my body through my spine. It was a soft feeling, quiet and gentle. And then I started thinking a lot about Atlantis. But I was thinking as if I was Fred!

I thought about the fact that the house is in Jenny's name and that because of this I/Fred didn't really take serious responsibility for anything material here and that I/Fred could not make a proper commitment to the place. I

started to worry a lot about what we'd planted in the gard-
en, what was growing and whether it would last the winter. I
worried about money - how much we had, how much we'd spent
and how much we could get. I particularly worried about
pregnancy and security for the child. I didn't like this
big house. I didn't like Burtonport. I didn't like the
main cottage on the island and all the visitors. I wanted a
new cottage that was mine and private and a private small
organized and controlled garden with plenty of carrots.

I was worried sick by all this, and felt like vomiting.
I was so anxious, I felt really isolated from everyone. The
anxiety made me feel that everyone else was stupid, had
no sense of reality and I could only trust myself.

Finally, I forced myself to turn on the light and
go downstairs and talk to Jenny and Ned. Ned searched the
house for Fred's body, but there was only his spirit present.

I was glad to return to myself and to be back in communication with everyone and to stop worrying about materialism, reality and security. Now that I've got out of that
dreadful state, I am freer to go and sow the carrots and
cut the peat.

Anxiety, Fred, is a frozen state in which you can
do nothing about the things you're worrying over.

Best wishes,
Love, Snowy."

*****

Some months prior to my recent pregnancy, I
had an idea for a reading that made me a bit
nervous. We'd dealt with death, and we'd dealt
with reincarnation, but what about a person
that does not yet exist?

Fred and I wanted to have a child together
and we were open all the time for this to happ-
en. Without telling her there was anything

unusual about the reading I was asking her
to do, I handed Becky a slip of paper on which I
had written, "Will you tell me and Fred about
our baby: Will we have one? When? What sex?
What will he or she be like as a person?"

I felt a bit guilty about giving this
reading to Becky, as I thought it might be
very confusing for her, or she might get nothing
at all and think there was something wrong
with her. But I answered myself, "Well, if
you don't leap, you don't get anywhere. Every
time we've taken a risk, we've opened up new
channels into the psychic."

I was sitting 'unconcernedly' crocheting.
Fred, who knew what was written on the paper,
was wandering round the room doing odd jobs
trying not to be too interested. Becky sat
very relaxed by my piano, one arm resting on
it. How on earth would she make sense of this
reading, I thought, even if she did pick up
sensations? I didn't have long to wait to find
out.

"I feel like taking in very deep breaths of
air," she said. "It's as if I haven't breathed
for a very long time. I feel that I have been
asleep for ages and ages and now someone is
nudging me from behind, saying, 'Wake up, come
on, it's time to wake up.' I'm not fighting
against it, but I'm a bit sleepy. I'll be ready
soon - I am definitely there you know," she
said suddenly, looking pointedly at me, so
that all the hairs went up on my spine. "But
I'm not in a hurry; I'm not about to leap.
I'm not here yet - I've just popped in for
five minutes now, and I'll see you again later."

That did it. I put down my crochet, gave
up trying to be cool, lay back on the bed and
heaved quietly. "Oh," Becky was saying, looking

at her hand resting on the piano lid, "I've
seen my hand before when it was really old,
when the skin was gnarled. Now I've got new
skin. I look young and fresh and soft. I feel
sensitive to everything. I can feel every little
ache in my body, and I like it, I love the
physical feeling of my body."

Then she stood up by the fireplace. She
looked in the mirror. "I am good-looking. But I
am not feminine. I am beautiful, but I am a
young man." [Well, she got this wrong - the
baby turned out to be a lusty, hardy little
Taurus girl!] "I am someone who doesn't like
any kind of brash noise. I love the sound of
this fire crackling and of the clock ticking,
but I hate machines and I wouldn't like fast
cars. I am a friendly person, very 'sorted
out' and confident. When I come here, I could
easily take over Atlantis. I would deal with
difficult visitors easily. As Becky, I have
no patience with them, but this person would
be able to look at any human being and take no
notice of their surface nonsense: they'd be
above that. They'd be able to be friendly because they would go right to the real person
underneath. This is someone really calm and
strong. And they would relate easily to you,
Jen, without any of the niggles and difficulties
that I, as Becky, have. They'd just respect
you and like you. I feel they have been your
son in a former life-time - they seem already
connected with you, and with me too. But you,
Fred, I feel this is a new connection for you.
You know, I have had a strong 'reincarnation'
feeling throughout this reading. I can't help
feeling that this is your baby, Jen, the baby
the two of you will have. He's older than you,
Fred, and wiser. You will learn from him; you

will learn from seeing him grow up without
being twisted. It's not that he won't need
you, he will; but he knows more than you."

The next day, still amazed by this reading,
we got my sister over from the island and gave
her the same reading to do, again not mentioning
that there was anything unusual about it. But
this time we switched on the tape-recorder
to catch word for word all that wisdom we were
sure would pour out. The occult, however, has
a mind of its own. Snowy surely did speak words
of wisdom, but they wouldn't reproduce too
well on paper being unaccompanied by the antics
she got up to: she spent the whole reading
playing with a box of 'toys' she found, having
a marvellous time, and causing the rest of
us to roll around in fits of hysteria as she
sat there in the centre of the room making
solemn pronouncements over the knick-knacks
she produced one by one from her box. She picked
out a penknife, pointed it at all of us and
said in a cowboy accent, echoing Becky the
day before: "OK you lot, I've come to take
over Atlantis." Later, finding a rusty old
key, she held it up and said in a deliberately
mysterious manner: "I hold the key to the future
- but the future is a secret. It's locked,
and I'm not going to tell you about it!"

*****

Those early days are over now, and although
we never become exactly blasé about the psychic,
it is true one acquires an air of amused relaxation about it.

My ten-year-old niece trotted into my
room dressed in high-heeled shoes, plastered
with make-up, and wearing a ghastly pink nylon

middle-aged woman's dress, her hair done up in
a gruesome hat, a white plastic handbag on her
arm. "Oh! She looks exactly like your mother!"
I said to the Irishman in the room with me.
He stared at me speechless, then said faintly,
"How do you know?" I had never met his mother.

But a few months later, this same Irishman
was doing excellent readings himself, so that
when a reading was being done of his elder
brother, whom I had also never met, and I started getting enthusiastic saying, "Gosh, Ned
is starting to look exactly like him," he simply
eyed me for a second, sighed, but didn't bother
to comment.

As I say, it gets just like porridge for
breakfast after a while - nourishing, and you're
always ready for more the next morning; but
it hardly evokes astonishment to note that
the porridge exists.

*****

PART TWO

In Which
Snowy tells her story
and THE READINGS are presented
interspersed with personal accounts of psychic
experiences from other friends and members of
Atlantis Commune

SNOWY'S STORY

At school, I was known as 'the girl who doesn't believe in God,' and treated with mixed horror and respect as a result. I wasn't interested in the wishy-washy nonsense of religion, nor in the abstractions of mathematics or physics. History was a bore because I couldn't touch it. I fell asleep in Latin and French lessons. I always hated 'abstract' art and felt angry with it as though the artist was trying to mystify me (which I am now sure he is!). I remember feeling particularly annoyed when I discovered some of Picasso's early work and wondered why, if he could draw so well, he chose to paint such disconnected rubbish. As a child, I had been given earthy explanations for everything, so there wasn't very much in my early years to indicate that I would become a psychic.

In my adult life, when through pain and difficulties in my marriages I sought help in therapy, I came in touch with many people on the fringe of normal Western materialism, I rebelled against them too. The therapy scene was scattered with various odd bods in long flowing Jesus-like robes with wafting hair and far-away spiritual smiles, muttering about third eyes and etheric bodies, carrying their I Ching like a bible and getting into 'good spaces' by 'going with the flow man.' As far as I was concerned, all I needed was to get all the pain and tension out of my physical body and use the two good eyes I had to see what was going on around me.

I was interested in guts not gurus and spent all my time getting in touch with my

body and feelings and did not try to transcend
them. The last place I expected my very gutsy
exploration to lead me was any spiritual or
psychic realm. I was more than content with the
practical magic of transforming my tension and
unhappiness into looseness and clarity through
the medium of crying, screaming, talking, and
physical movement. I was busy exploring all the
dark mysterious corners of my relationships
and feelings and found all the Eastern mysticism
that I kept coming into contact with irrelevant
and boring. I discovered the power of words
alright through Gestalt and encounter work,
but my words were very earthy: "I hate you"
and "I'm angry," and I never found any need
for muttering any mantras in foreign languages.

Then came a turning point. Through therapy
groups, I became involved emotionally with
a man who was not only attending encounter
groups but was also going to development classes
as a medium. At first I dismissed this as a bit
weird, until one night he persuaded me to go
along to the Spiritualist Association for a
'sitting.' There was a large group of people
awaiting the arrival of the 'medium' and I
sat there feeling very separate and superior.
When the woman walked in, I somehow 'knew'
that she was going to speak to me first. And
she did. She picked me out, hidden towards
the back of the room, and described in detail to
me my mother's appearance and her recent death.
She said that my mother knew I was going through
emotional turmoil and that she came to offer me
a flower and her sympathy. I thought: "How
bloody typical. She can't even leave me alone
when she's dead and of course she would try the
soft soap approach." I was so incensed about my

mother's interference that I didn't stop at
the time to ponder how exactly this woman who
had never set eyes on me before could know
so much about me.

Well after that, a few strange things did
happen to me alright. I'd be walking through
Holland Park looking at the flowers and trees
when I'd have an overwhelming sensation of
my mother's presence, just behind my left shoulder. [In psychotherapeutic work, it is common
to associate the left side with 'mother,' the
right-hand side with 'father'] I could almost
feel her and heard her voice in some inner
ear, comforting me and apologizing to me. The
last thing on earth I wanted was her consolation
- I'd had an overdose when she was alive -
so I certainly was not looking for her help,
but I had to admit that something out of the
ordinary was happening to me. At this time, I
was quite used to speaking to absent or dead
people in therapy groups; we all encouraged
each other to energetically clear out 'unfinished business' with parents, past lovers, family
members, teachers and bosses. There was nothing
crazy about talking to a cushion as if it were
your father or mother because such activity
would take place in full understanding and
communication with other group members, and
it had a remarkable effect. Old, stuck, dead
relationships which I previously thought had
to be buried and forgotten could be revived,
developed and cleared. I had discovered that
much of my bitterness towards my (now dead)
father, for example, had been melted by this
method and I began to feel some acceptance
and understanding to replace the blame. So
it was not too much of a leap for me to imagine

that my mother, wherever she was now, should
be attempting much the same thing, and the
strange energy that I experienced might be
times when she was focussing on unresolved
feelings towards me.

So I took this in my stride and absorbed it
into the terms of reference that I could accept.
But it certainly was not enough to make me become a spiritualist or want to become a medium
or get involved in all the weird astral travelling and rituals that my boyfriend was doing.

Then some time later, this same boyfriend
took me along to another medium's 'sitting.'
By this time, I was spoilt and expected to
be the first person picked out and was quite
surprised to be left to the end, when the medium
pointed to me and said she'd like to talk to me
privately. She then told me that she had a
message from my 'son in spirit.' Well, I had
two very earth-bound daughters, but as far
as sons went... I'd obviously caught her out
there. Then she reminded me - she reminded
me - that several years previously I had had
an abortion. It had been a very straightforward
affair with no doubt or guilt on my part. I am
a very practical person and I felt that it
would be criminal for me to have a very much un-
wanted baby at that time. However, the medium
surprised me by informing me that I was feeling
guilty on some level and that 'my son' was
picking this up and just wanted to let me know
that it was fine with him and he was growing up
well in spirit. This medium was completely
un-witchy and in fact looked like somebody's
comfortable Auntie Maud giving me motherly
advice on bringing up my children.

Well, that set me thinking quite a bit
about death. I had always accepted my parents'

teaching that you died and were buried and
the worms ate you and the plants fed off you and
the animals ate the plants and so life went
on. After all, that's what happened on my compost heap and I supposed that all the religious
theories about an after-life were developed
to help people deal with their fear of death.
"Religion is the opium of the people" I had
been taught, and quite obviously right too.
But now I was being told by complete strangers
who had absolutely nothing to gain from the
telling (the sittings were free) that two people
very directly connected with my body, who were
dead and should rightfully have been feeding
the daisies and minding their own business,
were prying into my deepest consciousness and
having thoughts and feelings about me. And
as if that weren't bad enough, they were actually having the cheek to set about communicating
their ideas to me. So what was this thing called
'death'? It suddenly seemed not to be such
a final sort of event at all.

    I once read an article in the London weekly
magazine 'Time Out' on a mortuary worker in
a big London hospital. He had worked with dead
bodies for many years and had some strange
stories to recount. But the thing that struck me
most forcibly was that through his direct and
everyday experience of death, he had a completely down-to-earth attitude towards it. He spoke
of people who after 'choosing to die' had 'changed their minds' and of them talking about
what they had experienced in their brief inter-
ludes in another world. Their stories were
remarkably similar. They experienced lifting out
of their bodies, floating away and meeting
other spirits and discussing the lessons they
had learnt or failed to learn in their life just

past and deciding when and how they should
return to carry on the lessons. Those who only
'died' briefly had seen that they still had much
work and learning to do in their recently abandoned body and so they 'jumped back in' quickly
to carry on with the good work. This mortuary
attendant took all this in his stride and said
that he had absolutely no fear of his own death,
except for any physical discomfort associated
with it, because he more or less knew what he
was in for. So much for the worms and daisies
theory.

Meanwhile, back at the therapy centre that
I was now running, I was learning massage as a
gentle and dynamic art form for releasing tension and helping people to open up old blocks,
get in touch with stuck areas of their being and
heal themselves. I loved massage because I
could use my hands to work directly with the
energy of another person in a very tangible
way to help them release and transform themselves. It was magic alright to see someone come in
stiff and tense and cut-off and go out an hour
later soft and open and alive, but this was
a sort I could handle.

I did, however, see something strange in a
massage class one day. I saw an experienced
masseur get her patient to lie down with closed
eyes while she massaged what she called the
'etheric body' which she claimed lay outside the
physical body. She never touched the actual skin
or clothing of her patient at all and yet she
put as much energy and focussed attention into
massaging the air above the body as if she was
doing an ordinary massage. I was a bit impatient
with this display of weirdness, but had to
notice that when it was over, the patient got up
looking as soft and relaxed as she would have

done after a physical massage. So once again the
boundaries of my understanding of the world were
being stretched. Death wasn't final and bodies
didn't end where they appeared to...

At this time I also came into contact with
psychedelic drugs. I never had any patience with
the spaced-out dope-smoking hippies who littered
the alternative scene and I saw drugs used
primarily as a means of avoiding awareness of
reality by entering a chemically induced fairy-
land where communication with real human beings
didn't take place. There was nothing that irritated me more than going into a house full
of dopey people dreaming off in their complacent
little bubbles, blissfully unaware of their
mucky kitchens, uncleaned toilets and carpets
littered with dog-ends and LP jackets – it
was invariably Dylan droning away in the background.

My contact with drugs took a positive turn
when I met a few people who had used acid as a
means of furthering their self-awareness and
breaking through certain difficult blocks in
themselves. As an aid to self-discovery, I
took several acid trips at well-spaced intervals
and experienced a new kind of opening in myself.
I found that I had 'knowledge' in me that didn't
come through the usual channels of thought,
talk, experience and understanding. For example,
I could look at a person while on acid and
see their essential nature immediately and if
I spoke out what I saw, that person would crack
up with relief at the accuracy of my seeing. I
also 'saw' myself with an astounding clarity
that was not comfortable but I had to admit it
was accurate and gave me in a few moments the
sort of insights that I often struggled for
hours in a therapy session to achieve. I too ex-

perienced the 'mind expansion' described by
the hippie drug-takers, but as I was firmly
rooted in the earth and my gut-level feelings, I
never saw any strange creatures or had bad
trips - I saw only my own personal devils and
felt the difficulty of my chosen journey with
magical clarity and power alright, but I experienced nothing that refused to fit in with my
already expanding consciousness of the world.

       And then I came to Atlantis where I've made
my permanent home amongst people dedicated
to an intense and integrated life of self-
exploration and growth. In my first week there,
I noticed how tools such as the I Ching, the
Tarot, palmistry and astrology were treated with
a practical humour, fun and excitement that
I'd never experienced before. I'd been used
to meeting people who when they used these
aids put on a special voice and atmosphere.
Precious attitudes, silk handkerchiefs, sitting
cross-legged facing North (or is it East?),
candlelight, hushed serious voices, and confusing generalized statements issued like readings
.from the Bible in school assembly, were the
norm amongst all the people I'd previously
known with a spiritual bent. But in Atlantis, a
Tarot reading would be an occasion for great
excitement and energy where no-one pretended
to know anything about what the cards were
meant to mean. The person having the reading
done would be invited first to interpret what
they thought the cards meant in their life:
"Hey, look, that man looks like your boyfriend
and that queeny character looks like you,"
would be the sort of remark. If a card seemed
irrelevant or mysterious, no-one would invent
meaningless mumbo-jumbo to explain it away.
Just a simple, "I don't understand that one,

maybe it will come clear later," and then on
to the next, more clear and interesting card.
The same attitude prevailed in relation to
astrology, the I Ching and palmistry: a healthy
energy, full of scepticism and fun, each person
exposing their own growth points, hopes, fears,
weaknesses and strengths to the whole group,
using the artistic channels of these psychic
tools. As often as not, a Tarot reading would
lead to someone having a therapy session about
some conflict which had been highlighted by
their interpretation of the cards and, equally
likely, that therapy session would be followed
by some practical measure to immediately remedy
the problem. It was not unusual for someone at
the end of an afternoon of happenings of this
sort to run off and pack a rucksack and hitch-
hike off in great spirits on a mission to see
someone in their family or an absent lover
with whom they wanted to resolve unfinished
business. So the magic of Atlantis had a totally
practical application and was never used in an
alienated way.

     So it happened that when Becky started
doing psychic readings, we immediately harnessed
her undoubted power for practical use. Through
psychometry, Becky gave us a lot of very interesting information about our lovers, friends,
and enemies. I can still remember looking at
Becky closely across the dinner table one night
after she'd been doing a series of particularly
accurate psychic readings and saying to her:
"What does it feel like to be psychic?" I think
I imagined she must be about to grow another
head. "Nothing different," she laughed as she
ate her dinner. But I couldn't really believe it
so of course very soon I had to have a go myself.

At first it was just a huge joke to me, going outside the room and waiting in the dark corridor excitedly to be called in and handed a sealed blank envelope. It was just like a children's party game. I've always been a bit of a clown and I was quite happy to dive into the spirit of the thing and start to 'do a reading.' What a joke. As far as I was concerned I was just saying anything that popped into my head and showing off a bit and acting the extrovert. Until everyone told me I was behaving exactly like Becky, speech, mannerisms, the lot, and it was her name on the paper. "Coincidence," I thought. Then I did other readings, lots and lots of them in fact, because they were fun and gave me a good excuse to take the stage and express myself. And then I could not help noticing that each reading had a very different 'feel' and that even if I was in a good mood to start with, some readings would bring me down, or maybe the next one would put me in a philosophical frame of mind, a further one would bring out my playfulness and yet another would make me feel upset and like crying. Some readings would be very easy to do because the sensations and impressions I got would be very definite and physical and could not be mistaken; other times I would struggle to say anything because I felt nothing in particular, or nothing very different from how I normally felt. I liked the ones best that affected my body because I knew how to express that successfully.

I did literally hundreds of readings, mostly in Atlantis at first, but later as my confidence grew I did them in other people's houses if I happened to be staying there; and I found that doing readings amongst strangers

was often even more exciting. Complete strangers
would give me pieces of paper with the names
of friends written on them and I would sometimes
be kept up late into the night doing readings.
I developed a skill which came from all the
therapy I'd done on myself, of being able to
offer the person I was doing the reading on
advice as to how to improve their life. I always
did this directly from my body feelings because
that was what I trusted.

To this day, I have no idea what this
strange force called psychometry is. Some people
say it's 'telepathy', as if that makes it any
less powerful or magical, hoping to explain
away the strong sensations by saying they 'just
come from another person's mind.' All I knew
for sure was that I enjoyed doing readings,
that they worked, and that the people I did
them for enjoyed them.

Sometimes I did readings at the psychic
fairs and exhibitions that suddenly proliferated
in England, but I hated the lack of depth and
radical help I felt able to give in such a
restricted environment. Also I found it very
embarrassing to call this type of public work
'psychometry' because with the person I was
'reading' sitting opposite me, any piece of
paper or necklace to hold was a total irrelevan-
cy. I only needed to glance briefly into a
person's face to read enough to keep me talking
for far longer than they would probably wish
to listen. Every line tells a story, the colour,
texture, and energy coming off a person's face
gives everything away. Not that that makes
it any less valid, but it made me uneasy to
have this sort of thing classed as magic –
it would be equivalent to praising a doctor
for his magical powers in diagnosing a case of

measles.

I have never developed the art of predicting the future for a person in a reading. I
can usually say what the likely outcome will be
if a person continues the way they are going,
because I can feel in my body where tension
leads. But I wouldn't know which bit of my
body to refer to for information concerning
what someone will be doing next Thursday.

I don't care for the repetitive little
flutters of proof that psychic energy exists
- it exists as obviously as sunlight (and can
equally easily be blotted out by clouds of
confusion and unresolved feelings). I simply
love the creativity and artistry of readings
and I value the way in which they deepen my
understanding of what it feels like to be someone else and thus extend my whole philosophy
of life.

That may sound a bit grandiose, so let
me explain. There are many exponents of Eastern
philosophies who will state mysteriously that
we are 'all One.' I have often found that these
people who would have you sink your ego into the
cosmic pool are some of the most egocentric
aggressive bastards around, with no facility
for even listening to and receiving another
person's words. However, through doing the
sort of ego-building work that therapy entails,
you can gain a large degree of self-confidence
and power which makes it relatively easy to
let other people in. I am sure this is one
of the reasons why I can do psychic readings
so easily: it is not at all threatening to
be temporarily overwhelmed by another person's
energy if you are fairly secure about who you
are and know that you can return to yourself
at the end of a reading. Thus, over the years,

I have been able to enter into the consciousness
of hundreds of people in depth and have found
that we truly are 'all one.'

People are very different from one another
on the surface of course. Some people have
most of their energy in their brains and think
and work out their reactions to the world.
Others feel everything at gut level. A simple
representation of a person in a reading is
not really satisfactory: after all, photography
does the job well enough. That's why when I
have scanned and represented the top level
of a person's behaviour and obvious mannerisms,
I always change gear and drop to a deeper level
of their consciousness. The results can often
be surprising.

I remember once doing a reading of a woman
I had hated for years. I was in a large group
and had no idea whose reading I was doing until
afterwards. I felt so much pain and struggle in
this person and cried some of her tears for
her; and I spent an extra-long time giving
advice. As a result, I came to have sympathy for
someone I had previously rejected as arrogant
and aggressive. Similarly, a person who is
apparently bright and energetic may well be
concealing the 'nasties' underneath. In fact,
this syndrome is so common that we have nick-
named it 'The Opposites Theory of the Universe'
at Atlantis - that is, the second layer of
a person's character is usually the complete
opposite of what they project on the surface.

So, through doing readings on such dispar-
ate subjects as an unborn baby, a dead man,
a murdered child, a pop-star and a sheepdog,
I have been able to experience consciousness
from practically every vantage point on earth.
But how does it work? If I had to give an ex-

planation, I'd say that everything in the world
gives off energy and that that energy can be
received and interpreted if your instruments
are finely tuned enough. I believe it is natural
to have opened up psychic abilities as a direct
result of doing years of deep therapy. In the
clearing process of emotional spring-cleaning,
I likewise have more energy for gardening,
helping my friends, writing, playing and learning new skills. Anyone who fails to develop
their psychic powers simply needs their energy
for sorting out much more basic problems. If
a person in emotional turmoil tries to do psychic work, it's as silly as trying to paint beautifully the walls of a crumbling house.

During the past few years, since we began
tuning in to psychic matters, we have had to
notice all kinds of happenings. One of the
most obvious is what we call 'materialization.'
This has become a source of amusement tinged
with awe in Atlantis. We play with the phenomenon by saying such things as: "OK, today we
need such-and-such, please Cosmos, would you
send it?" We always deliver these 'prayers'
in the form of a joke, but the number of times
they are answered isn't funny. From plasterers
arriving just when we need plastering done,
to a piece of plywood drifting past our boat
of the very size, shape and quality we just
mentioned we needed to make a table, to finding
just the right amount of money in an odd place
for some important purchase - there are so
many examples over the years that it has become
a routine matter requiring the development
of all sorts of expressions such as 'It's meant'
to deal with the strange feeling of being 'help-

ed' in our work by some outside force.

Telepathic communication amongst ourselves in the commune is proving very useful where there is no telephone linkage! One day last spring, Becky went to the mainland for some shopping, leaving me on the island preparing the garden. While she was away I thought to myself: "Damn, I forgot to ask Becky to get seed potatoes." I carried on gardening and later had the same thought again. Then, even later that morning, I berated myself once again for my forgetfulness.

When Becky returned from the mainland, she had with her not one, but <u>three</u> sacks of seed potatoes. "I hope it's OK," she said slightly embarrassed, "but when I was in the Cope, I just got the idea that you might want some; and then later a man was selling them off a lorry up the road and I thought you might need more. And then when I was in Dungloe, I thought again that we hadn't got enough, so I bought another sack."

Three thoughts from me, three ideas in Becky, three bags full...

But one of the most extraordinary experiences for me personally was what I have termed my 'psychic abortion.' I still think this is completely way-out, and wouldn't blame anyone for disbelieving it. I would disregard it myself if it had not happened to my own body.

Last year, I became pregnant, and after a long and intense series of discussions and sessions with other commune members, I decided that I really wanted to use my energy for things other than babies at this point in my life. So I went to London to one of the abortion clinics. But the evening before going there,

I spent with a friend of mine who is very interested in practical magic. "Jeremy," I said
to him, "I really hate the idea of going into
that anti-septic clinic full of strangers in
white coats - you wouldn't like to try and
'magic' me unpregnant, would you?" "Why not?"
said Jeremy, who always did fancy himself as a
bit of a wizard.

Then followed a really beautiful evening
in which he got me to relax completely while he
took me through a 'guided fantasy,' that is,
he would say things like: "Imagine yourself in
a place where you feel absolutely at home,"
and I would respond by quietly imagining to
myself a cushioned place with classical music
wafting through the trees, a strong fatherly
man sitting behind me, bowls of fruit and incense burning. Then he asked me to imagine in
detail exactly whatever I wanted to happen.
I pictured myself having a miscarriage with
lots of blood coming out of me. Afterwards,
I was quite disappointed to return from the
wonderful state of peace and rich imaginings and
to simply go downstairs and make us a cup of
tea.

Next morning I was still pregnant, so
I went to the clinic - where the doctor who examined me declared that I was not pregnant. This
did not surprise me unduly as I had been repeatedly told during my previous two pregnancies
that I was not pregnant and had nonetheless produced two very alive babies. I knew this time
that I was three months pregnant because everything in my body told me that.

I went out into the noisy London streets
feeling confused. I felt aimless and missed my
garden, work and friends back home. Without very
much idea of what would happen, I determined to

leave London immediately and hitch-hike back
to Donegal. Once home, I lay down with my boyfriend, relieved to be back in our emotionally
warm environment after the contrast of London
tubes and buses.

I then immediately started to have a very
violent and painful miscarriage. I bled extremely heavily, losing huge clots, and experienced
severe cramps and rhythmic contractions similar
to those of child-labour. This lasted about
twenty-four hours altogether and I was extremely
grateful to be at home with support and famili-
arity around me.

Looking back on the whole event, I explained it to myself that somehow my work with Jeremy
had immediately 'materialized' so that the
doctor sent me home, but that I waited for
the actual physical symptoms to occur until I
was in a better environment! Maybe there was
some kind of time warp or maybe pregnancy isn't
just a physical phenomenon to be measured by
science.

As if all this wasn't enough for one life-
time, my sister handed me Edith Fiore's fascinating book You Have Been Here Before, all
about reincarnation memories of her psychothera-
py patients in New York. I read it in one sitting and identified with her attitude that she
didn't really believe in or understand something
that in fact she was working with every day.
And then my friend Ken started to irritate me
by complaining that he never slept at night and
so was bad-tempered and tired all day when we
worked on our boat together. I wanted him to be
in good form, so I said, "Ken, Edith Fiore says
she deals very successfully with insomnia by
using reincarnation therapy. Do you want to
have a go?"

So Ken lay down and tried to relax (almost impossible for him) while I sat with Edith's book open before me, repeating phrases she uses in order to take Ken deep into his subconscious. Eventually, I got him to start relating a story of his past life and death. He told me that he was a gold prospector, a bachelor working on his own for himself. He had heard of a lucky strike several days' ride away from the small North American town where he lived. He set out alone on horseback, not wanting a companion because then he would have to 'share his spoils.' After a few days' ride, he fell from his horse and injured his leg so that he could not walk. The horse bolted off leaving him exposed in the sun. He soon ran out of the food and water he had carried and managed with difficulty to crawl to a nearby stream to drink. But his leg worsened, he was sick with hunger and heat, no-one passed by this lonely road. He felt himself dying but each time he relaxed into death, he thought to himself, "I'm not ready to die yet," and pulled himself back to consciousness by force of will. This happened repeatedly over a period of a few days: Death coming to release him from suffering and Ken resisting, feeling unprepared. "Why, I haven't even had a woman yet," he said at one point. "I've never really enjoyed myself or lived at all. Surely I can't die yet."

But he did die. He felt himself float upwards and look down at the thin bedraggled body sprawled beside the stream.

Ken did not feel at all flattered by this 'past life' of his. He was extremely difficult to work with, and I had to really push him to come out with any information at all. He delivered his story with great reluctance as it

didn't fit any of his preconceived images of
himself: he wanted something more glamorous.
"I thought at least I'd be Julius Caesar," he
complained. But for me, who knew him well, I
could see that his present life followed on as
a natural growth from the past life story he
had recounted. Every detail matched exactly his
present-day problems. Ken is a person who cannot
give in; he doesn't have a woman or any pleasure
at all it seems; he is a loner, a hard Scotsman
in this life, and he is totally obsessed with
food, which makes him a very good cook. In
Atlantis, he is having to learn the value of
other people's help, to share and be open,
to relax and have fun, to build nourishing
relationships and become more easy-going about
his material possessions.

If this past-life regression was 'just
fantasy,' it certainly wasn't a fantasy Ken
approved of. Where did it come from?

All I know is, boundaries seem to be breaking down. A new area of mist opens up between
black and white, between 'death' and life.
New possibilities appear. Old definitions re-
cede. A new dimension presents itself. There are
more things in heaven and earth that were dreamt
of in my philosophy...

"Nonsense," says rational atheist material-
ist. "Stuff and nonsense. Delusions, hysteria,
wishful thinking. Vain imaginings. There's
a reasonable explanation for everything. You're
making it up. Exaggerating."

"Perhaps," says Surprised Newcomer to the
psychic. "Perhaps it's all a dream and I'll wake
up in a stainless steel world of computers,
motorways and frozen foods.

"But somehow I hope not..."

*****

CHAPTER EIGHT: READINGS ON MARGARET THATCHER,
   IAN PAISLEY, RONALD REAGAN, JOHN LENNON,
                and JIM JONES

   In the second part of this book, we present
for your amusement, amazement, disgust or dis-
approval some of the readings on subjects of
wide interest which we have taped over the
past few years.
   At first I typed these readings up religiously, word for word, hiccup for hiccup. But
this didn't work as reading material - especially not Becky's, as she goes in for masses of
repetition to carry her from one sensation
to the next, and noises and faces are <u>per se</u>
non-reproduceable on paper. So most, though
not all, of the readings in this book are short-
ened, some radically. What I have never done,
though, is <u>add</u> anything. Everything you will
read is what came out of the mouths of people
who had nothing to go by but an unseen name or
series of questions written on a folded piece
of paper.
   Interspersed between the groups of readings
are short accounts by other people in the commune, or associated with us, of how the psychic
phenomena they witnessed affected them. My
hope is that this will have a grounding effect.
I know that throughout the making of this book,
I have often feared my head would fly right
away with all this airy stuff, or at very least
that old friends would look at me after reading
it and say, "Oh, Jen, whatever happened to
you, where did you go wrong?" It is comforting
to refer now and again to other flesh-and-blood
humans and check out, "This <u>is</u> happening, isn't
it?"

If you want factual, technical information
on the subjects chosen for investigation here,
then the place to look it up is in a biography,
or a history or geography book. Our readings
are always done from a 'characterological',
feeling point of view - even when the 'character' is Stonehenge or the Moon. That's our orien-
tation, it's what comes naturally to us, and
of course we find it valuable or we wouldn't
be doing it. Thus, if you don't like Margaret
Thatcher's politics - I certainly don't like
the nuclear weapons bit - and want your prejudices confirmed by the reading on her, you'll
be disappointed. Readings pick up the 'human
being' in a person, the subjective core. It
took me some time to accept that one, especially
when I really wanted to hate someone.

Doing readings on famous people isn't
something we've indulged in much, mainly because
it's the people close to us that are interesting
but also because of the frustration of not
knowing whether the intimate psychological
details of the Big Names are right. Nevertheless
here in this chapter are readings on five famous
people, three alive, two dead at time of writing
for your interest and assessment.

*****

MARGARET THATCHER: A Reading by Jenny

Right. Well, whoever I am, I have a great need to
be understood and for things to be clear and for everyone to
know what is going on, and to explain myself. I haven't any
very strong feelings in this reading. I seem to have the
kind of consciousness that deals with generalities and
wants to make connections and put things together and tie
them up. My attention is unfocussed, generalized, in-the-
head, scanning. I notice that I am not looking at anyone
in particular. I am noticing my stiff neck. Let me see,
what am I picking up about my posture? I'm either male
or yangy - yang energy.

I want something to get my teeth into. I am sort of
striding around: my spine is very straight. I'm posturing
- my body seems to fall naturally into poses and I'm very
relaxed in it.[At this point in the reading, the baby puts
her hands in some dirt and I rush off, get a dustpan and
brush, and busily sweep it up, singing a marching, galloping
tune as I go.] There's a lot of energy in this reading.
It's generally out-going athletic, busy - I feel very fit.
And I feel like a man, or like a man must feel - really
strong, capable of anything. I am the sort of person who
feels very strong about doing external things that I can
have an effect on. Definitely not inward-centred.

I feel good. The more you gave me to do, the better I'd
like it. Tasks. I could do a lot. I am underused at this
moment. But I don't feel confident about the 'Moon side'
of life, about darker things, soft things. I don't feel
confident about intuition. I feel confident that I can
clear up, clean up, fix up, do up, shove things around,
but I would be completely out of my depth if I had to do
a reading for example!! As soon as I focus on the inner
part of me, I feel quite awkward.

If I allowed myself to, I would actually whisper a few
little questions and ask for a bit of help; I'd say "Is this
right?" or "Am I alright?" What I really need is reassurance,
help, guidance, leadership, direction, but I very much

doubt if I'm ever going to show that. I'm also quite worried as soon as I get still or quieten down, about being boring - whereas I was completely at ease in that whole business of cleaning up the fireplace there. In fact, I'd like the chimney to go on fire, so that I could go up and pour water down it.

If this is a man, I really understand how men feel, that they want external things to apply themselves to and change and have effect upon because they don't feel confident in the interior regions. (I'm going to feel an idiot if this turns out to be Marilyn Monroe.)

Snowy, will you point me in directions that will bring more out of me?

Snowy: Yes. What sort of parent would you be?

Jenny: Efficient, energetic. A child would get a lot from me because I would push the swing up higher than most grownups would dare to. I would be kind of sporty. I'm a mixture of physical confidence and emotional jitteriness. I would provide an energy source for a child, a fount of energy; but I wouldn't be ever so sensitive to the subtleties of its feelings. Businesslike, goodnatured. I wouldn't be tentative. I'd be a bit like me (Jenny) only more so.

Pete: What is it you want out of life?

Jenny: I'd like a physical task to use up all of me and to stretch me. And I'd like to get help, in a very simple way, nothing deep, simple guidance as to how to feel more sure of this bit of me inside here. I am someone who understands and likes myself and that will probably mean I'll go quite far because I'll choose people who are on my side; I wouldn't be into self-flagellation at all. I'd probably keep to a good course. (I start speaking in a posh British accent.) Yes, I'd steer a clear course and navigate well in my life. And if someone was guiding me right, I'd be very flexible about altering course. I'm open to suggestion. If someone said to me, "The answer to your problems is down behind that typewriter over there," I'd have a look (I bend over and peer behind it!) I have certain prejudices against veering off my own course, you understand, but

I'd have a look just for the sake of being open.

Snowy: What age are you?

Jenny: In development, I would say latter thirties, that is, with a lot of youthful vigour left, with a lot of development still to do, with a fair amount of experience behind me, but not yet the worldly wisdom that comes at a more mature age. I am someone who has developed in my life: I can feel this because I've changed since the beginning of the reading. I've become more open and more friendly and more human and I have more richness and colour in my life; I feel closer to everyone through having laughed with you all and through having had to expose myself a bit.

Snowy: What nationality are you?

Jenny: I feel tall and slim and lithe and educated. I would say Northern European. (I start posturing, stretching my spine and standing tall and strong.) I have a really good body feeling, not sensuous, but more the Olympic Games sort of health.

Pete: I want you to look at each person in the room and say what you think about them.

Jenny: Well, I'd get a bit stroppy with you for starters. I'd stand up to you. My little bit of lack of confidence makes me proud in a good way. If you overstepped my boundaries, I'd start getting at you. You are looking at me and annoying me. I have the feeling you want something and you're getting quite nasty about it and therefore I will not do anything for you!

Snowy: What are your politics?

Jenny: I feel middle-class and humanitarian, but not in a wishy-washy way. I would have policies which took account of individuals and cared about them. For instance, I could be right-wing, but it would be the sort of right-wing that would be old-fashioned conservative that really minds about the rights and creativity of the individual, that kind of thing. (The audience is smiling, as if to end the reading) Hang on, don't tell me who I am, I want to find out for myself. Will you set me some task, Snowy?

Snowy: Let's see. How would you go about improving this room?

Jenny: Right. Well, that's very easy. Clear that shelf of all those books, get a wet duster, clean that dirt off. Consult the owner of the books as to what he wants with them anyway. Once this is ascertained, have respect for his wishes, as it is his place, and ask him whether he could not give some rough categorization (speaking very pedantically now) for the different sorts of books so that I could put them in rows. Would he like them alphabetically, according to subject, in batches of red and green books, paperbacks and hardbacks? Generally, we'd get this sorted out in no time at all. What else? Right, I'd put that table straight there, get rid of that bit of frippery there, I don't approve of it. I'm afraid this chair has seen better days and needs something doing to it. I would generally push the walls back quite a bit, and the ceiling upwards, and quite honestly, I'd like a big, much more ornate fireplace with a nice big log fire in it. I'm afraid it's all rather petty bourgeois in here, not grand enough altogether. I'd like large windows, open curtains, let the starlight and the frost in...

(The audience, amused, indicate they've got what they want out of the reading)

Oh well, what do I want? What I want is to be right. Let's see - am I a man?

Pete: No.

Jenny: I'm not a man? Oh, then I'm a Margarety Thatchery sort of a woman.

Snowy: Yes, almost sort of exactly precisely a Margaret Thatcher sort of woman..!

*****

THE REV. IAN PAISLEY - A Reading by Becky (who'd never
heard of him even when she was subsequently given the name!)

The first feeling I had as I walked in and picked
this up is tht I am quite bright and breezy, and very organized - a feeling of planning everything, organizing the
work. I'm into keeping everything in order and this includes
every aspect of my life, my personal cleanliness, my clothes
and fitness, the running of the house, everything.

I've got things so well tied-up that I'm thinking
"What next? Where's the excitement?" A feeling of wanting
more involvement. There isn't any real upheaval going on
at the moment [end of November 1980]; the work's getting
on well, everything is moving along, but I'm slightly agitated and frustrated. I'm quite impatient, a feeling of "I
just want it to happen."

Jenny: Could you put yourself mentally into a situation of
more challenge and see how you would react?

Becky: Well, I don't think, "Oh, we've got to be careful."
I feel like charging along. I feel very English: "Right-
o, chaps, come on then, all get your boots on, off we go! I
hope you've all got your sandwiches packed. Off we go!
Ten press-ups every morning. I hope you all realize this
is going to go on for a few years!"

I'm the sort of person who doesn't like being told what
to do. I know what I want to do with my life. I've done an
awful lot and I know about an awful lot of things. And
it's ever so frustrating when someone tells you not to
do something. Very frustrating. I am completely immersed in
my present situation and I'm not the sort of person who can
detach myself and think about something else.

My body is really upright and my shoulders are back. I
stand to my full height. I feel as if I've been in the
army. (She starts acting like a soldier.)

Jenny: Face yourself mentally with stress, problems, crisis
and see how you react. Represent it physically: move up to
that big cushion over there so that you can't go any further.
(Becky barges up to the cushion and speaks in a very milit-

ary voice:)

Becky: Excuse me, who do you think you are and what do
you think you're doing? I don't want to get aeriated about
anything but I don't normally have people standing in my
way, so would you mind budging? I've got plenty of time.
I'll just stand here till you grow a pair of legs! I don't
want to get physical or anything. I can wait. I'll just
wait here till I go over the top, till I pop. And then
I'll kill. Well, I wouldn't kill, not for something like
that. But I might get a bit aggressive (kicks the cushion).
Move along please! I'd make a good policeman. Shove on!
Time for moving along please, closing time! I said Closing
Time! Will I have to repeat myself?

It doesn't seem to be moving. Well, I'd move it. I'd
pick it up and move it. Unless of course it was bigger
than me. In which case I would be very verbal. I would
use my indignation. I'm thinking of someone who has a wide
vocabularly and is very educated and would use his head. He
is very bossy and very intelligent; he can use speech and
could get quite a long way by being pushy in that way.
If I couldn't win physically, I'd try that. Then, unless it
was a matter of life and death, as long as I felt I'd won,
I would then say, "Right!" and leave whoever it was to
it.

Jenny: And if you did feel it was a matter of life and
death?

Becky: Well, I've got a lot of pride and I would want to
fight the battle on my own. But if I really had to get
other people, I would if I could. I had the thought, "Would
I use an instrument?" And I thought, "Oh terrible, terrible.
I wouldn't do a thing like that." But I think I've got
enough pride and feeling for standing up for myself that if
I had to use an instrument to protect myself or somebody
else, I would.

I have the feeling now of being on a demonstration
where, say, I am at the head of it in some sort of big
posh parliament house and that perhaps the police are trying
to get into it to get me to take me out for some reason,

and I would stand at the balcony and say, "Excuse me, chaps, this is private property, do you mind going away?" I am aware of how I'm acting a part: that I exaggerate my feelings to get my way; I make them more theatrical. "We're having a private meeting up here, go away please!" I imagine the police battering away at the door and trying to get in, ringing the bell and getting horses and dogs and me saying, "Excuse me! That's my front door. Go away! I'll come down when I'm ready. I've rather important business going on. I didn't invite you all for tea you know. It's awfully impolite of you! I say chaps, what are you getting so aeriated about? Are you looking for somebody? Oh, it's me you're looking for! Oh, jolly good. But I won't be able to shake hands with all of you, there's an awful lot of you down there. It seems I've become famous. Oh jolly good, I must ring my mother, she'll be awfully pleased. Really this is getting too much, boys! Hey, you lot down there, you lot in the blue coats, you fellows with the funny hats on! Definitely English police. Cheek of it!"

Just because they are policemen, they think they can do all sorts of things to me and quite honestly, they are a load of bovver boys shoving their weight around. I've got a very keen sense of what's just and what's not. Just because they're in uniform, I wouldn't say, "Oh, you're a policeman, alright then do come in and walk all over the place."

I've got really strong feelings about everything, but I keep my head on. I like being important. The reading is reminding me of meetings where there are M.P.s present. I have the feeling of being smartly dressed and fiddling through papers and files and pulling things out and talking away. I get lots of sensations of meetings and everybody starting to talk at once and I say, "Ahem, excuse me!" I'd quieten everyone down and organize it so that one person speaks at a time. I can imagine being anything from a teacher in school to a judge in the courts. I like the feeling of having the power to shut people up, looking down on everybody and saying, "You do this and you do that." I

feel I've worked through things in my life so that I have
got that respect. I know what it's like to be at the bottom
of the pile and shouting my head off to try and get someone
to listen to me. And I didn't give up, I kept on going
and going and now I've got to the age where I can just
stand there and command attention. I've achieved what I
wanted: respect and position in whatever I'm engaged in.
Rob: How do you feel about people who strongly disagree with
you?
Becky: I listen to their side of the argument, but at the
end of it, I still believe in my own ideas. I'm not very
shaken - my ideas won't be changed by someone disagreeing
with me.

*****

Not long after he was elected President of
the USA, we gave Becky a reading to do on:

RONALD REAGAN

My first feeling was that I wanted to open the paper
- it was curiosity. I thought, "Oh, I can't be bothered
to do the reading, I want to know who it is."

So I am someone who wants to know what's going on,
and I want to know who I am. I'm impatient. I can't wait.
Energetic. Agitated. I feel as if I'm about to explode.
I feel like a bottle of fizzy lemonade. I just had an image
of being like an old banger going along the road - Chitty
Chitty Bang Bang! Or like a laboratory, all sorts of things
churning up and popping out all over the place, turning
different colours all the time. I'm quite a lot of fun.
It's lovely just making noises! Well, I've got to speak
haven't I? You've got to get yourself across loud and clear.
(Makes noises) Are you receiving me?

I'm a strong, dark, upright, goodlooking individual.
I've got a feeling of moving and shaking myself up; I need
to stretch myself. I'm aware of a pain in my stomach and of
bits of me that are a bit stiff. I'm very changeable,

there's lots of different sides to me. I love using long
words or new words; I like it when I use words that other
people don't know - it's a way of getting on top of people!
So I'm a person who is concerned with winning and weapons to
get on top of other people. I like interaction; I want
a fight. I'm looking at faces on the wall and imagining
making faces at them and amusing myself by talking to them
and imagining that they are real people and provoking them
and them provoking me. I want to get my teeth into things
and people. I feel pushy and aggressive. I would stand
in front of someone and say, "What do you want?" Even if
they hadn't said a thing, I'd say, "Who do you think you're
looking at?" Just to provoke someone; just for the hell of
it; just to fill a spare moment. I have Mars energy, to
do with fighting. I feel very sure of myself, quite laid
back, very confident; I feel I can allow myself to relax
physically because I have this verbal weapon, a very sharp
mind, and quick with words. If someone comes at me, I have a
quick answer for everything. My eyesight is very clear;
I feel bright in myself. I like making sudden movements
and noises. I really enjoy looking at myself in the mirror
- I have a lot of love for myself. I am in touch with all
the different aspects of myself. I feel like I've had a
lot of training, though it comes naturally to me anyway.
I'm imagining films with Brigitte Bardot in them, a gang of
women all on horses, fighting and shoving their weight
around.
      I'm very conscious of taking in information and ideas;
I want to balance everything. I like to make things fair.
But I'm not wishy-washy, I'm definitely not wishy-washy.
I don't want to shout about it BUT I'M NOT WISHY-WASHY.
I can get really het-up even just looking at pictures on
the wall and seeing what's going on in the world.
Jenny: How would you handle a really bad situation?
Becky: I feel I would keep calm, and keep calm and keep
calm and then suddenly crack! and I could imagine getting
suddenly really angry. I would get quite indignant about
things. I imagine a situation where shitty things are going

on with the other side and that there would be enough
strength amongst us just to remove ourselves from the
situation. I have a feeling of being very independent and
not staying with things if they're painful.
Jenny: Earlier on, one of the things you said was that
this person was looking for a fight. How do the two parts of
this character fit together?
Becky: The feeling of wanting a fight wasn't just brutish,
just 'out for a fight.' It was a feeling of having fight in
me, of having a feeling to fight for myself, and of wanting
interaction. I suppose it's a feeling of 'If there's shit
going on, then let it come out,' and I'll have a good old
bash at sorting it out. Removing oneself is in an ultimate
situation, a dangerous situation. But if there were enough
of us to deal with Them, whoever they are, I would fight.

As I'm sitting here now, I feel quite tired and a
bit uneasy. I feel less of a fighter and more of a coward:
I don't have the feeling any more of fighting to the death.
The feeling in my body was very different at the beginning.
I feel more down in myself now, sort of deflated....

*****

About a week after he was shot dead in New
York, we gave Snowy a reading to do of:

JOHN LENNON

Well, I've been holding the reading for a few minutes
and haven't felt much yet. I feel really sick, consumed
by obsessive thoughts; I feel horrible, sick with myself and
with the world. Uninspired. All those material things;
just getting and spending. I feel really blocked and that
I want to block. It's like there's no incentive to unblock.
There's no excitement or forward-looking. I'm not depressed,
it's not like that. Just going on and on and on and on,
and do it again and the next day and the day after that.
That's the way it is, that's the way everybody's life is

- that's life. Everybody's like that. Well so am I, and
that's the way it is, and what more would you expect? No,
I'm not depressed, there's nothing wrong with me, it's
just the way it is. I've never heard of any other way of
being. I mean, there's holidays and Christmas, those are
the nice times, but I mean that's just to make it bearable
to go on with the on and ons. And on and on and on. That's
where we live isn't it? That's where most people live.
Don't you live there? Well I do. On the on and ons. And
you get old later on, that's part of the on and on and
ons, getting old. And then you don't have to work any more;
they look after you a bit when you're older. Then you go
on and on a bit slower, and then you die. I'm not looking
forward to that very much, so I don't think about it. That's
about it, isn't it? I'm not depressed though, there's nothing wrong with me. It's just that that's where it's at
you know. Every now and again something happens that's
a bit more out of the ordinary, get a letter or something
like that, but basically, it's just the on and ons. Well,
it is like that, isn't it? And I'm just part of it.

          You ask, has it always been like that? That suggests
there's a different way and I don't like that question.
Have I always been like this? Well, I was young. That's
the time when you have a bit of a fling isn't it? I had
a bit of a fling. It's alright. I've got a few memories.

          I got stuck on something. I got stuck around the age
of eighteen. I'm only young now but I feel ever such a
lot older. Personal relationships? The usual. You know,
the way people are. I can't bear questions at all. You're
just a cheeky bugger, you come in here and you say what
about my personal relationships. Who are you? What do you
mean? You can't ask questions like that. I don't have personal relationships, and if I did, they're personal. You
can't ask me about them. My feelings are my feelings. Not
the sort of thing you can flaunt around in public, are
they? Well, I don't know what you get up to in the set-
up you come from. But when in Rome, do as the Romans, and
at the moment, you're in my Rome.

Oh, I'm scared. I'm very very scared. I want to faint.
I feel sick with fear. I'm a person with strong feelings who
has to put a lot of energy into controlling them. It's
making me ill. In my head and my stomach. I hate it. 'It'
being feelings. It's like jumping off a precipice. I haven't
any landmarks or hope. It's just horrors, complete nightmare. Don't let me go down. Guide me back to safety. I'm
seeing you like a woman. He must be under to a woman. I
can't bear you. I've got no patience whatsoever. I hate
you. I hate everybody. I don't want to speak. You're just
trying to draw energy out of me. You're going to have to
put energy in if you want anything out of me.

I'm defending myself from being overrun, from being
taken over, from getting hurt. I have to withdraw to protect
myself. It's a necessary defence.

Ken: Have you ever felt better than you do now?

Snowy: Yes. This is just something I'm going through at
the moment. But this person is not getting the help they
need. This person has not got friends around them.

*****

From someone who was shot, to someone who
shot himself:

JIM JONES: A reading done by Snowy

Quite a lot of power here, but I don't think I know how
to change gear: I'm sitting here to find out what to do
with myself next. Every time I come to a turning point
in my life, I lose my clarity and my vision completely.
I don't know where I'm going at all. It's like I keep all
my controls in my brain and if I move out of my normal
groove, I lose any sight of what I'm doing at all. I'm
the sort of person who would go somewhere where you've
got to put yourself under a lot of stress in order to break
your defences. I hope you all know that I'm working very
hard indeed, and I'm extremely serious about what I'm doing.

I'm putting myself through an awful lot of pain, but I'm not getting very far. I feel sorry for myself. It's a real uphill grind for me to get anywhere. I'm not the sort of person who can just go leap, jump, bound on to the next thing - I really have to work at it.

My main physical block is in my pelvis; my eyes are in a very bad state, and my head ought to be amputated! I don't ever move myself. Not that there's any pain; there's just a feeling of general stuckness and coldness and thickness and deadness which amounts to not having any real sexuality or creativity; not really having any life-force. I am basically a very dead person, extremely dead.

I have the impression that in my family, my father was on top, and that means that the Rational was on top and that it was all Peace and Love shit in the house. The shit came out but it was expressed through father being very heavily attentive and 'loving,' and that was the way the oppression took place. "Now dear, you've got one of your nasty turns, you stay in bed today and take a nice pill and I'll look after everything." That really heavy "we'll keep it all under control, right dear?" sort of heavy love shit. I've got my rational on top pouring honey and syrup to push down my own aggression. I think of nuclear war and how that's going to bust open all the shit that's going on in the world. There's a nuclear war inside myself. If everything mushrooms out of me, there'll be clouds.

This person has an absolutely superb mind in some respects and knows an awful lot. But when I look at myself and feel how my energy is - forget it. I'm just out of it. I wish I could cry.

I am someone who can only achieve through picking and picking away. I do move - it's imperceptible, but it's there. Having been set on my path, I'm on it, and I'm going along it. I'm very religious, I'm a very faithful person and a very straight person. I'm capable of curing and healing. I have some beauty; I'm not just a boring dead person (she is nearly crying at this point). And if it's possible for me to improve, it's possible for anyone in the whole world, because you couldn't meet anyone as damaged as me in that horrible dead way. You couldn't meet anyone more deadened and flabbed-up and crunched and blancmanged and liquidized.

But now I've got to the point I was most scared of: I've been successful and now I'm scared that I won't be able to progress any further. OK, well, I'm down. But by god I feel better than I did in the beginning. I am getting nearer towards what I'm going towards, which is Death. Ah well, that's encouraging anyway.

Jenny: How do you think other people would see you?

Snowy: I think people would have a lot of respect for me. I don't think they would particularly seek out my company for pleasure - I think that's very unlikely. But I think I would be a meticulous helper of other people. I wouldn't be an inspired helper; but I've got persistence and a sort of steadfast courage that would be very reassuring.

I can feel that other people wouldn't see me in as kindly a light as I'm feeling this person from inside the reading. I am sensing the struggle of this person and identifying with them and caring for them. But I've got a feeling that outsiders wouldn't see that at all and would just think of me as a pedantic old fool, dead. I'm thinking of someone I know: he's obviously on some incredibly serious purpose of his own, but if you go near it, it stinks! It's not something you'd care to share or go along with. He's obviously doing something with his life which he is very very serious about. But there's a sort of madness in that kind of seriousness which blots out contact with other people and it could be that I'm going up a gum tree.

Jenny: How would you handle other people?

Snowy: I wouldn't like too much life and energy. I would avoid anything which moved too much. I wouldn't be interested in anyone who was into being a victim; I would have very little sympathy. I would handle people quite silently. I wouldn't be into talking personally much at all. I've got the feeling of something political, theoretical, maybe

teacher-like; fitting things into some kind of theory and
presenting that and that being my way of relating to people.
I'd have some format for my experience and I'd relate via
that. I've got a feeling of having a few special people,
I don't know if they're my disciples or if I just think
they are, but people who I think are taking me seriously
and who I approve of and who I'd help. I don't have a picture of having anybody I look up to - I feel very alone.
But I don't think that makes me a leader. I've got no verve
or inspiration.

I keep wanting to tell you that I'm not suffering.
That's interesting. I wonder if it's just that I'm avoiding
all the suffering. I'm the sort of person who would actually
have to intellectually work out whether or not I was in
pain. I would have to get my mind to look individually
at each part of my body and make an analysis or decision as
to whether or not I was in pain.

Jenny: That reminds me of a boyfriend I had who said he had
to look down to see whether he had an erection or not!

Snowy: I don't like you saying that, thank you very much.
So I've just eradicated it.

Well, where to next? I've got quite deadened again. I
feel like eventually I'd just slow right down and stop
and give up. This person has quite a hard time of staying
alive, of actually just staying alive.

Jenny: What would be the attraction of this person, if
any?

Snowy: If you got into this person's heart, you would stay
there. It would be hard to get there, but once this person
takes someone to them, they are very very faithful.

Jenny: At one point, you said that this person isn't a
leader; but that isn't right.

Snowy: Well, if I think of a leader, I think of a Leo-type
person who has colour and imagination and drama and movement
surrounding them; and this person hasn't got that. So why
would people want to follow me? Well, in a crazy world
where there are no anchors, I'm incredibly steady, picking
away step by step. Everybody in the whole world is going

bonkers and looking for some sort of rock on which to depend and I've certainly got that. But I can't imagine how I'd get to the point of giving it out to the masses: maybe I'd just make tape-recordings. It's funny because all the gurus today are boring and dead. I just thought I couldn't be a leader because I didn't have any flow. If I think of a leader, I think of someone with a big banner waving in the wind saying, "Come on chaps!" I'm not like that. I'm the sort of leader who would just sit and make very pedantic speeches.

Jenny: What would be your solution to sudden crisis?

Snowy: Sudden crisis is a solution somehow. Sudden crisis just needs handling and dealing with: a steady reaction, a feeling of calming, of rock-ness, of picking up pieces and saying, "Right, you've got two arms and two legs left, you've got one arm and one leg..."

Jenny: Well, I've given you a reading of someone about whom there is a very definite consensus of opinion, and ....

Snowy: Is this Jim Jones?

Jenny: Yes. But even though you now know who it is, I still want to carry on for a bit. You said he'd be methodical in a crisis. Well, in a weird, macabre way, he was: 'A cup of cyanide for you and you and you...' And evidently, he had got his followers to practice the whole death ritual on many former occasions over the years.

Snowy: Complete insanity. He was in his own bubble totally.

Jenny: Yes, but I want you still to be Jim Jones and answer questions. What was your motivation in taking with you all those people and killing yourself?

Snowy: To stop people being hysterical, to stop the world going mad.

Jenny: You chose death to stop people going mad?!

Snowy: Yes, everybody was getting in such a paddy about it all. To calm them all down.

Jenny: That was a very effective way of calming people down!

What is your attitude towards death then?
Snowy: Well, there isn't any fear in me about it.
Jenny: Why not?
Snowy: I think it's because I don't experience pain myself.
Probably because I feel so much deadness anyway that it
would almost be like a slide, a slipping into death. It
wouldn't be a jolt or a break.
Jenny: And why would those nine-hundred-odd people want
not to see that he was mad - why should they want to be
even madder than him by killing themselves and their children at his bidding?
Snowy: They must have lost themselves a long time before
that; they must just have handed themselves over so long
before that.

*****

An interlude now before we take the next leap into
somewhat freakier readings, for

ALEX'S STORY

As a computer-brained, logical Virgo,
I have always tended to pooh-pooh the occult.
If you can't see, taste, touch, smell or buy it,
it doesn't exist.
My first realization that I could have
these dreaded psychic powers came sometime
around 1977 when I was dossing in a squat in
London. One evening around eight o'clock, I had
an irresistible impulse just to crash out and,
of all things, to put on a record of a Requiem
Mass. I found out a few days later that at
that same time of evening, my girlfriend in
Ireland was contemplating suicide. At the time
of my listening to the record, I was actually
wondering if she was feeling suicidal and I
felt terrible myself, as though surrounded by
blackness.

"Oh my god, no," was my reaction to all this. Not the dreaded psychic invading my encapsulated logical world. Get away please.

Once when coming down off an acid trip, my girlfriend handed me a glass prism. When I looked through it, it was as if the prism opened up and I went into it. I saw myself at the time of a motor-bike accident I had had back in 1971. It was all there: the desperate haggard expression on my face, the split-second slowing down of everything before the crash, the car and the occupants' expressions, the crash itself and the street lights spinning.

In spite of this, I was still a determined non-believer in the occult, though I kept on having a lot of these 'everyday' experiences of, say, watching a girl come into a room carrying a flower, yet 'seeing' her carrying a machine-gun; or of a guy coming towards me and me 'seeing' a heavy elephant; or the more pleasant event of a girl stating that she hated me, and me actually feeling loved. All these things border on the psychic: seeing and hearing what people are really saying and doing as opposed to what they appear to be doing.

Also while on acid, I've seen people's auras and literally watched a girl turn green with jealousy; and I've seen people's bodies twisted up by their inner tensions, or seen the amazing fleshy aliveness and vitality of a healthy body.

So when I came back to Atlantis after being away for three years, during which there had been an immense flowering of the psychic aspect of life, I already had some experience of psychic phenomena, though as usual I was outwardly denying this. I walked around shit-scared of all this psychic stuff – but what I was really scared of was that people could see through to all the nastiness in me.

The kind of thing I regularly saw happening in Atlantis was where someone would do a 'reading' on someone who had blocked off to suss out what was actually going on in him and bring it out into the open. I have always found this a liberating and relieving experience and I've had it happen to me a few times and have done these kind of 'readings' on other people. It's fascinating and creative and can help unblock stuck situations.

The first 'blind' reading I did was on Hitler. Everybody in the room was in hysterics as I goose-stepped about the room planning world domination and destruction and listened to the Blue Danube by Strauss. I also said I wanted to invade Poland and was obsessed by Baltic women, including one Eva Braun. When somebody asked me how I felt about the Jews, I had to stop in hysterical laughter.

I had been given this reading because it is said that I have a Hitleresque streak to my character and should have found it easy. I then went out of the room again and while people were writing down 'Flash Gordon' on a piece of paper, I was having clear images of space ships and solar systems outside the door, and was thinking of Flash Gordon. But I couldn't accept the possibility that I was picking things up correctly, and so I fluffed the reading.

Once I was handed a piece of paper that had Jenny's new-born baby's name, Louise, on it. Upon holding the paper, I was overpowered by rolling waves of sensuousness, sleepy darkness and I just wanted to lie down and curl up like a foetus; and at one time I made the strange

comment: "This baby didn't want to be born."
[The birth was in fact very long and difficult.]

I have had a reading done on me which
had a very strong effect on my life, changing
dramatically people's attitude towards me.
My outward mental patient act was no longer
taken as the real me, people stopped feeling
sorry for me and began to demand a lot more.
Life has never been the same for me again.

Of the readings which follow in this book,
the one that affected me the most was the Bhagwan reading because it voiced my own suspicions
of my involvement in that movement. It wasn't
very pleasant to listen to, but it was all
there: the vain attempt to change one's personality by wearing orange clothes, the strained
attempt to 'have fun' but not really feeling it
inside, the desperate attempt to convince myself
that I wasn't just an 'ordinary person' by
my involvement in outlandish techniques; but
all the time knowing that underneath I was
really no different from everybody else, but
was actually quite conservative and even boring
with it all, just trying to hide the fact that
I felt I was running out of juice and not finding much in life. As was said in the reading,
after all the 'hoo-hooing' [the sound of a
noisy 'meditation' used in the Bhagwan movement]
was over, we all looked at each other and knew
that in spite of it all, nothing in our lives
had really changed and we were no different from
anybody else: no talk about going to Poona or
doing 'dynamic meditation' could change that
fact.

At another time, I was also heavily into
Buddhism and the reading on Buddha completely
blew my mind - in essence how Buddhism pretends

to be a jovial, life-loving religion - the image of the smiling Buddha - but in fact it is one of the most negative, life-hating doctrines on the market, killing off all spontaneity and facial expression in the name of the eightfold path and Yogic and meditative austerities. Superficially it's nice, with all its talk about loving, but underneath there is suppressed anger. I've always been puzzled by how all these peace-loving Eastern philosophies manage to produce the most deadly fighting systems like karate and aikido!

The image of God presented in the readings as some kind of super-human being with work to do and lessons to learn just like us but on a larger scale, and with correspondingly larger responsibilities - the Earth and Solar System being his areas and growth points just as my relationships on this planet are mine - I find a completely liberating relief. I don't give a damn if it can't be 'scientifically' proven - it makes more sense to me than all the religious garbage I used to believe in from Christianity to Buddhism.

What 'Atlantis Magic' is about for me, apart from fascinating reading with some frightening and thought-provoking illustrations of the Law of Karma and Reincarnation (if you get past the bit about the reincarnated vivisectionist, you'll read the book!), is that deeper truths about people and events can be elicited by personal intuition or 'psychic' powers than can be arrived at by logic, reason, analysis and the scientific method. For me, who fancied myself as a logical-brained person, this goes a bit against the grain: to have to see that it is possible, when the artificialities of so-

called modern civilization have been stripped,
to tap deep into the cosmos directly, without
any need for anything like laboratory investigation; and that psychic powers, telepathy, clairvoyance, are in fact perfectly normal powers
which we have lost and which, by living in
and being affected by a place like Atlantis,
you can recover.

                                    Alex Cunningham

                    *****

CHAPTER NINE: THE GURUS
BUDDHA, JESUS CHRIST, TM, BHAGWAN, HARE KRISHNA

One of the most common characteristics
of mankind is wanting someone, a leader, a
teacher, a master, a guru, a daddy, a guide,
a god, to take over and show the way to a better
life. So we decided from time to time to take
a look from inside at some of the people who had
offered themselves as religious leaders. The
results were more than a little embarrassing as,
atheists or not, we were ingrained with certain
prejudices in favour of cultural respect.
One day, my publisher and my poet, Peter
and Jeremy, handed me a reading on:

BUDDHA (by Jenny)

My eyesight is beautifully clear. I am really seeing
and letting everything in. But there's a feeling of shyness.
I was going to say I've got no gigantic hangups, but then I
realize I don't look at you.

I'm either a child or a childish person or am childlike in the good sense. I have a taste for enjoyment. I
like people, but they're a bit problematic.

OK, here I am, and I have this energy and brightness in
me, but what shall I do with it? We could have great fun -
but has anyone else got the ideas? The thought of food is
good - I quite fancy the old omelette and chips idea that's
cooking out there, but I'd like to do something that made me
feel not so loth to look up. I'm stuck because there's
some step I don't take. This person, in order to deal with
something very painful in their lives has put a shell around
that thing to get rid of it, and having done that, they've
said, "Ah, well, now we can..." But unfortunately, now
we can't.

I have this belief that I am sunny, I am smiling,

I am light; yet I have to notice that I am not moving forward.
It's a passive position, a waiting for something to come
from someone else. Although I think that I am quite alive
and ready, the fact of the matter is that the centre of my
life-force lies outside myself, because I am not initiating.
Peter: Tell us something about your beliefs.
Jenny: Well, the thing I'm noticing most throughout this
reading is that all the time I've got a kind of smile on
my face, a potential smile. And I must believe in beauty,
because when I look at this room, I see beauty and colour.
But I don't feel like a very belief-y sort of person. I believe it ought to be possible to do anything, but I get depressed as soon as I think of what I actually do do. Having
encountered my block, I'm starting to find things like sleep
rather attractive.

       Yes, this person has an inflated idea of how positive
they are. What I'm actually doing is waiting for stimulus
from outside, which is absolutely negative - it's not-doing.
Not using the life that is given to me. Something's got to
jolt them heavily, hasn't it? They're not as creative as they
think. Just being ready for someone else to throw a ball
to you, where's that at?
Jeremy: Imagine you are in a position of great power and
influence...
Jenny: Well, immediately I get the picture of a kind of smiling Buddha, and I like the person I'm doing the reading of
much less. In fact, I don't like them at all. Because the
feeling of this reading is so shallow and childish and basic,
that if in fact this person is in a position of power and
influence, it must be based on pandering to the superficiality
in people in some way. It must be based on pandering to the
nicey-nicey-nice in people; pandering to a kind of superficial
positivity that isn't really rooted. I keep getting this
picture of the smiling Buddha, the constant smile of the
film-star, or the constant positive spew of the politician
or the constant reassurance of the religious guru or the
constant good mood of the pop-star. I'd use my power and
influence to convince everyone that I was absolutely life-

giving and life-loving and life-ly and I would want to be
seen to be encouraging that in others. I'm ostensibly people-
oriented, but when it gets to real contact with them, there's
a strong headache in the way, extremely strong.

I'm going to use my image of the Nice people of this
world. I'm a complete phoney, I must be. I must be extremely
hostile and negative inside if I need such a powerful pro-
life image. There is so much negativity in this world, it is
so important for us all to be so terribly positive, isn't it?
We must encourage life-force because there is so much blackness. I philosophize on my own bad feelings. I extrapolate
and externalize. I make out that this is a crusade towards
the positive and we must not dwell on the bad, for where
would we all be, I ask you, if we went that way? Can you
imagine it? No, don't imagine it, it's too awful.

Jeremy: Go on, this is fantastic.

Jenny: Aha! A bit of encouragement from the populace and
you'll never hear the last of me. It's not the bleedin' Pope
is it?

Peter & Jeremy: Not far off.

Jenny: Absolutely typical mass-leader syndrome - speaking to
that which everybody can easily recognize to be good; on a
safe ticket. Compare it with Atlantis for example, or any
movement which encourages people to look at the black and the
bad. I ask you, who's going to do that? I am like the writers
of the Omo ads., appealing to that which is obvious - the
Right, the Righter than Right, and the Rightest of all. I cannot lose. But actually, I can't win, because I can't get
through to my real self. It's funny how I felt that smile all
the time. It's so fixed that if I were lying fast asleep and
someone shone a torch on me, I'd be smiling in my sleep! It's
become an indispensible, inseparable part of me - Sweet Positivity Ruleth, OK? And so do I as representative thereof.

Peter: Do you know who you are?

Jenny: No. Well, Jeremy gave me the strongest clue to myself
by putting me in a position of power and influence: that
immediately gave me something to relate the sensations I had
to. When I felt myself to be a frippery trippery child just

seeing beauty everywhere, it didn't mean much, just being
a ten-year-old kid a bit spoilt, but the minute you put me Up,
I knew the sort of person I was. I could be someone who led
people into a religion and made all things shining and beautiful and let's all love one another - it could be one of these
love and peace religions where you never really butt up against another person; or it could be a political leader who
takes people like lemmings straight over the cliff because
they say, "Look at the shining economic sunset over there."
Or it could be something more obviously false like the complete charade of the pop world or the film world or the Omo
world. This person would, for instance, make a good jingle-
writer for a product. It's all the same kind of character
structure needed - the mass popularity syndrome; (as opposed
to the Atlantis mass unpopularity syndrome!)

Peter: Well, that's enough. You're Buddha.

Jenny: Oh!

Becky: Is he the one that always sits cross-legged with a fat
belly?

Jenny: I thought he was just a china idol on a mantelpiece.
Did he exist as a person? I thought it was just a concept
- 'Buddha-like.'

Jeremy: No, he was a person. Evidently, according to legend,
he was born a prince, led a rather sheltered childhood, and
when he went out into the world as a young man, he was so
saddened by the misery and sickness he saw everywhere that
he gave up being a prince and went out into the wilderness
and sat under a Bo tree, which is a thing they have in the
East, and then he suddenly received Enlightenment and set out
on his mission to save the world.

Jenny: I do remember there being something about him having an
inscrutable smile, a benign smile for everything and everyone
always, which made me sick straight away.

Peter: Oh dear, another idol dropped.

Jenny: It has to be. If there's hundreds and thousands of
people following one thing, there's got to be something wrong
with it, because if it was good and there was that number of
people following it, the world wouldn't be going the way
it is.

Peter: "If you meet the Buddha on the road, kill him."
Jenny: Who said that?
Peter: It's the title of a book. [by Sheldon Kopp]
Jenny: By someone who's seen through it all?
Peter: Yes.

*****

And now with some trepidation, we offer the
words Becky delivered when handed a reading on:

JESUS CHRIST

This reading is a big energy source, because it has the
effect of making me want to breathe deep and stretch and
expand myself, open myself up. It's like the energy inside me
is so huge that I have actually to expand my body and my
being because whatever I am is very big. I'm looking down at
the floor and I feel like I'm looking down on the world and
all these little specks of dirt are things on earth.

There's something conventional about me. I'm imagining
myself as being like a nurse in a hospital and having a uniform on. I care. My hands are really feminine and I feel
like I have lots to give. The clothes I have on are grey
and black and white. I feel physically really strong and
sturdy and solid. I'm getting loads of the same feelings as
I had in the reading when I was doing 'God': a feeling of
being huge and of being able to do anything. I feel I could
just reach out of that window and pick that man up in my
hand and he would yell and his legs would be kicking in the
air, he'd be screaming and panicking and I'd be saying,
"Don't worry, it's only Me. I'll put you down in a minute. I
am only experimenting." It would be the shock of his life. I
could put out my finger and tickle him under the chin and
he wouldn't know what on earth was going on.

I feel as if I've come back to a place after I've grown
up, like perhaps gone back to a classroom that I was in when
I was little and the chairs and tables and everything seem so

small and I feel huge. That's the kind of feeling this person
has. I've got incredibly good balance. I could walk around on
tiptoe and I'd never fall over or go off-balance. I have
tremendous power and strength and I feel like I could just
walk across stepping stones across water, and I'd never fall
in. I'd just go from stone to stone and I'd never trip over.
I'm ever so tolerant too, ever so patronizing: I look at
people and know they are just like children; I don't look
down at them as nothing, but I do look down on them. They
don't really know what's going on and they don't understand;
they're just learning.

I can imagine being the main nurse in a hospital, and I
would have to be completely tolerant and patient. I wouldn't
get mixed up in all the little nonsenses of all the little
people. I don't feel nasty about this - I'm just needed as I
am, above it all. I love the feeling.

But I don't feel physically healthy. I feel pale and
under a certain amount of stress. There's a lack of bounce in
me, a lack of joy and excitement, a lack of pleasure. I'm
taking things too seriously. I can laugh for five minutes,
but then someone will say something and I'll be completely
distracted. If I could play around with every situation, then
I would be able to survive, but there's too much sensibleness
in me, I listen too much and try to understand too much,
and it messes me up; it throws me and puts age on me. I'm
like an old woman. I need to learn to enjoy myself instead of
destroying myself and putting knives into myself and hurting
myself. I'm still whole inside, but my actual physical being
is grey and drawn and in distress. I'm very conscious, awake,
and ready, but I'm quite boring.

Jenny: How do you think others would react to you?

Becky: People don't notice me, that's the feeling I get.
They don't actually know that I'm around, they don't feel my
presence particularly.

Jenny: What is your purpose in the world?

Becky: Oh god, purpose in life? Oh Jesus. I don't know what
to say. I think of the millions of people in the world and
it's like saying why are they all here? I'm very strong -

my purpose is strength. I'm powerful, I'm solid. But my mind
is a pain to me. I keep getting the feeling of wanting to
give up. I feel alone, I'm on my own. I'm not in relationship
to anyone. I feel like some sort of martyr; I'm suffering
and punishing myself and feeling sorry for myself. I'm a
big energy force, something really huge, and yet I feel somehow I've made a mess of whatever I was meant to do. I haven't
taken charge as much as I should have done. I keep feeling
that my purpose in life is looking after people. I've still
got the fantasy of being the main nurse in a hospital, the
Big Nurse, and that instead of using my authority over people
and telling them what to do and organizing them, I'm mucking
around with experiments in the laboratory, making things
pop and set on fire, and meanwhile the patients are dropping
dead around the place. I'm not taking charge and everything is
just getting into a complete mess. Oh god, I feel really
guilty. I am very bogged down. Something big happened. The
only thing I know that would get me out of this is something
really extreme; I'd have to really fight for myself. There's
something that I'm going to have to fight with: something
is going to challenge me.
Jenny: What sort of effect would you have on other people?
Becky: Not a good one, because if I have the kind of power
I feel I have, it means that people are following me, and
that means they will end up like me. I am someone who should
have been more like a parent; I should have shown the way
and have people follow me; and people are still following
me, and yet I am in a mess myself. I'm giving the message
that it's OK, go ahead and be comfortable, you'll be looked
after. I'm not giving the message that you have to survive
for yourself. What I'm saying is, "It's OK, you're all little
children, you can all stay in your playroom and play." I'm
forgetting to tell people that they've one day got to grow up
and look after themselves.
Jenny: How do you think people would feel about you?
Becky: I feel they'd have their heads down and they would
listen a bit for a while and then they wouldn't really bother.
People won't really respect me, not really. It's like listen-

ing to the priest in the church on Sunday: everyone goes
there and pretends, it's something everyone does on Sunday,
but no-one really looks up to the priest. If anyone's really
in distress or needs help, no-one's going to turn to the
priest, no-one's going to take him seriously. They all hate
getting up on Sunday morning and they don't really want to
go to church and hear a boring old voice. Everyone's kidding
themselves, everyone's pretending...

*****

So what about some of the more modern hopes
of guru leadership? Here is part of what came out
of Becky when she was handed the name of the
Maharishi Mahesh Yogi, guru of the Transcendental
Meditation movement ('TM'). It was rather difficult to transcribe from this tape for reasons
that will become obvious.

TM by Becky

Er (yawn) sinky sinky much much sink. I feel completely
heavy. Spaced out. OK, right, pull yourself together. In
a minute, I'll start. (She begins talking in jumbly language)
Yes, in a minute, I'll begin (repeats this over and over
again). Right, right, in a minute I'll start, in one minute,
start, start. All I feel like doing is (makes noises) ..
I'm confused, fushed, fused, confushed (etcetera, repeated
many times). Completely confused. Fused wire, burnt out,
kaputt, finish, haven't started, got nothing to start with.
I'm fused out, fushed, finished, empty, going insane (laughing) going, going, gone. Definitely gone (giggling). End,
end, end of the end. Fini fin fish fin finished foshed fashed
flished fished floo fly flee fum, I'm completely fin, splash
splosh splish (helpless with giggles) Finnegan, Michael Finnegan beggigan begin again oh god Michael Finnegan threw it
back in again. I'm completely empty (snores); nothing left at
all. No conclusion, no hope, splash splish oh my god I can't
stop. STOP!

A nutter, but I feel good.

Look, if this was a sensible professional reading, I wouldn't be able to sit here going like this (makes more blabbering noises). I would have to put this confusion and splish splosh into sense. (Starts speaking in a posh voice) Now, I am the sort of person who em (giggles) wants to repeat things again and again. And again. I mean just once after the last time, and then again. Yes, I am the sort of person who has something in my mind I want to say over and over again, a constant humming (bursts into giggles). Yes, as I was saying: now from here I do not know where to go, because I always want to go back to the beginning once again. But just in order not to bore you all to tears, I will try to push myself forward. Yes. Perhaps I am the sort of person who has got up at eight o'clock every single morning, walked to my office with my briefcase, had dinner dutifully packed by my wife, had my shirts washed on Sunday, come back at six o'clock in the evening, got into the car, had a crash - could not cope. Now, if this was a reading for a businessman and I had to be sensible, I would have to put myself across very properly. Now how would I do this? I would put my hands in my pockets, take a deep breath, stand up straight, and talk very proper.

Jenny: -ly.

Becky: Properly. I'm a person who probably spends a lot of time dancing around repeating things. Does this make sense? No of course it does not. I'm afraid I'll have to tell you that I am definitely not the sort of medium who picks up things as they should be. I am rather the sort of medium who picks up things as they shouldn't be. This means that you have to make up your own conclusions.

Yes, I would say this person needs psychiatry, primal therapy and mental hospital. They definitely need to be tidied up, packed up, packed away, sent off and never brought back again.

But I think I am perfect. Absolutely wonderful. Very communicative titive titititive. Confusion from an early age. Perhaps beforehand as well. Perhaps a broken family. Per-

haps no parents. Perhaps had psychiatry. Perhaps gets out
of wrong side of bed. I fancy a nice cup of coffee and a
cigarette. That's all I can say for this person I'm afraid.
That'll be ten pounds please.

Fred (who came to Atlantis straight from the Cork TM centre):
What sort of place would you like to live in?

Becky: Quite a bare sort of house. Perhaps just one bed;
white walls; no carpet; perhaps one chair, one table, one
fork, one spoon, one knife, one pen, one pencil, one piece
of paper and one envelope and one pence to buy one stamp.
One light bulb with one light switch; one door for one person.

Fred: Why are you talking to me in this way?

Becky: It's the only way I can keep sane. Slightly. Shall
we go through the questions once more? I think we should
go through it once again so that you know exactly what you
are doing. I'm very polite and proper and do the right thing
even though we are all going insane.

        And now I'm stuck. I have said something and I don't
know why I've said it. I will go back to the beginning again
and repeat it once again just to make sure you know what
I said.

        When I start acting 'proper' I feel bad. I have now
succeeded in losing all the sensations I had. I have become
completely sane but I have lost all sense of fun. Now I am
completely blank. Therefore, sanity solves everything. Which
means you are left with nothing, which means that you have
no problems because you have to communciate with nobody about
nothing.

        I have an awfully tight jaw from talking the proper
way. How will I ever get all this across to an audience of
the average sort? Of course, I get no answer. Which means
I have to answer it myself. The answer is: Blank. Well you
can't say blank to nobody, I mean to everybody. My god. This
person has a bit of their brain missing which means that
after a few minutes, they come to a piece of their mind which
goes blank. Which means they have to reel back again to see
if they've missed out 'blank' next time. But this space of
Blank never gets recorded which means it's awfully tiring by

the end of the day and you feel like giving up.

Fred: Do you sleep much?

Becky: If you mean sleep meaning slumber, no I don't. If
you mean relax, no I don't. If you mean dream, no I don't.
If you mean put my arms around another of the other sort,
no I don't. But if you mean close my eyes and go blank, yes
I do. And in the morning, I feel awfully blank.

This person fancies himself as a speechifier. I can
imagine being awfully priestly or being the judge in a high
court. The bit I like about being a judge is having a hammer
(bangs on the table). That in fact appeals to me more than
anything. Being a judge and saying, 'Case Dismissed.' And
then the others have to sort it out...

*****

Being somewhat concerned about the justice
of this reading, I consulted my sister. She
came up with the following tale from her own
experience:

Many years ago, I had a very brief affair with a man
who did transcendental meditation. One morning, he asked
if I would like to meditate with him. I agreed out of curiosity. He told me that the idea is to blank out all thoughts
completely. The way to achieve this was by counting out loud
and concentrating only on the numbers themselves. If any
other stray thought cropped up, I had to return to number
one again. He demonstrated the method out loud for me: he
sat cross-legged on the floor and in all seriousness began
counting: one, two, three... oh, one, two... uh, one... one,
two.. one, two, three etc. He never got beyond 'three' because
thoughts would cross his mind which he had to blank out by
penalizing himself, that is, by going back to the beginning
again.

He took the whole exercise completely seriously, like a
teacher marking work, crossing it out each time a 'mistake'
occurred. As a lover, I found him very dead, which didn't sur-

prise me when I discovered how much effort he put into blank-
ing himself out. I didn't bother to continue the relationship
after this episode.

*****

Another time, we tried Becky on the guru of
the 'orange' movement:

BHAGWAN SRI RAJNEESH

Well, the first thing that comes to me is that I don't
mind if I wear a long dress. I like being scruffy and hippie-
like. I like that image of myself, really loose and brown.
So I'm the sort of person who has felt what it's like to
be tied up and conventional and now I feel more alive wearing
'cosmic' clothes. I've got a sensation that one day I'd go
out in a three-piece suit with my black shiny shoes and then
the next day I'd go out in some flowy trousers with a cloak
and dingly dangles from my ears, and bare feet. I quite fancy
myself I suppose. I want to be different, though I have to try
quite hard actually. I have to deliberately wear different
clothes to be a different person. I do it very consciously.
Now what kind of different person am I?

I feel controlled in my speech, like a machine-gun.
I feel very sober. I've got this rhythm in my mind like music.
Not that I'm particularly musical, but I believe in music.
Music makes me relax. I feel I'm quite a tight, stiff person,
and music helps me to loosen up. I wear particular clothes to
make me a particular person and I listen to particular music
to make me a particularly loose person. I'm very conscious of
everything I do, and I do it in order to be a certain type of
person which I think it is a good idea to be. That's me in
a nutshell.
Fred: Goodbye.
Becky: Goodbye? Definitely not goodbye. Don't say goodbye to
me. I feel very hurt. I have come here today to speak to
you (she speaks in a strange stilted, staccato foreign voice).
Oh dear, I'm a very toned-down, quite boring person actually.

Here I am, flat out, bored out of my mind, wearing my particular clothes, listening to particular music and to the tick tock of the clock. Well, I am someone who keeps at something until I get it right. I keep on chugging along until I reach whatever I have to reach. I don't feel any joy or laughter. I'm waiting for something exciting to happen. I'm impatient and annoyed when everything doesn't go right.

I'm a serious person desperately trying to have fun. It's a Good Idea to have fun, yet it feels terrible, really empty, tight and strained. I feel glum. I've got masses of time and space to myself: I've organized it that way. Everything is white and clean and plastic and smooth. I couldn't cope with things being a mess. But now I'm left with nothingness. I've put myself on the outside of it all and I'm not involved. I don't relate personally to anybody. I've got other people to organize the others and I'm left bored with headaches, backaches, leg-ache and arm-ache.

I don't know if I'm picking it up right, but I was thinking of Bhagwan, how he talks, and how I imagine he must organize himself. The feeling is of stagnation, really old and decrepit, hard, fraught, dried-up. I've lost the pleasure of the taste of food. I'm going to die of cancer. And I've done it to myself.

I'm aware of the stillness of the sky, of the ticking of the clock and the slow winding of the tape-recorder. In other readings, I have been all jumbly and messy and enjoying myself, though not knowing what the hell was going on. But in this one, I am very sensible and together and grown-up, a bit like a grandfather who's got it all sussed, but there's no joy in it. I'm really sane and proper and I know where it's at, but what am I left with? I could sit for hours and do nothing. No physical sensations, no good ones anyway. I've got really weak legs. And I've got a kind of smile on my face, my lips are turned up, I'm turned in on myself. Yet I feel grumpy. I could act out anything. If the done thing was to sit here making a certain noise, I could do it. Do you want to ask anything?
Jenny: Yes. What effect would you have on the people around

you?

Becky: I suppose people would think I'm a good idea. I give out speech and thought and intellect. I imagine a hodge-podge of ideas written down, so anybody who'd just come out of university, anybody into ideas and books, would listen to me. I'll just use my image of Bhagwan: I'm thinking of a girl that was here, how she used to go on about being in love with him and thinking he's something amazing - but where does it really get to? I've got rheumatism in my legs, my stomach feels bloated, I feel lazy. I started off with a big idea and I've ended up with piss all. I'm sitting in a boring old office, with a ticky old clock and piles of papers. I've got nothing else to write about or talk about. I'm a dried up old stick so I end up despising everybody and I just feel rotten and miserable. I'm near my death-bed, my death-day is coming shortly. I've done millions of things, but I don't feel which is a big mistake, because feeling is the most important thing in the world. I do know what is going on though. In other readings where I was enjoying myself and laughing, I needed a bit of knowledge as to what was happening, a bit of sanity. In this reading, I am very sober, slow and together, but there's no joy. I would appeal to intellectual type people who want everything to make sense: if you do certain things, you know what's going to happen. You all get up at a certain time in the morning and you all go 'hoo, hoo' and you feel cosmic. But there's a lack of 'umph'; there's no good aggression.

Jenny: OK, I think we'll leave it now.

*****

So what about the Hare Krishna movement? You know, the bald-headed ones with the one tuft of hair hanging down their backs who make a song and dance in the streets and rush around thrusting glossy records at you, insulting you if you don't buy them, who set up extraordinarily glittery ('Woolworthsy' my mother would have said)

stands at exhibitions, flamboyant temples at
festivals, and give away plastic cups of very
nicely done foods. They claim to be entirely
spiritual, removed from this world. They are
not allowed to have sex either outside or within
marriage, except for production of the next
little Hare Krishna chanter - and even then,
to make sure they don't enjoy it, they have
to chant 'Hare Krishna' before, during and after
the act.

HARE KRISHNA by Becky

I'm looking in the mirror and it's just like looking at a
painting of something Victorian; there are flowers and everything is proper and old-fashioned. It's very beautiful, but I
wouldn't say that I _feel_ beautiful. I'm very calm, as if
I've been through some sort of exercise or study. I've got
a straight neck, and my eyes, skin, hair, everything is just
perfect. I feel like an actor on a stage; there's a really
big director and he's put me in the right place and the action
is about to happen. I've put all my effort into this moment
and now here I am, and I'm hardly breathing. It's the modern
day, but I'm sort of old and I've got a special hairdo, and
I've got an image to put across. I'm holding myself like
a ballet dancer and all my energy has gone up into my head;
I'm floating. There's no depth to me. I find it really hard to
breathe into my stomach and relax.

I can imagine spending all my time doing myself up -
my eyes and my hair and my earrings and my pictures - and
I wouldn't have any time left to sink into myself. I'm completely involved in talking about the Proper Way and the
Thing to Do and the time to do it and the place to do it. I
find it hard to get into the feeling part of me. I've gone all
up to the surface and I'm skimming around.

I've got taken in, taken in all day long: from morning
till night I'm completely dolled up and perfumed and lit up.
Every minute of the day, I'm sitting here posing and driving

places and going out for meals, and there's nothing real
left. At half past such and such we'll be doing this and
at another time we'll be doing that, every day. Everything is
image and my body has gone dead. I'm starting to lose my
character. It's all glittery, shiny, glassy; little drinks
thoughout the day, not a hard day's work and then a meal
and solid, down-to-earth living. It's a social pressure I've
put on myself. I know how to get rid of it: I'd have to take
my hair down, shake my head, stick my legs in the mud and
run around the garden barefoot, milk the cows and scream
my head off, punch pillows, kick around and let go completely.
That's all I'd have to do to loosen up. But at present, I'm
completely in my head. I'm glued together, my wig is glued
to my head and my brow is tight. I feel as if I've been scrub-
bed up and given clothes and talking lessons and language
lessons and music lessons and I'm living in a middle-class
atmosphere, and quite honestly at the end of it I might as
well be dead.

Jenny: Why would people be attracted to you?
Becky: It's a feeling of clannishness, of sticking together,
of all being hoity-toity together. I feel very narrowminded
and clinging to whatever I've got. I'm not worried about
the world. It's like a priest or a church, something to fill
up people's emptiness, something for them to cling to.

*****

     Several people in our commune came from
backgrounds where hope was pinned very firmly on
to some deity. Here is how someone from an ultra-
conservative, Irish Catholic background survived
exposure to all this pagan witchery:

FRED'S STORY

     I remember very well my reactions to Snowy
James suggesting to me on one of the first evenings I met her that she do some readings. As soon
as she mentioned the word, the connection I

made was with fortune-telling. I was much taken
aback as she delivered into the room a representation with all manner of idiosyncracies of a
flat-mate of mine of six months' standing whom
she had never met.

Over my first months in Atlantis, I witnessed many readings. To me they showed that there
must indeed be connections between all things in
the world and a basic similarity in the way
people are made up, just as in music all the
tunes in the world in their various tones and
shades of emotional expression are built on
just a few basic notes.

Each time one of the readings came uncannily
close to how I imagined the subject to be, I
used to doze off. I would be nudged back to
wakefulness and teased about trying to avoid the
stunning effect the readings were having on
me. I made brave efforts to breathe deeply and
keep in touch with everything that was being
said, but it was all too startling and spooky
and soon I'd doze off again. I am thinking now
particularly of readings done of my own child
who was at the time not even conceived.

I could for much of the time dismiss the
"reader's" words as inaccurate, but as a reading
continued I would often be shocked into the
realization that it was not so much the words
being used that were important as the manner
in which they were delivered. I am remembering
a reading of my mother where Snowy turned into
a demure, carefully-spoken, lethargic woman.
It was her facial expression and 'speed' of
speech that spooked me. Likewise when Ned, a
fellow communard, did a reading of my brother
- no particularly accurate words from Ned describing him: what was astonishing was to see Ned
seem to shrink from his usual five foot ten to

the smaller stature of my brother. Ned folded his
arms in the manner my brother always did, and
marched up and down with a lively energetic
air, very dogmatic manner, suspicious and careful
in his scanning of the people in the room, all
physical and emotional characteristics of my
brother. I meanwhile started to cringe with
embarrassment at having my relatives thus brought
to life in the room, and felt like folding up and
going further into my shell.

The main thing that gets to me about readings is the drama that unfolds; it has its own
shape and form, though carried on the vehicle
of another person's emotional makeup. I know
that the times I've been most shocked by a reading have been precisely when I've stopped saying
in my mind, "Now I wonder what that could symbol-
ize?" - when I stop looking for the meaning
'behind' what the person is saying and simply let
myself be affected by what is coming out. It
is then I realize that the meaning does not
take time to come across: it is immediate and
is in the playing with words or in the facial
expression and body movements of the "reader."

Readings of places and 'things' make me
wonder at the connection between everything
in the 'uni-verse' - a 'unity that is always
turning,' in which energy is never destroyed but
changes form, becoming sometimes 'inanimate
matter.' Material 'without a soul'? I wonder.

Fred Moloney

*****

CHAPTER TEN: READINGS ON
DOG, GOD, INISHFREE, SOUTH AMERICA, LONDON

When it came to writing up some of the readings in this book, I was so nervous about much of the strange material that had emerged that I asked my sister Snowy to write something to lead the reader gently into this often meta- phorical, poetical world. She wrote:

"If, dear Reader, you are tempted to think that these readings are the result of a power- mad woman projecting her crazy delusions into other peoples' minds in order that they shall speak out her insane notions and not have to take responsibility for them herself, then per- haps you are right..."

Thank you Snowy. The moral of this tale seems to be: don't ask your younger sister to be your public relations officer.

Meanwhile, guess who was first to attempt that most outrageous of all subjects, a psychic reading on 'God' who, as all good atheists know, does not exist...

SNOWY ON 'DOG' AND 'GOD'

On a boring ferry crossing from Stranraer to Larne with Colm, I said, "Let's do some psychic readings to pass the time."

Then followed the most exciting ferry crossing I've ever had over the Irish Sea.

The first piece of paper Colm handed me had our sheep- dog's name SNIP written on it, though of course I didn't know that.

"I feel mindless," I began. "Brainless. No thoughts.

I want to climb over the table and sniff you. I'm all teeth
and nose. As I look around at the passengers on the boat,
all I see is their feet and ankles and up to their knees.
I don't notice anything above the knee."

Such was my impulse to climb on Colm, that I didn't
resist. I sat on the seat next to him and sniffed and nuzzled
up to him. He looked alarmed. "What do you want?" he asked.
"I feel as though I'm trying to get your approval because
you're bigger than me, but really I hate you and want to
get even. I'd like to sink my teeth into you."

When I opened the paper and saw our dog's name, I was
incredulous. I'd only ever done readings on people before
and this was a completely new departure. How far could we
take this amazing game?

It didn't take long to find out. Colm then, unbeknown to
me, wrote 'GOD' on a piece of paper and folded it for me.

"I feel like a crazy professor," I began. "I'm a maths
professor. I've got all my plans and equations well worked out
on paper. I'm very intelligent and very neurotic. Extremely
high energy. Although I've got all my sums done, I'm very
worried indeed."

I looked nervously across at the hot water machine ominously hissing and spurting steam behind the cafe counter.
"I've set up an important experiment. And I'm afraid that
it's just about to explode. There's nothing I can do now.
I don't know what I've done wrong, but I must have made a
mistake. It's all going wrong. It's going to blow up."

*****

Well, after this exploit of Snowy's, of
course a whole new world of possibilities of
how to use and experiment with readings opened
up.

We have known for a long time now that
we want to move from Europe. We want to go somewhere really primitive, probably mountains in
South America. But meanwhile, we are very sorry

to leave our beautiful rocky island of Inishfree
and all the carefully tended gardens and green-
houses we have built there. We take very seriously all the astrological, political and psychic
predictions about this civilization coming to a
catastrophic close this century and we want
to 'go back to the caves' under our own steam
rather than be blasted there by bombs. But I
still wanted to know how safe Inishfree was.
It is a very flat island, and the slightest
rise in sea-level would make it disappear over-
night, and that would be another Atlantis under
the sea.

So I decided to give Becky one of her first
'thing' readings. I didn't tell her there was
anything different about it, so she was bound
to deliver the reading as if she were a person,
and I wondered how I would interpret it. I didn't
have to wonder long.

That day, Becky happened to be dressed
unusually soberly in a white blouse and neat
pair of black trousers. I had written on the
paper she was holding: "Inishfree: am I stable?
How long will I last?"

Becky stood neatly and still throughout
the reading - very unusual for her. She was
upright and prim. She spoke gently and simply.
"I am a conventional person," she said. "I am
conservative and proper. I am very very clean.
I do not get upset. I am not uptight. I am kindly. It would take a very great deal ever to
make me explode, years in fact. I might go
through a whole life-time and never ever explode.
I do feel things though; I am not at all dead.
But I simply wouldn't express myself like that."

I was crying softly with relief and love
- love of my daughter standing there so fresh and
perfect, and love of our windswept island.

People in the commune naturally wanted
to know more about what was involved in my crazy
plan to transport the whole lot of us to South
America. So Fred and Snowy gave me a reading to
do one day, not mentioning that it was not a
person. On the paper was written: "Jenny, will
you give us an idea about the following: Where
will we end up? What sort of place will it be?
How soon will we settle there?"

Of this reading, Snowy writes:

Jenny's reading on our emigration to South America
gives a picture of the journey itself rather than a very
specific description of the arrival place, which is what
I asked for on the paper. Thus I am given a philosophic message, as well as a practical one: the journey is the thing.
As Don Juan says to Carlos Castaneda, "There are millions
of paths, and they all lead nowhere. The important thing
is to choose a 'path with heart' and stick to it."

At Atlantis, we make a point of pushing ourselves and
each other to find a way of enjoying everything NOW. People
who meet us are often amazed at how much zest and vigour we
put into the simplest tasks like washing up or cleaning floors
- but living in Atlantis is no insurance against pitfalls
of negative thinking, and this reading had a little joke
on me: I was having an anxiety about the future, and so it
told me off and brought me back to enjoying the present.

THE JOURNEY TO SOUTH AMERICA by Jenny

Usually when I'm about to do a reading, I get a feeling
of slight nervousness, of "God, I can't do this." But this
time I feel like no longer messing around. The feeling now
is, "Right, that's it! Off we go!" I just feel like rolling up
my sleeves and getting on with it. There's business to be
done, we've got loads of work to do, and it's changed the
whole quality of everything in our lives.

I feel very willing to dive in, but not terribly sensible

about it. A lot of energy. I feel very physical and capable,
but all over the place. I am very aware of my legs and of
having done that ten-mile walk yesterday - now isn't it amazing that I could transport my body all that way through space!
I really need to walk around everything in the room. (I jump
up on to the table, then to the top of the piano, across
cabinets and down on to chairs.) I would like to be without
a body for this reading - just fly around the room and land
on anything. I need an Aldermaston march! I could go on for
days and days and days. Nothing could be too much or even
enough. With the right shoes on, I could walk forever.

        I feel as if I am just Energy: you can use me how you
like. Here I am, I stretch out in all directions. I'm huge.
I could never be tired. I've never had a feeling like this in
a reading before. It's such a sort of 'everywhere' feeling.
You could present me with any difficulty at all and I'll
just sort it out. I'd like to do really dangerous things
like stand on rocks and just dive off. I think I could swim in
air. It would be worth a try, because then I'd find my own
limitations. Let's do an experiment: you use me Snowy for
the next five minutes and see what happens. Give me a task.
Snowy: OK. Start that side of the room and go right across to
the other side of the room slowly and en route tell me everything that happens, and when you get there tell me what happens.
Jenny: Well, I can't do it very slowly - it's a bit small,
isn't it? (I leap in one go right across the room) Now if
you said do that all the way to the cottage at the bottom
of the garden, right straight through the window and over
the rocks, that would be a bit more interesting. (I get up
on the table again) I find it easier to imagine when I'm
up here looking down on everything; this way I've got a bit
of distance and can see everything a bit better. I want to
go further. I would jump up on the piano, but it's a bit
wobbly. I wish everything in this room was stable so that
I could just jump on it and land. (I jump off the table)
Oh, that was lovely; I'm heavy and nice. And I feel much
better right in the middle of the room. Or right Up.

Snowy: Get to where you feel right, and tell us what it's like.

Jenny: I'm afraid that's rather difficult because I find all sorts of things wrong. We've got to be outside for starters. I definitely do not like the feeling of these walls. Definitely definitely not indoors. This whole house suddenly seems like cardboard, extremely flimsy and dangerous. Absolutely not here as it is, it's just wrong. I like that word NOT, especially NOT THAT (I sweep away with one gesture all the buildings in the village!). Not, NOT, not the rocks.

Snowy: Not the rocks? What then?

Jenny: Grass. Lots of it. Very long and warm. I want to take us little lot out there. I want to sweep the rocks and houses away, sweep everything until there's incredibly lots of Smooth for a long way around; so that it's green as far as the eye can see. Just really long lush grass for a long long way. And us little group will get together in the middle of that grass.

I feel a little bit tired now for the first time. I'm not sure whether it's the thought of being able to expand and expend my energy in that great big Savannah, or the weariness of fighting against these walls and restrictions in here. But I feel good whatever mood I'm in; I just feel completely and utterly capable. And that feeling of tiredness didn't last very long. It was a very small pathetic little tiredness! I just be-ed it completely, and it was gone.

(Looking out of the window) Oh! I'm going to kill that child next door because he's just locked our puppies in the barn! I feel quite cool about it. I would simply exterminate him if he did something wrong. And I would enjoy it, move on, and forget about it in two minutes. I'm ever so sorry about this, but absolutely everything seems to fill me with pleasure. Hey, I hope I come out of this reading, else I shall never be able to go to bed again or stop walking around or do anything ordinary - I shall be forever surveying and walking across furniture and exterminating intruders!

Snowy: I feel very satisfied and amused with the reading. You could end now. Do you know what it is?

Jenny: Well, I'm definitely not a person, am I? I never once
felt like a person. I could be an element or a concept; abstract rather than tangible. I'm a force or a source. I'm
energy of some kind. Am I the move to South America?
Snowy: Yes.
Jenny: Oh, and you must be asking me where to go. I don't
see how I could possibly have answered a question as to where
we're going!
Snowy: Yes you did. We're going to be nomadic, live in the
open, have a look everywhere, and end up in the middle very
high up. And it mustn't wobble!
Jenny: Oh, that's silly! Where's the reading? Let me see what
you wrote.
Snowy: You've had the reading on you the whole time, twit.
You put it in your sock!
Jenny: Oh yes.
Snowy: Right, we'll know not to let her carry the map.

*****

    And back in Europe, what is going to happen?
Here are Snowy's comments on the reading which
follows:
        Becky's reading on London brings to the fore an
over-riding theme in all our work: What is the ultimate result of the way things are going? London is obviously bent on
self-destruction, reaching the ultimate of nuclear war predic-
ted in the reading. People argue about whether or not nuclear
war will happen, but it seems to me that living on the brink
and under the threat of it is no way to live at all. The
very possibility that it may happen is quite enough for me
and tells me that we are facing the wrong direction and ought
to look for radical alternatives.

LONDON by Becky

    The first thing I feel is agitated. I have no outlet.
I feel really hot with lots of energy. I can't stop moving

all the parts of me. I'm sweating all over. I feel cynical,
suspicious, not completely convinced by myself. I desperately
want to find the proper box to put my energy into, and the
right way to let it out. I'm holding on to myself tightly.
Oh Jesus, I'm so confused. I don't quite know who I am. I
get completely taken over by other people's personalities.
I'm going mad with surplus energy. My eyes are open and kind
of wild. I'm trying to fit everything together and nothing
seems to fit. I'm desperately trying to block everything
up and the more I try to box it up, the madder I go, because
I can't do it, I can't get everything under control. I'm
annoyed that people's moods change. I can't keep track. I
didn't get it all written down and damn it, it's all changed
already, so I have to throw it away and start again.

     My whole energy goes into being badtempered. I enjoy
being badtempered. I'm completely irritated, pickly and messy
- one minute I think I've achieved something, then I go along
the road and I find out there's about ten different ways
and I'm walking along every single one of them. Phew! I don't
know where to go from here. I've done all sorts of things in
my life, dangerous things and interesting things, bad things
and good things too. I can talk about them, but it's not
enough: I want more and more. I keep getting this feeling
of trying to consume everything. I think, "Quick! One day
I'm going to starve and so I've got to eat as much as I can
and I've got to get as much as I can and gather it all into a
box and take it with me. And yet I can't bear it when there's
masses of things. It annoys and irritates me.

     I've got a whole headful of what's right and what's
wrong and who's who and where everyone should be and what you
should do with your energy and if you haven't got any energy,
what you should do to get it. I can't bear it. I feel like
something is crawling all over me: I'm going completely mad
with it. I actually think there's a creature walking on me,
something itching me. I want it all to stop; I want to get
off.

     I've gone wrong from the very start. I've been working
on myself for years now and I'm turning into a complete mon-

ster. Before I started, I was perfect. Now I don't have any
friends at all. Now I just chase everybody away. I've turned
into a Dalek. If anyone comes near me, I say, "What do you
want? Eff off!" I don't like people, they drive me insane.
I'm going to start a new world and get rid of them all, and
start all over again with only Me. I've tried hard to be
nice - that's what you're meant to do, isn't it? And you're
meant to like me how I am. This is me (she grits her teeth
and snarls)!

I've been changing for years and I've achieved - this!
My god. You didn't expect this, did you? Well, this is what
has happened. After all these years, I have no further to go.
This is the Ultimate Me and I'll never come out of it. I
feel completely mechanical. I don't want anything to be loose
- I want everything packed tight and wired together and switched on and off. I feel like a machine trying to compute
everything. I've got lights switching off and on in me. I
look at that picture up there and all I see is splashes of
blood and electric storms and there's a man being electrocut-
ed by the storm. He's got, I've been got.

I feel completely shut in and clamped and everything's
metal and hard. I am walking along one long dark corridor,
and I just keep on going. The image I have in my mind is
of having steel boots on and steel clothes and being like
a soldier, clicking - the noise of clockwork as I walk; just
the noise of my steel feet walking on the steel floor; clang,
clang, I keep on moving forwards, but the corridor never
ends.

Something is getting to me. I'm scared it will eat me
away (starts yelling). Everything I touch turns to insects,
everywhere. I'm eating them. I'd rather die than feel this.
It feels really sharp and stinging; it's driving me mad.
It's not imagination any more, it's happening, I'm sure it's
happening (she's really freaking out now, hysterical). Something is eating me and I'm eating something else and that
something is eating something else and we're all joined together in a big chain going round and round and round. I've
felt like this a million times before. This is the place I

always get stuck. I don't know what I do when I get stuck
here - I've got a feeling I just kill myself off normally
because I can't bear it any more [this section becomes clearer if you allow for the concept of reincarnation - even of
whole cities or civilizations].

I'm very affected by blood. I'm desperately trying to
calm down. "Everything will be perfectly alright." But I
don't feel alright at all. I'm going blank. I'm panic-strick-
en. I feel I've let myself in for something horrible, like
I've joined the army or something, because I thought it was
good for me.

All through this reading, I feel I'm in a complete
little world of my own. I keep hoping it's just a dream,
something that will pass over. It's only a reading, or something bad I ate at dinnertime. Oh god, tell me I'm asleep
or it's just a bad trip. I don't want this to be me. My mind
is full of horror. I'm like a mad nutcase in the middle of
Birmingham. I feel like a machine. I've got buttons: you
press the buttons, and I'll do it. The only button I have
missing is the Sanity button. Doesn't anybody mind or care?
Jenny: We have actually got the message of this reading,
Becky, if you'd like to stop. Unless you want to do a little
bit of prognosis.
Becky: Prog..?
Jenny: Future.
Becky: Oh god, the future. Well, this is the future. This
person is definitely going to turn into a machine and everything is going to be clockwork, washed down with Ajax, painted white and filled with glittery tin switches. Something
awful is going to happen - oh, I know, this person is going
to build a big hospital and is going to take in millions of
people, wrap them in lovely white sheets and chop them up.
I'll inject everyone with water, I won't bother having proper
drugs. Dried grass made into green pills and water that's
coloured red with clothes dye and I'll squeeze it into everybody and 'cure' them. And I'll be paid billions of pounds for
doing it. There you are.
Snowy: I can't wait. Anything else?

Becky: More? You want more? Well, the only thing I think of
when I think 'future' is blackness. And the blackness is
full of all my fantasies of the Inbetween - of the world
when you die. It's horror. Everyone's going mad and the only
way to deal with it is to go mad yourself. Everyone is just
black faces and mess and bodies. Everyone is letting out
shit and madness. Everything is let loose because there's no
cars any more and no solid things. So all the madness of
the world is let out in the space Inbetween, and it's complete chaos. God save me if I ever reincarnate.
Jenny: God save us if you ever reincarnate.
Snowy: Tickets please! Anyone for the next train to London?

*****

Since you got me here I see
You're trying to steal my soul:
Your army's trying so very hard
To find for me a goal.
But where's your quiet pastures
Where there's time for me to be
Nothing else but what I am
That's what you seem scared to see.

You cover up your emptiness
With brick and noise and rush
Oh I can see and touch you
But you don't owe reality much.
Have mercy, I cry,
City, you're all upon my mind
Sometimes I think you keep forgetting
That you don't know me.

Send another carriage
Chugging down your chokey tube;
I hope it makes you happy
'Cause it don't do my health much good.
Your slowly killing fumes now
Squeeze the lemon in my head

Make me know just what it's like
For a sindrenched christian to be dead.
Ah, show to me your glitter
And your flashing neon light.
You see I think that only the sun
Knows how to be quietly bright.

Hey city, what you been doing?
All these years, what you been doing?
Who would believe
That what you been doing
Would make such a ruin of you?

MERCY I CRY, CITY

Song by the Incredible String Band

*****

From a reading on the City, to a man from the City:

JEREMY'S STORY

I am not like most of the people you will meet in this book. I am the total twentieth century man. I love aspirin, water closets, pre-packaged food, electronic games, aeroplanes, flashy fashion clothes, the whole technological thing. You are very likely to find me walking down the street with a cassette player hitched around my waist pouring music into my ears through headphones. I have never explored myself via therapy and unlike the vegetarian folk of Atlantis, put down meat with an enthusiasm which Dracula himself might envy. Nor do I share a lot of the beliefs of Atlantis — I do not believe in the end of the world for example. And as for existing in a total therapy environment day in day out for years as they do, the very thought makes me so nervous I have to have something with a lot of vodka in it to soothe me down.

But there you are, one of the delightful things about Atlantis is that it embraces all sorts of anomalies and contradictions, and I have in fact been visiting Atlantis for years. Many Atlantis folk have stayed in my house, which is a kind of Atlantis Embassy in London, and quite a few of my poems have appeared in the various Atlantis books Jenny has written.

I am appearing here to say to all you twentieth century rational scientific people like me: don't worry. Come on in, the water's fine. I know the whole thing is ridiculous, but nonetheless, it works. I know the whole idea of doing psychic and occult things regularly and casually and finding them helpful and easily accessible is totally way out, but nonetheless, it is possible. I've done it. And there's no use in saying pigs can't fly when you see them catching swallows.

One evening at my house, Snowy rang up in answer to an advert offering courses in developing one's psychic abilities. "Oh, hello, you don't know me, my name is Snowy James," she said. "What's that? Hilary James?" asked the man at the other end of the phone. 'Hilary' just happens to be Snowy's 'real' name, the name on her birth certificate, though she has practically never used it. Even I, who had known her some years, knew nothing of it.

The man she was phoning was called Joe Friedman. He told me that people fear their psychic powers greatly. He said that even people who have paid good money to develop these powers are often frightened when they begin to emerge. All through history, he says, people have 'scape-

goated,' that is, they have put their power
on to priests, magicians, shamans and gurus.
"You be magic and all-knowing. We are afraid/un-
worthy/too lazy/too scared." But we are all
priests, magicians, shamans, gurus, if we are
willing to let ourselves be. All you have to
do is open your own door. Psychic powers are
always within us, but when our rational selves
are strong and operating full blast, they are a
little shy, just as the stars are always there,
but are obscured by day by the much greater
light of the sun.

So this is a final avowal by this twentieth
century scientific person that he believes in
magic, it works, and that you, the reader, can do
it. Why not have a try?

Good luck,

JEREMY WARD

*****

CHAPTER ELEVEN: READINGS ON
IRELAND, ENGLAND, RUSSIA, USA, CHINA, THE INCAS

We wondered what would happen if we wrote
down the name of a whole country: would it be an
impossible task for a medium to give a 'feel' of
such a vast subject? We started small - with
Ireland.

IRELAND by Becky

Well, the immediate feeling is of everything being unorg-
anized and there's noise and mess and people everywhere.
(Laughter from the audience) Look, will everybody please
be quiet. I don't want to get too annoyed about it, but I'm
someone who would like a bit of respect. I have a sense of
authority, but I don't want to raise my voice.
I feel slow and relaxed, like I'm sinking. I'm being
drawn and dragged into the ground, pulled down and down.
I could actually pull myself back up, but I don't know whether I'm bothered. It's a feeling of something calling me slowly to my grave. I feel like snoring and falling asleep. That
woman over there, whoever she is [I was tidying the room -
JJ] is like a neurotic housewife. I feel so different from
that. I am so peaceful and quiet; I like taking things very
very slowly. Just you moving around looks like a film speeded
up to me. I am a very comfortable person, easygoing. Perhaps
it's just that I'm very old and my body has slowed down.
It just doesn't respond as quickly as my mind, which is still
going very quickly. If I was just myself, I wouldn't talk at
all. I feel like an old person who can't lift themselves
up. I move one leg and then the other and then get the crane
out to lift me and get the oilcan to move my joints. I get a
picture of dinosaurs - I've heard it said their colossal
weight made them move really slowly, as if they were almost
too heavy for their own strength.
Jenny: How did you get like this?

Becky: Well now, let me see, I'll take this very slowly. How did I get like this? I got like this by being laissez-faire. It was my natural way to go.

Jenny: What are the effects of it?

Becky: The effects of it are that I don't move very much!

Jenny: And how does it make you treat others?

Becky: It makes me have a lot of patience and understanding and a lot of time to give to people. [I can confirm this through living seven years in Southern Ireland in an outrage-ously flamboyant atheist commune stuck slap bang in the mid-dle of a fishing village, population: 200. In spite of sensa-tionalist press reports and our fair share of hassles, we have in general been treated with the utmost respect, accept-ance, and eventually, solid unostentatious friendship by this 100% Catholic community - JJ]

I have the feeling of a really patient teacher who has plenty of time to go through things really slowly. I would be very helpful.

Jenny: And how does this cause others to treat you?

Becky: People are a bit snooty with me and tend to ignore me and try and talk over my head. Because of my slowness and quietness, I don't get as much respect from people as I would like. People don't listen to me as much as they should. But it's their own loss.

Jenny: And what way are you going in the future?

Becky: There aren't going to be any big changes around me. I am who I am and I'm not going to suddenly change unless some-thing changes me. And I don't think there are many people with the power to change me.

Jenny: What can you teach us? If I had the time to listen to you, what would you teach me?!

Becky: Anything you want to know. I feel like my main lesson is caring - teaching people to be a bit like me, that's what most people teach, isn't it? I teach people to take things slowly and to have a lot of patience with others. I'm like an old priest talking to everyone at Mass and saying, "Love Thy Neighbour" and if you don't, well, such-and-such will happen. I've told you before and I don't have to tell you again. If you will go throwing bottles around, what do you expect to happen? If you drive a car before you've passed the test, you can't expect not to have a crash, can you? If you get drunk and start throwing your weight around, well, there you are..."

I feel I am something very solid, somebody very strong and sturdy in my ways and very wise. I imagine teenagers and young people battering away at me and hating me and rebelling against me and throwing abuse at me, and I say, "Yes, well, that won't get you anywhere you know." I am completely untouchable basically. People try every way to get at me and slag me but I'm just so sure of myself it doesn't matter somehow. Children these days! You would know, Jenny, don't you?

Jenny: What would I know?

Becky: The hooligans you get these days - these young ones that throw their weight around. No wonder there are so many accidents. They don't listen to me.

Jenny: What is your sureness based upon?

Becky: My first feeling is that I've been through an awful lot, that I've been a hooligan myself in my younger days. I did all those things when I was young and it didn't get me anywhere. I just feel that I'm very wise and very old and I know an awful lot about life.

Fred: Do you feel you're going anywhere? Do you feel like you're moving?

Becky: It sounds like you're worried about something. I'm quite happy where I am at the moment actually. I'm not particularly panic-stricken about moving on somewhere else. I'm quite content with the way things are.

Jenny: Can you guess who you are?

Becky: I'm him - Fred.

Jenny: In a way. But not exactly. Try again.

Becky: The Pope, or something like that.

Jenny: Something like that, yes.

Becky: The Church.

Jenny: Something like that!

Becky: IRELAND!

*****

So many men have come and tried to change us
To stop us from being what we are
But you might as well go chasing after moonbeams
Or light a penny candle from a star.

> From the song
> "If you ever go across the sea to Ireland"

*****

Across the water, then, to the country that has done most to try and 'change' Eire. What aspect of our own overcrowded island would Becky pick out?

ENGLAND by Becky

I feel embarrassed about expressing myself; I don't regard myself as a professional yet. I'm just not confident about myself. I'd like to be on stage with a microphone, but only if I could take the piss out of myself. If it was serious, I'd get too uptight and stiff. I set myself such high goals, I feel I've got to get to the top of the ladder quickly and I forget I'm not quite fit for it, so I fall off the ladder half way up and break my neck. I don't give myself time to enjoy what I do know and I try so hard, I'm puffed out before I start. I don't allow myself the space to sit back and learn and take life slowly. I'm like a young kid who was born with loads of lovely energy and magic, then the kid's energy is crushed and there's no more room for growth or excitement; and so it ends up growing up into a suppressed adult.

I haven't got any strong feelings in this reading. I don't feel very grand or exceptional. I feel quite mundane and normal. There's nothing extra-special about me. I've got a picture in my mind of Birmingham or Manchester, and

you go along the motorway and you see hundreds and thousands
of houses that all look the same; there's thousands of people
living in them and all the people have a TV, they all go to
- the same shops, they all read the same newspapers, all their
kids go to the same schools, none of them has any individuality, none of them have fought to get any fame or to do anything good in life or to lift themselves out of it. They're
all sitting back and allowing everything to happen around
them, waiting for the news and for everything to go their way
- for the food to be brought to them, the music, the entertainment, everything is given to them, and they've all got
jobs handed to them to click in and out of.

Jenny: What's in the future?

Becky: I'm an example of what not to do. I can't feel what's
in the future for me, but it's much more serious.

Jenny: What is the worst possible thing that you could do
at the present time?

Becky: What me? I wouldn't do anything! I'm innocent! I am a
person who doesn't like being accused of anything.

Jenny: I wasn't actually accusing you of anything!

Sally: It sounds like you are very guilty of something.

Becky: The minute you said that, I immediately thought: The
most terrible thing I could do would be to cause a nuclear
war. That was the immediate thing that came to my mind.

Jenny: How could you do that?

Becky: I don't know.

Jenny: You're clairvoyant, you've got to know!

Becky: This person doesn't feel they've got the power to
do anything.

Jenny: Oh yeah? And yet when I said, "What's the worst thing
you could do?" you said, "Cause a nuclear war."

Becky: Yes. This is somebody who has an awful lot of power,
but doesn't use it. They make out to be smaller and more
stupid than they are. I make out to be little and powerless.

Jenny: Well, I still want to know the answer to my question:
How could you cause nuclear war?

Becky: I suppose the way I would do that is by handing over
responsibility to somebody else.

*****

The Campaign for Nuclear Disarmament (CND)
has always argued that Britain, although geo-
graphically small, could have a large influence
on world politics by being the first nation
to unilaterally give up the monstrous illusion
of 'defence' through owning nuclear weapons.
In the '60s, the Labour Party (in Opposition)
finally adopted a policy of unilateral nuclear
disarmament, but this was later 'unilaterally'
abandoned by the feneigling of its leaders.

In 1982, there are few people left (there
were many in the 1960s) who would argue that
the USA has any very altruistic motives in encouraging us to saturate our 'Offshore Island'
(the title of a book about nuclear war by Margh-
anita Laski) with nuclear weapons and targets.
Our only hope ever was and is, firm withdrawal
from the whole obnoxious business. It is astonishing to me that Becky, who not only did not
know the nature of the reading she was doing,
but wouldn't have understood the political significance of it if she had, should pick out this
fatal abdication of responsibility on to the
shaky shoulders of 'Big Brother.'

*****

And so to Big Brother himself, the USA.
This reading, given to Snowy, is one of many
examples where our life-long prejudices (in
this case, extremely anti-American) were by
no means properly reflected in the reading. My
sister's delivery is highly philosophical and
metaphorical and responds to the vast diversity
of the United States. We have often noticed that
the very best and very worst, in people or situa-

tions, often go side by side. The USA has, on the
one hand, reached the ultimate in the Awfulness
of the twentieth century, but on the other hand
has spawned a whole bevy of growth movements
bringing some hope back to the world.

My publisher hated this reading, thought it
was the 'worst in the book' and at first wanted
me to leave it out. That's because it doesn't
say: "This is a reading of a country composed of
x number of States, with mountains over there,
lakes up there and such-and-such a history."
No, it certainly doesn't say that, nor anything
like it. What Snowy zooms in on is far deeper,
far more difficult to understand, and finally,
far more rewarding. She grasps briefly the energy
of the the entity 'USA' and treats it just like
we treat ourselves and one another at Atlantis:
what are we here for, what are we like, how
do we behave, and what is our real nature at
core; what do we teach, what must we learn,
where have we come from and in which direction
are we heading? To think of a whole huge country
in these terms was new for me, too, at the time
of this reading, and is something we'd probably
never have thought of doing if my curiosity
hadn't led me to put the US into my sister's
hands. I feel that she has come up precisely
with two major aspects of the USA: firstly,
the top layer of revolting Pepsodent toothpaste
smiles, the bonhomie and Good Intentions, the
Bighearted Caretaker (the South Americans would
have a word or two to say about that) - but
also the genuinely positive side of this charact-
eristic in the real openness, searching, explora-
tory nature of sections of the North American
population. And then, when all the bright cheesy
grins and golden handshakes are over, there is
the darker nature: a mean little mole squirreling

away (sorry about that) his assets, digging
tunnels to prepare for blowing up the world; the
capitalist instinct, the protective, visa-demand-
ing acquisitive side of the US, so familiar to
all its enemies and victims.

Over to Snowy:

(It needs explaining by the way that the
entire walls of my room in which most of the
readings in this book take place are entirely
covered in a picture-collage of cuttings taken
from a dozen different sources. These pictures
provide a very useful 'scrying' focus for anyone
doing a reading.)

THE USA by Snowy

I feel as though my eyes are really wide open. I'm scanning everything. I'm looking at that wall and it's full of
images, full of colour and life and I'm seeing it all. I'm
seeing the journeyings and the travellings and the peoplings
and the relatings and the dyings and the lovings and the
hatings and the work and the creating; I'm seeing psychic
things and children's things, practical things and intellectual things and artistic things. If I'm a person, I'm one who
has a broad overall vision, and almost an obsession with
it. It's like I'm desperate to oversee everything. Maybe
it's that I've got a responsibility to keep my eye on everything. Yes, I feel that I'm a person or entity that is used
to responsibility, used to being in control of the situation,
and I find it hard to abdicate [Vietnam!].I want to know and
see everything. I want to be in charge. I'm superior. I'm
somebody who has far-ranging interests and activities: my
energy spreads over a wide area. I feel as though I'm handling things quite well most of the time, but sometimes it's a
bit much. I'm someone who people are completely jealous about
and want to possess and gobble up. But actually I don't feel
threatened because I'm ever so sure of who I am; my boundaries are clear. I feel tremendously arrogant, but my arrogance

seems well-based. I've just been so many places and seen
so many things.

Jenny: Could you say more about your role?

Snowy: My role is to keep things clear and bright. My role is
to disinfect. I'm a cleansing device. It sounds as though
what I've said means I'm a force for complete good, but I
don't feel saintly or angelic or goody-goody. I feel ever
so involved in all the mess. I feel as though I've got my
hands completely dirty; I am completely in it. It's almost
like I'm a disinfectant down the toilet.

Whatever I am, obviously I need to develop and improve.
And when I ask myself, "What is my growth point?" I get the
exact opposite feeling to what I had at the beginning of
the reading, which was tremendous eyes staring: Now I feel
blind. It would seem as though I have been very blind and
I'm having to learn to see, but not by desperately scanning
everything. It's my destiny to find some sort of balance;
neither obsessed with overseeing everything, nor blindly
closing my eyes.

At the moment, my eyes are closed up tight and tense.
I'm a curled-up little mole, underground, a velvety black
mole just sniffing my way through tunnels and not ever caring
or wanting to know or see anything. I feel quite strong and
independent, but mole-ish and sniffy and underground. I'm a
hoarder and I'm private. I have tunnels blocked up with
things and I don't want anybody to come in and I don't want
to go out or even to have a mate. I'm barricading all the
exits up; I just have my little store in the corner and I'm
sniffing along to make sure nothing has come in and patching
up all the holes where the earthquake has come in through the
roof. I feel tough. I'm a real tough little creature, ever so
selfish. I'm hidden under the earth and I don't give a damn
about anybody or anything, except in so far as they intrude
on my space. I'm not going to let them. I'm very badtempered.

Jenny: I want to know the good things about you for the world
and the bad things about you.

Snowy: OK, the good things. Whatever my teaching is, it has
come through experience. I've got my knowledge through in-

volvement. I teach people that coming into this world is
a matter of getting involved; it's no good locking yourself
away or getting on some cosmic trip, because if you were
really on a cosmic trip, you wouldn't be down here on Planet
Earth.

Bad things - what's bad about me? Well, although I'm
saying that I get my hands dirty, I don't actually feel emotionally involved at all. There's too much blandness and
positiveness about me, and that can't be right. It can't be
all bloody clarity and light and brightness - there's something peculiar going on. It's something to do with loving
'humanity' but hating people. This person is making it all
seem too easy and nice, and it's not. This person is pretending it doesn't hurt; but it does. Oh - two pictures on the
wall which I've never noticed before stand out now. One is
of a large bird with its wings outspread [ever looked up
to the top of the American Embassy in London?]. It looks
like a bird of prey, and it's coming straight towards the
camera. It could be a vulture type of creature that has come
down to get a body. And next to it is a picture of a skele-
ton. What am I getting from that? That you've got to hurt.
That death isn't just passing on into another life. Death
is to do with pain, sickness, a long time, confusion, decay,
nasty things. It isn't just a matter of turning over the
page.

I'm a trickster. If I were the only way in which you
learnt about what the world was, you'd think it was some
sort of nice jolly ride that you went on and you had little
lessons written out on tablets before you. Number One you
learn this and Number Two you learn that. You'd get under
the illusion that life was easy and you would be completely
mistaken because life is not easy. I keep getting the word
Trick, that I'm a Trick to make you think everything's OK.
All that bloody clarity stuff. I'm as confused as anybody
else. I mean, am I going to keep my boundaries so bright
and clear that I can't actually relate to anyone? Am I going
to be so principalled and upright and perfect that I end
up with nothing?

I'm at some sort of turning point in my career where I have to take all the learning from my vast seeing of patterns and start to apply it very specifically. What is going to happen? The first thing I get is that there's got to be a big clearout. I would have to get rid of excess, and draw together just certain elements that I wanted. There would have to be a big pushing away of everything else.

Jenny: What would happen to all the rest?

Snowy: Gone. They would just be gone. Thrown away, put on the compost heap. I get a picture of that bit in The Six O'Clock Bus [a book about the spiritual significance of the world shakeups expected during the rest of this century] where the authoress [Moira Timms] says two thirds of the world's population is going to be wiped out, and she talks about there being select communities or scattered groups surviving. I keep getting a picture of those scattered groups and my feeling is to help them to communicate with one another and to show them why they have been chosen to survive and how we're to put all the knowledge of all the shite that went before into building something a bit cleaner and brighter. I feel much more down-to-earth when I'm talking like this. This person that I'm doing the reading on is now at this stage much saner.

Jenny: Well, you're the USA!

Snowy: What! Oh, then, the reading's far too positive!

Jenny: Maybe. I think what you've picked up is the big sell of the 'easy life' - happiness through possession of material goods. Obviously the US has reached the limits of 'growth' of this nature: there needs indeed to be a 'big clearout' but of course there's little chance of sufficient enlightenment for a whole nation to realize that in time and turn back towards simpler living. And so the inevitable will happen when the cancerous growth of 'things' chokes the main body to death in the all-time explosion of nuclear war or natural catastrophe forcing all the rot off the face of the earth. I don't know about those 'select surviving groups.' Maybe. Round and round we go till the lesson is learnt....

*****

Russia is a country I feel I know nothing about, having discarded the glossy absurdities of my Commie background propaganda. Of all the non-personal readings, this one upset me the most. I kept wanting them, the Russians, to turn a different way. I pushed my questioning of Becky in the hope something more positive would turn up, but no way could I bend reality – the strange vibrational reality of readings – in order to fit in with my desire for a 'Happy Ending.' The message remains stark and depressive.

Immediately prior to this, Becky had been doing a reading on the rightwing politician, the Rev. Ian Paisley. When handed 'Russia', she jumped right across the bed to the other side of the room and said:

RUSSIA by Becky

Well, in relation to the last reading, I'm on the other side. I look at things from a different point of view. I don't need to sit up there on a big chair like that last fellow: I'm quite comfortable sitting down here. (She starts speaking in a working-class accent.) I'm short, with a bit of a pot belly - a belch here and there and a pipe hanging out of my mouth, a pair of glasses on. In the last reading, I thought I was for the community, but in fact I had to lower myself an awful lot to try and please the public; but in this reading, it just comes naturally to me. That last fellow would have his meetings in grand white houses and everything would be posh - I think he fancies himself as the Queen. But I would be in any old local hall and everyone would be sitting around smoking fags. I imagine having a long moustache and twirling it and sitting there taking the piss out of the other side. I mean it's been going on for years, hasn't it? As long as I can remember. The man next door is trying to take it all over.

I've got a feeling that I'm waiting for something to

happen; and I haven't yet taken my position. Whatever is going to happen isn't going to be very nice and I've accepted
that. I haven't got any solutions. The other side seems to
think they have a solution, but I don't know what to do.

I feel on the outside of everything; I don't feel enmesh-
ed in what is going on as much as the others are. I feel
like I have a lot of power; people listen to me. I see lots
of different things going on outside myself, but I don't
see any of them as being particularly good. I don't see any
of them being the right way. I mean, it doesn't work, does
it? War is still going on. I'm a bit disappointed by my own
wishy-washiness because I'd like to feel fierce about what
is wrong. But actually I'm more worried than the other side
is. They're up there and they've got one track, and they're
charging along. I don't think they're really concerned about
what the outcome is going to be. They don't question themselves very much. I feel I take a lot more responsibility on
to myself. I look at what's going on and I see it's not working and I think, "Oh my god, what's going to happen?" and
"What am I going to do?" and "Who is going to do what?"

And while I'm worrying about what's going on out there,
my own personal life at home might be collapsing. I'm organizing everyone else's life, but my own life needs repairing
from time to time. I can imagine sitting up for nights on
end worrying about things, writing things out and being at
meetings, and I might forget to wash my teeth or shave or
brush my hair, and my clothes would be getting dirty and
I wouldn't have time to change, I'd be too involved with
what is going on out there. And my wife might be threatening
to leave me because I hadn't given her enough time.

Jenny: What if you were faced with a really critical situation?

Becky: Well, I don't want to think about it because I would
not want to face it. I would keep away from danger if possible. I feel quite scared actually. I don't like what's going
on and I'm not all that sure of myself. I think I'm much
more likely to withdraw from things. I feel wary. I suppose

it's partly to do with the fact that I don't feel I've got as
much power as the other side. I'm a bit more given-up than
them. I'm more affected by the terribleness of everything.
Jenny: What do you think has gone wrong for you?
Becky: The minute you asked me that, I looked at that picture
up there with loads of skulls on it, lots and lots of death.
What has gone wrong is loads of destruction. It's been going
on for so long and it's so complicated, I just don't know
where to start or what to do.
Jenny: But if you had to make decisions?
Becky: I immediately thought, "I'm a peacemaker." But even
when I say that, I don't think that's the real answer. I
don't want to be pinned down. I don't want to have to make
any decisions. I can't bear it. I would hate to say one thing
and then have to do it, because I've got the feeling I would
turn round the next minute and realize I'd done the wrong
thing. Then I'd want to back-track, start all over again
and have another chance. But I know I wouldn't be able to,
it would be too late. For me to make a decision just feels
like the end. It doesn't matter which way I turn, I'm going
to die anyway. I've got a really short amount of time left
to make a big decision.
Jenny: And if you have to make it, what's going to happen?
Becky: I'll repeat something I've already planned in my mind.
I don't think I will come out with anything original. It'll
be something that's already been decided and I'll just come
out with out of the tension and strain of the moment. Then
two minutes later, I might completely regret it.
Jenny: What makes you react like that?
Becky: It's because I've got grudges against somebody. I'm
so annoyed about being put in this position in the first
place, having this strain put on me, that I've blocked from
letting anything positive occur to me. I have a lot of different possibilities and they're all negative. I only have to
choose one of them. Everything has speeded up and got really
sour and bitter. I'm saying, "Well, blast the lot of them
if they're going to behave like that to me. I just don't

give a damn any longer. Let's put a finish to the lot of
it. If none of you are going to listen to me and you're all
going to have a riot all over the place and none of you are
going to be sensible or take responsibility, then I don't
care any more, it's only my life I have to lose."

    And yet I'm not sure of myself.

Jenny: What is the effect of this insecurity?

Becky: Panic. The outcome is to give up and throw everything
aside, throw in the towel, that's the way my energy goes:
give up the fight to live, the fight to keep anything in
the slightest bit clean or clear. I have the feeling that
whatever I will say is the ultimate. I suppose it must just
mean war, that's what it must be. I just have to say one
thing, and that's the end of the world.

*****

    If I knew nothing about Russia, I knew even
less about China. Some time after the following
reading was done [in 1980], I met an Irish merch-
ant seaman who told me that 'Red' China was a
place he'd often visited − just the ports of
course − and he gave me several titbits of information, including the fact that no Chinese woman
is allowed to marry until she is TWENTY−SIX
years old; that marriages are arranged − the com-
rades may well not even know each other, i.e. no
love, passion or sex please. He said that men and
women all wore the same clothes, light blue
shapeless overalls, and that this was regulation:
women were absolutely not allowed to wear anything which emphasized their womanliness. He
said that in spite of this, the people he met
said they were happy.

    I remember well the atmosphere in the room
as Becky delivered her picture: the energy was
such that I slumped into a heap, nearly fell

asleep and never wanted to hear another reading
again. Worried about the extreme negativity of
the 'China' reading, I asked my publisher if
he knew anything about the country, whether it
really was so bleak and grey. He told me about
the 'Cultural Revolution', about the banning
of Western music and all things colourful. But
WHERE did <u>Becky</u> get this energy from? All she
had in her hand was a scruffy piece of paper on
which was written:

CHINA

I was frozen when I came in. As I started the reading, I
looked in the mirror and was very acutely aware of my hair,
which is dark, and my eyes which are dark. (Becky is talking
in a punctuated, staccato voice, the words very separate.)
I have a dark complexion. I am aware of my hair being in
a parting to one side, combed with a 'flick' (she is speaking
very stiffly and formally). I cannot bear things not being
done properly, perfectly. I want everything to be organized;
it is very important to be proper. There's a way to do everything: there's a proper way of preparing food and of preparing your body and for doing your hair. There's a way to do
it, and that's the way you should do it, so there you are.
      Ever since I began this reading, I've had a pain.
<u>Jenny</u>: In the very middle of your stomach?
<u>Becky</u>: Yes.
<u>Jenny</u>: The minute you picked up that reading, I got a pain
there.
<u>Becky</u>: That means that something in my life has got hold
of me and is stopping me from expressing myself. Although I'm
not aware of it most of the time, it is always there and
if I were to move in certain ways, it would hurt me. I immediately think that it's a feeling connected with sex and dancing and self-expression.
<u>Jenny</u>: How do you interpret all this?
<u>Becky</u>: There are all sorts of aspects of my life where I'm

cowering down. I have been brought to my knees to obey certain rules in my life and they're not particularly good for
me. They give me pain because it's not healthy. I've got a
picture of my parents above me, looking down scowling at
me, and me standing at a mirror brushing my hair, and it's a
feeling of being told to behave myself, control myself, be
careful, don't be loose, you mustn't enjoy yourself, you
mustn't laugh, be happy, dance or have sex. You mustn't,
you mustn't, you mustn't. Just letting this out has made
the pain go away.

Jenny: Yes, mine's just gone too.

Rob: How did you get into this state?

Becky: I don't feel in a state.

Jenny: Well, you were just now!

Becky: By obeying rules that were set out for me. People
putting out rules to stop good energy - the pain was from
obeying.

Jenny: So which way are you going in your life?

Becky: I feel I'm going in the direction of giving up. I've
already done it in fact. I'm already saying "Yes" to all
the things that have been put out before me, all the rules
which say: be normal and don't really enjoy yourself. We're
going to dismiss you if you don't obey our rules. And I feel
I've said, "OK, I'll obey." I want to be right and proper
because I want security.

Rob: Have you always been this way?

Becky: No. Something I keep wanting to say is, "In my country
we .." do such and such. In my country, no, we haven't always
been like this. In my country, we used to be a lot more outgo-
ing and happier and a lot more flamboyant. But there's not
much of a flow left to me any more.

Jenny: Which way are you heading?

Becky: I feel like I'm clamming up more and more. I'm stiffen-
ing. And I feel that the more I clam up, the more I'm hated.
I'm going to be destroyed, that's what it feels like. I'm
going to allow myself to be walked over, trodden on, killed.
Any goodness or life that I did have will just be blown away

in the wind and forgotten. It won't be carried on by anybody.

Jenny: What does it feel like being you?

Becky: Horrible, really horrible. Very hostile.

Jenny: Towards?

Becky: There is hostility coming towards me, that's what it feels like. Whatever I represent, or whatever I am, an awful lot of hostility comes towards me.

Jenny: Why?

Becky: It's a feeling that I haven't stood up enough for what I'm doing, for who I am; that I haven't been confident enough in who I am and what I'm doing, and so people are interrogating me and I've allowed myself to be interrogated. It's obvious that I must have some huge guilt, some huge thing is already going on inside me.

Jenny: What is it?

Becky: I've allowed myself to believe in something that's greater than me supposedly, and I've allowed it to take my life over and I'm completely in horror and in awe and tension the whole time. I've given my life over. I had beauty and I didn't value it. I damaged myself by handing myself over.

Rob: What are your relationships with other people like?

Becky: Terrible. They're cold. Oh dear, I'm so negative. Everything has really turned sour and my relationships with people are sour. I have no self-respect any more and so people don't respect me. I feel a seriousness about the place, and a coldness in people. There's no passion left, no hot feeling any more. And quite honestly, if I'm going to have a cold feeling, I'd rather have the cold feeling of killing everybody rather than lying at the bottom of the pile and being killed.

Rob: What are your ambitions?

Becky: My main ambition at the moment is to stop this horrible reading! So that means I've no respect for my own life. I'm waiting for other people to make it better for me. I desperately want an end to come to it all. A feeling that I've made a big mess and done all sorts of things wrong and I'm still scrabbling around and making a mess.

Rob: How do you react to other people's advice?
Becky: I think I'm quite defensive. I have a feeling of block-
ing people out. I don't think I'm very open at all.
Jenny: What do you achieve from that?
Becky: Not very much!
Jenny: Yes, but what do you think you achieve?
Becky: It's a sensation of hoping I'll manage to stop contact. I hope I'll be able to get out of responsibility for
everything.
Jenny: What if you didn't lock people out, what are you scared of happening?
Becky: I'm scared of being exposed, of my weaknesses being
shown. This is the ultimate feeling of someone who's cut
off: feeling very insecure and thinking that by pushing people away, blocking off, I'm somehow going to manage to survive. I'm completely paranoid. This person likes to think
that they're OK, that they're quite communicative and happy.
They think, "I have problems, but I sort them out. I'm a
good person." But from the feel of the reading, I would say
this is not true: that I'm completely the opposite - guarded
and defensive. It would take somebody really powerful and
strong to open me up or to get into me. My defensiveness
puts people off, people turn their heads away completely
and don't want to know me. It makes me feel cornered and
horrible and more and more isolated.

*****

After this depressing reading, we tried
somewhere completely different: the Incas of
Peru. At the time of the reading, I knew so
little about them, I wasn't quite sure whether
it was a surviving tribe in South America, or
whether the Spaniards had destroyed them entirely. Since then, because of our intended move
to that part of the world, I have attended a
brief course in Quechua, the language of the

Andean Indians, at St. Andrew's University,
during which I had access to and crammed into
myself a whole range of books on the highly
organized Inca civilization. I discovered that
'Inca' really only refers to their kings - the
Indian population was as subordinate to them
as it later was to the Spaniards. Ornate decora-
tion, imposing costumes, elaborate rituals,
facial masks, theatrical behaviour and customs,
were all very much a part of the Inca's way
of life, just as Becky picks up. And the naive
way the Inca King handed himself over to be
chopped by a bunch of impudent Spaniards is
one of the incidents in history that is hardest
to believe.

As with all these readings of such vast
subjects, only a tiny sample emerges; what fasc-
inates me each time is the 'vibe' emanating
from a mere written word. Did we somehow put
all this into Becky? Well, here's what came
out:

THE INCA CIVILIZATION OF PERU by Becky

The minute I picked this reading up - before I picked it
up in fact - I had an image of opera and theatre and masks
and costumes, really grand costumes and face-masks, like
cats and devils; everything grand in big halls, with high
ceilings and chandeliers, with tables of fantastic food,
wine, the whole lot. I have a feeling of being very tall,
sturdy and strong; a feeling too of drama, of learning off
amazing spiels, learning things off by heart for a play,
and speaking in old-fashioned language. [The Incas had no
written language whatsoever.] I am very aware of my posture,
the way I stand: I am making sure that my shoulders are very
square. I have huge padded shoulders to my clothes to make me
look really big [drawings from the period confirm this detail
precisely]. Being very strong really matters to me. I'm very

stern. I imagine myself having a Roman nose.

(At that moment, she accidentally bangs her elbow) Oh, I'm the sort of person who hurts themselves and then makes drama out of it: "Wound, O Wound." I've got a feeling of theatre and clowning. I have images of plastic knives that you stab yourself with and they disappear into themselves and you don't really get killed, but you can have the drama of it.

I'm not sure where to go from here - I'm the sort of person who has a sudden burst of energy, a sudden flash of brilliance, but after that, I kind of collapse, and find that I'm waiting at a busstop for the next bus to come along and take me away. It's like a young person becoming famous suddenly and having a great time and really doing things well, and then perhaps one of my parents steps in, or an elder brother, and I fall back. I give up I suppose. There was a burst of youth and happiness and joy and everything was flowering and happy at the beginning, and then bang! there was a flattening of everything.

Jenny: What was your weakness?

Becky: Not fighting for myself. I didn't stand up for myself. I allowed people to undermine me.

Fred: Have you any message to give to the people in this room?

Becky: That it's very important to be individual, to have your own spark, to start things yourself; because the trouble with most people in this world is that they all follow each other, nobody stands out, only a few people really stand out above everyone else and just be different.

Rob: Are you trusting of other people?

Becky: I suppose I must be because I've allowed myself to follow other people. And I've learnt to be guarded, not actually closed, but not to just go along with anything at any old time, but to really question things and to know if something is really worthwhile or not. I didn't spend enough time finding out if things were real or not, and how much basis there was in what people were saying to me.

*****

CHAPTER TWELVE: DEATH

As three of the readings in this chapter are
of an eighteen-year-old girl whose life ended
abruptly in a London fire, it is very relevant
to give space first to her father, Mr. David
Boadella, to comment on the one evening of readings he spent with us.

DAVID BOADELLA'S STORY

When Jenny and Snowy first started writing about their
psychic experiences, I thought they had gone back to old
traditions of Irish witchcraft. But they emphasize that anyone who can tune in to spontaneous feelings can pick up some
kind of 'psychic' communication.

It was, to say the least, remarkable to see Jenny per-
plexing herself with the problem of feeling into the body
style and personality of a confident man who liked order
and believed in leaving a strong imprint on others. We had to
tell her the person we had in mind was not a man. "If I'm not
a man," she said, "then I must be a Margaret Thatchery kind
of woman." The name on the paper was Margaret Thatcher.

When we wrote 'UFO' for Snowy, she started to go all
skittish and flutter her fingers. She felt she had bells
on her, and coloured lights. She kept looking upwards and
zooming her head around. She behaved like a comic caricature
of a character from Close Encounters. "I don't know who I
can be," she said. "Unless I'm a UFO."

When Snowy tried to tune in to my daughter, who died
tragically in a London fire two years ago, her mood changed
totally. This was not a seance, nor was reverence expected,
nor did Snowy know that the name on the paper was of a dead
teenager personally related to someone in the room. But she
became much more spiritually aware and answered questions
about life after death. I was told that if I emptied my mind

more, it would deepen my life, which is true, but more important was that the whole atmosphere of the room deepened greatly, with Jenny asking many crucial questions about death
and the after-life that were not themes I'd heard her raise
before.

So what is happening? Nothing spooky or occult. Just the
ability to relax mental muscles and tune in to a level of
sensation and imagery deeper than the personal. Of course
whatever is said also reflects qualities in the person of
the agent, as well as the subject who is chosen as the focus.

I don't want anything to do with seances or puerile
communications: I know, however, that when I quieten inside
and step out of the rush of life events a little, I feel
Eilidh, my daughter, very much alive still. I don't think
she 'spoke through' Snowy, but that Snowy was some way in
touch with a mood and style of being that does connect with
Eilidh.

From the day of Eilidh's death onwards, I knew we are
evolving in two worlds and that this is only one of them.
The world we see with eyes shut is immenser than the one
we see with eyes open.

There is great danger that the occult movement gets
a monopoly on the answers and drives people away from their
own truth, their own anxiety, and their own search for greater trust by mass-producing cliche answers about death and
what's after.

Arthur Guirdham wrote a book called <u>We Are One Another</u>.
After the deep play of one evening of Jenny and Snowy's very
ordinary and non-melodramatic but always surprising variety
of 'psychism,' I move several steps nearer to realizing that
the world of myself is not contained within the skin.

DAVID BOADELLA

*****

When I was twenty-two years old, I had
a very posh (Harley Street) but illegal abortion.
I was with the doctor for only four hours and
he was in a hurry to get me sorted out and packed
off. The anaesthetic he used was gas.

I fought against the gas-mask and was terrified out of my wits, feeling that it would suffo-
cate me. No amount of reasoning could convince
me I wasn't being killed. As far as I was concerned, I died.

My next moment of any kind of consciousness
is difficult to describe, because 'I' didn't
exist. I was disembodied consciousness. However,
from this state of non-being, I witnessed what
seemed to me a horrific scene. I saw a clumsy
two-dimensional oblong-shaped wheel, a bit like
a gasket from a car engine, and it was flicking
monotonously, erratically round and round in
circles, attached to nothing, related and connected to nothing, all alone in a dim black void.
On this wheel were flat silhouettes, just head
and shoulders, of various beings, people, spread
around it at intervals, faceless, pointless,
lifeless, joined helplessly and hopelessly forever to the wheel. I was observing the sickening
monotony and aimlessness of this scene when
suddenly, in a split-second 'flick' of the wheel,
I was horrified to find my perspective had changed: I was now on the Wheel. I was one of those
figures I had so recently pitied from my grand
distance of blessed non-being. I'll never forget
that most miserable moment, the appalling realization that I had been condemned to participate
(probably the abortionist was shaking me, trying
to bring me through to another 'level' of wakefulness). If for some 'birth' is a joyous thing,
all I can say is, it was far worse for me than

the 'death' I thought I had just experienced. Dying had been physical, terrifying surely, but this was a mental horror of realization that I had been 'claimed,' dragged inexorably onto a wheel I wanted nothing to do with.

As the doctor, through alternately slapping me, hugging me, pleading with me and calling my name, eventually pulled me through layer after layer of thick resistance to coming to, I remember - apart from being sick all over him, and driving him to distraction by sobbing uncontrollably - crying out, "please don't make me come back, I was happy being dead."

*****

Being born, giving birth, dying. Difficult, painful, inevitable, frightening. Each a mixture of fascination, horror, wonderment, and sometimes - rarely - joy. Death I have been obsessed with all my life: thinking about it, worrying about it, later philosophizing about it, reading and writing about it, trying to come to terms with it. I'm still trying. Our psychic work has opened up an unexpected avenue of exploration of this highly-charged subject.

What does it feel like to be faced with death? to die? to be dead? to die 'before time'? Some of our readings have given us glimpses of the answers.

A friend of ours in Ireland witnessed some of the readings being done in the commune one day and immediately asked us to do one for him. He wanted to know more about a local suspected murder. It was an eight-year-old girl who had disappeared several years previously in the area and her body had never been found.

We gave the reading to Snowy to do. She
had just come over from our island and knew
nothing of the nature or subject of the reading,
nor who was wanting it done.

At first, she picked up aspects of the
child's character structure. But soon she said,
as she sat on my floor looking at her hands,
arms and legs: "There's something funny about my
skin. It's white and pale and lifeless. Oh!
I'm dead!" We who were listening neither confirmed nor denied this information and attempted
to contain any flicker of a reaction. Snowy
then said, "Let me see, how did I die?" and
she began systematically to try and discover
what had happened, while we listened, hardly
daring to breathe.

She said she could see a point in front
of her which she was moving towards, moving
too fast towards, much too fast, being rushed
towards it in fact. Everything was happening
far too quickly for her; she was getting panicky,
struggling and upset. Starting to cry, she yelled, "Oh! It's my death!" I was crying too by
this time, as quietly as possible. Snowy was going through all the distress of being forced,
fast, horribly fast, towards this inevitable
point in front of her. She felt roughly handled,
by more than one person; she felt bundled -
into a car? She felt something over her head.
She felt something bashing her on the back of
the head.

"I'm not ready," she was crying. "I'm too
young."

*****

We were shocked to hear of the death by fire
of the daughter of our one-time therapist, David
Boadella. Eilidh had left home for the first

time the day before, travelled the several hundred miles from her village to London to begin
residential work in an old people's home, and
twelve hours later, she was killed, along with
several other people.

We have done three readings on this girl
to try to come to terms with what happened.
The first time, her name was given to Snowy
on our island where there is no electricity,
so the reading could not be taped. We were sitting round our peat fire one evening in our central cottage. My sister of course had no idea
who she had been given.

At the very beginning of the reading, Snowy
said, "I feel this reel of the film is finished.
It is time to put in a new reel now." She depicted someone very bored and fed up. She said looking at us all, "Well, you lot think everything
is new and exciting, but I can tell you, the
world's not like that for me."

Snowy was sitting on a table staring down
into the peat fire. "I am going right into that
fire," she said. "I can imagine dancing and
melting with the flames."

Several weeks later, I gave the same reading
to my daughter on the mainland. This time, I
plugged in the cassette recorder. Here is part of
the very long and harrowing material that came
out:

EILIDH BOADELLA by Becky

I am boiling hot. I feel like I'm suffocating. I've
got pain in my chest. Oh god, I feel ill, I feel as if I'm
going to faint. I feel hot and sweaty, like there's hot air
all around me. I feel kind of mindless. (She starts breathing
short, deep breaths) I keep feeling I'm pumping myself up,
taking in air, trying to take in lots and lots of air, but

there's still not enough air. I feel like I'm going to pass
out any minute. I feel like I'm floating around. I'm in a
panic. I'm in a hurry to get everything out, to explain everything, to tell everyone what's going on, to show you that
I'm here. I'm suffering and I can't cope and I'm boiling
hot and I'm about to melt down. I'm going to conk out any
minute and give up and start all over again. I want to scream
something out of myself. I'm gritting my teeth and holding
on desperately. My mind and body are rushing at tremendous
speed, going round and round and round, I'm zooming and shooting through space at a million miles an hour, just shooting
round and round. There's no time to rest or relax, I just
keep on going zoom zoom, round and round. I've got no time
to think or feel, I'm just being hit off something all the
time and going round and round. The air is really thick.
Everything's really sticky and sweaty and hot and horrible.
I keep squeezing on to myself, holding on really tightly.
I'm holding on to a thread, just a tiny thread, and it could
snap so easily.

I'd love to be like an aeroplane, something with wings
so that I could fly and make a noise. I've got a really tight
feeling in my chest as if I'm being crushed, as if I've been
punched in the stomach and winded. (Breathes strangely) I
keep wanting to stop, to give up on myself. There's a rushing,
swirling, hot feeling in my stomach, like hot water. I feel
completely insecure, like I'm not attached to anything. I
feel like a spinning top in the middle of space, spinning
round and round. My head's going round and I can't get hold
of anything at all for definite in my mind. I'm getting all
sorts of images, like I keep thinking I'm just a little planet
going swirling around in the middle of space. I'm a little
blob just swirling around in blackness. I'm completely wrapped
up in myself, caved in, curled up.

I keep feeling like crying. Who am I? What am I doing?
Where am I going? Who do I belong to? Why am I alive at all?
Why am I suffering? Who's in control of this situation? Who
is going to tell me what to do? Who's going to make sure

that I stay sane, because I'm going insane. (Crying now) I keep thinking, "I've got to be sensible." You're meant to stop yourself from crying, you're meant to keep really calm in the situation, you can't start cracking up now; you can't start going soft now. You've got to keep your strength up. You can't start falling apart at the seams now. But I want to curl up and go to sleep and cut off. I don't want to know any more.

I feel like a coiled spring, ready to burst. I feel completely distorted and screwed up. Can I end this reading? (She is crying) I feel like I'm in a nightmare and I can't come out of it. I want to stop everything, kill myself. I can't bear life any more and I want to end it. But I know even if I do die, it won't end. It'll be worse if I die, it'll be even more horrific. I want to put the reading down and let go and come out of it. I can feel the blood rushing up and down my body and all my veins are going to burst, my blood pressure is getting higher and higher, everything is going to pop.

Now I feel like I'm in the waiting room, waiting for something like ... the end. In a waiting room with lots of other people like myself, just waiting, for Doomsday. I feel light in my body. I'd just love to be asleep, wandering, dreaming, floating around. When I first picked up this paper, I got a hot, hot feeling. Now I feel almost like water. There is something quite magical about me. I look in the mirror and I'm moving and I don't look solid. I'm rippling, moving like waves in water, or like smoke, and I've lost my panic now. I feel very very calm. There is something very mature about me. I have a feeling of going away. I'll be looser than when I'm here; I'll be freer. I'll be dancing and dancing. After all the trouble I've gone through, I feel quite confident about dealing with adventure on my own. I feel really calm, sober, mature, alert, ready for the next storm.

Jenny: If you look back on what you went through, what do you feel about it?

Becky: I've got a feeling of cleansing. It was something I needed to go through and I went into it and through it.

✻✻✻✻

The third reading using the name of this young girl took place in front of her father. It was now about two years since the girl's death. The reading was done late at night in my publisher's office, with him present, and it was done by my sister Snowy. It was the quietest, calmest reading I have ever witnessed.

EILIDH BOADELLA by Snowy

(For the whole of the first part of this reading, Snowy concentrates entirely on the piece of folded paper containing Eilidh's name. She treats it with great care and reverence, keeping it clean and neat.)

A nice square piece of paper folded nice and clean. Discipline is something that concerns this person or entity. A slow start on this reading. I am a person or something that finds it hard to get started. I'm going round and round and round and round. I'm like an engine that can't start. I need a kick start, I need someone with jump leads, I need some help. I'd really like to have my own engine ticking over. But I'm scared of messing myself up - I like the nice white smoothness and the tight edges. I like the neatness and whiteness, but it keeps bothering me that there's writing on the inside. I don't really want to see it, I ever so much don't want to see what's inside. I very much don't want to see myself. It wouldn't be proper, it wouldn't be the right thing to do. The right thing to do would be to get that wheel going round with no false start, just to get going.

I must be careful not to squeeze this piece of paper, really careful not to screw myself up. I must keep it smooth and disciplined and white and narrow and straight. I feel a lot of friction and warmth when I rub this, it's a good alive warm feeling. That's better - maybe there'll be some chance of starting if I just rub and get warm and just get everything ticking over and humming and purring. I am looking at this reading as if it is something important and valuable.

I am something of value, something that's important, and
I have to be preserved. In fact I should be in a thing like
that musical box over there (it has a perspex cover). I must
just be careful of myself, I must make an effort to preserve
the paper just as it is, and underneath there will be a little brass plaque with writing on it which will explain the
date and where I was found and people will come along and
there'll be a glass case over it all and you will look
through and they'll get their glasses and look me up in the
catalogue and say, "Oh yes, that was found in blah blah.
Very interesting." And I'll just sit there and be clean and
unchanging. I have the image of thousands of years from now
just disintegrating into dust, a neat little pile of dust
just lying at the bottom. Preservation seems very important.
I am totally and utterly static - no wonder I couldn't get
the engine going, there's nothing to go. I did have something
that worked once, but now it doesn't work; it's preserved,
on show, there to be looked at, like a beautiful old steam
engine polished, but the lines I'm standing on don't go anywhere. Men in suits come along and dust me and you have to
pay to see me. I am completely useless, but I'm important
nonetheless. I give people a sense of history; people need
a sense of understanding where things come from, how things
developed, and that's what I'm for, to give people a sense
of stability and understanding. I feel quite beautiful in
a funny sort of way. I think there might have been a time
in the past when I might have been of use. Then it would
have been different, then I would have been more used in
those days and things would have been a lot more hectic,
a lot more dangerous. There would have been risks and dirt
and damage and trials, and there would have been things to
encounter, winter and cold and snow and ice and dust. I'm
sort of in retirement and that's why I couldn't get started,
I couldn't get the wheels turning any more.
     There will come a time when I'm used again. It's silly
the way things are, it's a shame I'm not being used.
     I've noticed that the only thing of any importance is

myself, but that somehow doesn't matter. It's not like being
selfish. There isn't anything else of any importance, just
myself and how you use me. You could relate to me, comment
on me, look at me, learn from me, ponder about me.

David: What were you used for?

Snowy: I can only think of transport really. If it's not
transport, it would be something to do with taking people
to far away places or out-of-reach places. Maybe that's metaphor for something. I am a vehicle for taking people to far-
away places which are quite inaccessible and through me you
will be able to enter physically into places you couldn't
normally enter into. You wouldn't be able to do it without
something as big as me. You would need me to protect you
and guide you and to look after you. You couldn't really
go there on your own. Wherever it is that I could transport
you to - I just have to keep using the same image - to some
distant place where there's no roads or facilities, shops
or civilization, nothing like that; where there's just air
and weather and elements. You wouldn't really want to go
there on your own, or I wouldn't want to go there on my own
- this reading isn't of Death, is it?

Jenny: Mmmm.

Snowy: Is it Death itself?

Jenny: No. But as you've said that, can you tell us anything
about death?

Snowy: I feel very serious but I don't feel unhappy. Death is
serious but it's not sad, not really, it's just an extension
of the journey. It's further than people normally go. I keep
on seeing this dusty prairie, I can't actually see what the
people are going there for.

Jenny: For someone like me who's always been very scared
of death, what would you say to me?

Snowy: Just sit down and relax because it's OK. It's just
further than you're used to going. There will be other people
there, you won't be alone any more than you are now; there
will be other people parallel to you going through similar
experiences, and you will still have help available. It won't

be a sudden blacking off into isolation, you'll have help
from both your peers and your superiors and your inferiors.
It isn't an end, it's not like a wall, you'll continue to
use what you have learnt; it's a carrying-on on a different
sort of level, but what you've learnt now, you'll be able
to use.

Jenny: But what about the actual passage into death?

Snowy: Well, there's always doubt about where you're going,
so that makes you hold back. You might need some force to
push you there because you might not go readily. You might
need to be shoved.

The past seems quite friendly to me in this reading.
The future makes me feel upset (she is nearly crying).

Jenny: Why is that?

Snowy: Because it feels like uncertainty and I don't like
uncertainty at all.

Jenny: How do you find the strength for the transition?

Snowy: I was thinking about being kicked or shoved - because
lots of people don't die naturally from choice, most people
are taken, rather than die.

Jenny: Have you any information about why death comes at
certain times to certain people?

Snowy: Each person has to find their own way, it's the most
important thing to find out what our nature or element is
and to really be true to it. You have to find your own way
of dying, you can't go with the crowd. There isn't a conven-
tion, you just have to find your way.

I feel very soft and quite open; slightly eerie - something to do with the lateness of the hour and just feeling
that there are other levels of things going on, and that the
softness I have through this reading has enabled me to open
to other things that aren't normally there. For instance,
when Pete walked by me just now I very clearly saw his aura
which I've never ever seen before. I didn't see a colour,
but I saw his after-image as he walked past, like there were
two Petes: you walked past, and just behind you, there was
another one. I didn't mention it at the time. It was very

clear 'clairvoyance.' Did you know there was something just
behind you, Pete?!
Pete: What does he look like?
Snowy: Just like you!
Jenny: Is it enjoyable by any chance - afterwards?
Snowy: After death? Yes, I am enjoying this reading very
much indeed, definitely. It feels like I could go on for
a very long time. I could live like this and be like this
forever and feel good.
Jenny: Could you look at each person in the room and give
them a message?
Snowy: You, Jen, I want to give you comfort. I want somehow
to take away some of your pain (crying a bit). I have an
image of pouring oils and balms on you and telling you just
to settle down and calm down and sit down and you'll be alright.' It won't be any better if you jitter around. Don't
be scared of dying. You're not going to be dead just because
you're quiet, or if you're on your own.
Jenny: Can you say where that wisdom comes from in you?
Snowy: I was feeling that I had been in a lot of pain. I
feel very old. I've had lots and lots of experience, and
it comes from there. I've known many forms and elements.
Jenny: Can you answer what form you're in now?
Snowy: Preservation. Still in good form.
        I have thought about Eilidh quite a lot during this
reading, because of the quality of the reading. (Facing David
now and finding it difficult) I'm really scared of breaking
something with you, David.
David: Just come out with what you're feeling anyway.
Snowy: I'm very scared of affecting you. I'm frightened of
the power of what I could do to you. You appear to be unaffec-
ted on the surface, but I think it would be really easy to
affect you. I feel more upset now than I have done for the
entire reading. I found it really easy to do up till now,
really lovely, but when I look at you, I feel really nervous.
I feel ever so powerful. I somehow feel that anything I put
at you is almost going to be an overload, too much. It makes
me feel really jittery.

Up to now in the reading, I've felt a humming coming through me as if from thousands of years, but now I feel very here in the room with you, with all the difficulties and embarrassments and tensions of having a physical body.

My message to you is: You need to use yourself a lot more. Come outside your framework and find a new way. It feels like you've got too much in you, and so you can't receive because you're too full. If you emptied yourself a bit more, you could receive, and then you could change.

Jenny: Do you know anything about this reading at all, whether you are a person or what?

Snowy: No, I feel as though I'm not a person.

Jenny: You're a dead person.

Snowy: When you tell me that, I think, "Hmm, well, then I've definitely been dead a lot of times because I feel much much bigger than just a dead person. I've got a very definite feel of a very long history and maybe my own uncertainty about the future is because I haven't decided whether to or how to come back next time. I really feel that death isn't final.

I feel solid, strong and calm and steady, as a result of having been really traumatized. After all the hysterics and panic are over and I have really been shaken up ever such a lot, I have come down and seen that in the end, when all that fuss and bother is over, it's not very important. I was talking earlier of being kicked to go through Death. I would come out of it and say, Bloody hell, I'm glad to have dropped all that off me, all that material stuff and all that clinging on and illusion, and just to have my solid centre core left.

Maybe I was somebody who had too many trappings around me and I broke free of them by dying. I said at some point the most important thing is to know what element you're made of, and somehow my death showed me what element I was made of.

David: And what was that?

Snowy: It feels like rock, something very firm, which I don't think I knew before. Maybe in my last life, I wasn't like that; I was ever so much less strong.

There was a bit of the reading I didn't develop at all. It's to do with enjoyment of death - being able to encompass more of the elements, of the cosmos, to take in more; growth of our own consciousness really. And that's really enjoyable; in fact I think it is the only enjoyment when it comes down to it. You talk about 'soul pain' yourself Jenny, and I know that the emotional pains we have aren't physical really. They are pains of consciousness.

Jenny: One last question: What would you say to someone who was mourning your death?

Snowy: Well, that's all part of what we've got to go through, isn't it? Really, their mourning isn't very much to do with my death...

*****

After hearing this reading, David told us: "When Eilidh left for London, she posted a card to a boyfriend. He got it next morning, the day she died. It said, 'See you next time around.'"

*****

The idea of having 'help' after death appealed to me greatly. Not many days after this reading, what should I chance to read, but the following account in Life After Life by Raymond A. Moody, from a woman who "died" in hospital and was brought back to life:

"... all these people were there, almost in multitudes it seems, hovering around the ceiling of the room. They were all people I had known .. but who had passed on before. ... It was a very happy occasion, and I felt that they had come to protect or to guide me. It was almost as if I were coming home, and they were there to greet or to welcome me."

*****

One day, we handed Becky a folded slip
of paper which inside simply said:

DEATH

I feel really stiff. Whoever I am, it takes a lot to
get into me. There's lots of barriers up. I feel I have to
struggle to get any air at all. (She is breathing deeply
and shuddering) I feel very big, like a robust woman with
a sneer on my face. I look down on everybody. I push my way
around. I'm sharp. There's something inside me that really
aches. I don't feel at all nice, not colourful or joyful.
I'm grey. There's no buzz to me inside, no fizz or bang.
There's no guts to me, no muscle. When I move, there's no
solidity, no shape or figure. I'm arrogant. I don't care.
I don't give a shit what I look like. I've got a sneer on
my face - one side of my nose and mouth is turned up. I'm
completely cynical and snooty. I'm saying, "Fuck you lot,
look at me." My face feels pointed and tight and sharp, my
fingers and hands and nails are really bitchy and cat-like.
All my energy goes into putting everything down and tearing
everything apart and snooting at everything and pointing
at everything and destroying everything. I knock everyone
over with my big bum. I shove everyone out of the way. My
elbows are poking everybody and my shoulders are shoving
everyone aside. I've got a sharp tongue and I put everyone
down and I don't give a shit. I just throw open the door
and walk in, shoving and kicking and walking on as if nothing
has happened. I walk around with my nose in the air. And
I'm really quick: if it came to a fight, I feel ready. I'd
just grab them and get them down, and that would be that.
Jenny: From the picture you paint, this doesn't sound a very
hopeful question, but is there any way we could enjoy you?
Or cope with you, or deal with you, or get anything good
out of you at all?
Becky: Well, I think of us when we are all laughing and playing around, or I think of myself in a dance-hall where there
are girls who shove their weight around and I want to kill

them, but instead I put my energy into dancing more wildly
and letting go and enjoying myself more and being more sexual
and holding my boyfriend - just doing everything _more_.
Jenny: So the answer is to be more alive?
Becky: Yes.
Jenny: What are you for? What do you teach?
Becky: Well, some people would learn not to be so stupid and
to keep out of my way. Other people would learn to enjoy
themselves more. I am a lesson to everyone not to behave like
me, to show them it doesn't get them anywhere.
Jenny: If I were to get past you in some way, what would
I find? - If I were to get through you, to the other side of
you?
Becky: I can feel that below the surface, I could be quite
likeable, softer. I'm quite receptive. I feel a really strong
urge to protect people: if there's something unjust going
on, I would just step straight in. But I wouldn't be a protection by putting my arms around someone; I'm not soft and
soggy. I'd encourage the person who was being trodden on
by saying, "Come on, you'd better stand up for yourself,
because I'm here now."
Jenny: My goodness, do you know the world is a poem?

                            *****

    I am the question that cannot be answered
    I am the lover that cannot be lost
    Yet small are the gifts of my servant the soldier
    For time is my offspring
    Pray what is my name?

    MY NAME IS DEATH
    Oh cannot you see?
    All life must turn to me ...

                                            from
                              MY NAME IS DEATH
                    a song by The Incredible String Band

SALLY'S STORY

I'm a very simple person. If I can see something, it exists. If I can't, then it doesn't.

I met a man called Liam who'd been to Atlantis. He gave me some leaflets. I read them and decided I'd never go there.

He told me about 'readings' and wanted me to try to do one. He spent ages talking to me and persuading me to try. So I did.

The main feeling I had before I started was nervousness. As soon as I picked up the piece of paper, I felt different. I felt stronger, I stood up straighter and felt immensely powerful in my body. I walked straight to the mirror and examined myself closely. My face looked older, more mature and more relaxed. My eyes looked softer. I enjoyed looking at myself, whereas normally I'd just check briefly to make sure my hair was alright. The rest of my body looked and felt different. My hips seemed wider as if I'd had kids. I felt like an older woman. I stopped at that point. Liam told me the reading had been on Jenny James, whom I'd never met, and he told me a bit about her.

I was then completely convinced that these readings worked and was pleased that I could do them. I didn't try to understand what I'd done. I still don't try. I'm completely happy to accept that they work because I've experienced them working. What difference does understanding make anyway?

I did a couple more readings for Liam. One was on an Australian man who'd been staying at our house for a few days. He was very depressed and talked a lot about his two-year-old son who had drowned a year or so previously. I didn't know who the reading was on. I talked for an

hour and it was the most amazing reading I've
ever done. At one point, I knew that I wanted to
die. I felt the urge to die so strongly that
I lay down on the floor and felt what it was
like to die. It was a beautiful feeling, just
lying there feeling death pushing down on me.
It was a warm, sad, secure feeling and I felt
very loved. My body felt lovely and relaxed.
There was no pain or tension anywhere. I would
have been quite happy to stay like that forever,
but I realized that I was actually an alive
human being experiencing what it would be like
to die, and that although the experience of
death was pleasurable, I had to get on and live.
So slowly I started to sit up and come alive.
I felt lovely for hours afterwards as the feeling
stayed with me. Since then, I have never been
scared of dying, and I never will be.

                                        SALLY WOOD

                    *****

Note: After completion of this chapter, the information has
come from the parents of Eilidh Boadella that the coroner's
verdict on their daughter's death was that she died peacefully in her sleep overcome by carbon monoxide fumes before
any heat reached her.

    This of course once again raises the question of where
the sensations, impressions and, occasionally, strong emotional effects, of readings come from. Was what Becky picked
up Eilidh's experience on some level of consciousness? Or
did Becky somehow get her material from my own below-
consciousness imaginings of what it would be like to die in
a fire?

    Either way, Becky certainly went through a very painful
and ultimately a very cleansing experience that day, insti-
gated in some way by the energy of our concentration on
Eilidh.

                    *****

CHAPTER THIRTEEN:
GOD; THE DEVIL; UFOs

And now, at great personal expense in terms
of white hairs, frown marks and general neurotic
worrying, the reading you've all been waiting
for - in fact, no less than TWO readings on
the Almighty himself - with profound apologies
to all atheists. I know exactly how you feel.
I know there <u>should</u> have been a deathly silence
from the medium, but I'm afraid what she actually
came out with does us all in, theists and atheists alike.

But first of all, a few words from Therese,
born and bred in Co. Kerry, as to how she was
affected by such pagan insolence as a <u>character
reading on Himself!</u>

THERESE'S STORY

Having been brought up Irish Catholic, I was naturally
deeply affected by the readings on God and Jesus Christ that
appear in this book. The one on Jesus made me laugh and feel
angry too. I felt angry because he could have achieved so
much but instead chose to stop and become the most perfect
martyr of all time. This is how I was taught to be too - take
everything lying down, don't fight back, there's no way out.
I thought of Ireland a lot during that reading on Jesus:
Irish people tend to be like him, feeling sorrowful and helpless and doing nothing to better the situation. Ireland has
allowed herself to be dominated many times over and the 'Paddy' is still regarded as the underdog wherever he goes.

Hearing these readings, I got a feeling of everything
fitting together for me: Jesus, Ireland, my upbringing. It
just all made sense for me, however outrageously unconvention-
al the picture presented.

The reading on God had a much softer effect on me. I

felt compassion for him. It struck me as being totally unfair
how everyone leans on him. I know that my parents and the
rest of my family still do. No-one wants to bear responsibility, so they pin it on someone else. All I know is that the
reading made me cry, cry for the fact that God is a lonely
isolated being reaching out as well. It was lovely to see
God as a human being who makes mistakes: he's not perfect
either. The reading brought all the abstract dogma which
I accepted in faith down to earth for me. I liked that. I
think that my father who's a devout Catholic would like that
too.

*****

"God can no more do without us than we can do without Him."

MEISTER ECKHART

*****

When we gave Becky the reading on God,
on the paper was written: "What or who is God? Is
God just the fantasy of a lonely species, or
is he a being, or a force? Did man invent God, or
does he/it exist outside of us and we sense
him? What mistakes have people made in their
understanding of God?"

GOD by Becky

Well, I feel I've got good balance. Straight away when I
started, I had the feeling of wanting to dance and move about
- I've got good co-ordination of the body, I don't blunder
at all. I could put my feet to anything. I want to stretch
all my body, and when I stretch, I want it to be as far as I
can go.

I've got a lot to say. I feel very serious about what
I'm doing. Even if all I'm doing is standing here and stretching my legs, I'm serious about it. There's nothing to laugh
about.

I'm very strong. I want to pick up everything, every
little last drop of everything. I want to gather every little
bit together and mix my fingers in it all and mess it all
up again and fit the puzzle back together again and put it
right the second time and mend all the pieces and put them
back again.

I feel bigger than just a person. My power and my strength are much bigger than that. I have my feet on the ground,
but they could be like two big steel poles, they could be
a bridge, a huge enormous bridge across a big lake or across
the sea. I feel stronger than just a person. There's something springy about me when I move. My legs feel really powerful, but it's not the kind of strength where I want to go
kicking things around or pushing my way around.

I've got a heaviness on my head. I hate this. I keep
thinking of the Earth and that I spend all my time fighting.
I don't regret it, but hell, it's hard work. I feel like
the sky is actually sitting on top of my head. The sky and
the clouds are heavy, there's something thick about the air.
Everything's sitting on top of my head. I am very strong
and solid and I won't be squashed, but boy, it's awkward.
And I ache, I pain. There's not enough fresh air and blue
sky for me to enjoy myself. There's not enough sun and warmth
to dance around. I seem to be spending my life having a heavy
time. I feel stunted in my physical size because there's
not enough fresh air. There's a smoggy thick feeling in my
lungs; the air is thick when I breathe it in. I can imagine
the air being so thick, that my arm just rests on it. I've
got a very strong feeling like I had on acid once: I felt
I was in space and that I was floating round the room. And
I didn't want to breathe any more because the air in the
room felt and smelt like gas. There's more to air than it
being just 'thin air' you know. It's not thin, it's thick,
and full of millions of things. You wouldn't believe how
many things there are in the air.

I've got the feeling I'm saying to people, "Mark my
words. You might think I'm stupid, but I know better. You

might look down on me and sneer at me, but mark my words,
I know what I'm talking about. I'm very solid and serious,
so don't sneer at me, it's not worth your while." There's
something very important that I want to say. I want to be
taken seriously. I don't want to be messed around with. I
have some important information and I know what I'm talking
about.

Oh god, I look really terrible if I look in the mirror:
I look stressed, my eyes are all brown round the edges, as
if I haven't slept. I've got an urge to look out of the window: I see people out there, but I don't want any of them
to see me.

Jenny: You don't want them to see you? Any particular reason?
Becky: I keep thinking I want everyone to get together -
it's a time for gathering. But I don't want to be seen, because I feel I'm only just learning myself. And yet I feel
really important and I want to be listened to and taken notice of. I know what I have to say is important and that
I'm going to get it across one of these days, but I don't
want to show my face yet. I want to be there, I want to be
present, I want to be watching everybody, but I don't actually want them to know that I'm around. I don't want them to
know that I'm actually a person. I've got my eye on everything and I'm sending out information. I am bringing everyone
together; I am actually doing it, but I don't want them to
know that I'm doing it. I want them just to experience it
and to have their little squabbles and their little affairs,
but I'm actually the force behind it, I'm the one who's pushing.

My body hurts. I'm struggling and I'm under stress.
Jenny: What's the trouble?
Becky: I keep thinking of God, that if there's a god, somebody up there, this must be what he feels like and what he's
going through. I've got a sensation of not having reached
my peak of maturity quick enough and there's a mess. I have
not been present all the time, and things have got really
messy and I'm here now looking at everything and there's

a general complete fucking shambolic bugger-up.
Jenny: I like the way you put it!
Becky: I'm here to clear it up.
Jenny: Oh, jolly good! Just what we need.
Becky: I hate the feeling in my face, really drawn.
Jenny: How would you want people to treat you?
Becky: I don't see that you have to treat me in any way.
I'm the one who's needing from you. I feel completely alone.
I'm thinking of two people in a relationship, and I haven't
got that feeling. I am completely on my own, and because I am
on my own, it's taken me this long to mature, because I've
got no-one to relate to. I'm going to use my phantasy of
imagining god, and he's a man who hasn't got a woman. And
he has to run everything and take responsibility for everything. But he needs a woman like any other man does, and
he hasn't got one, which means that it's taking him ages
and ages to grow fully, because he's starving of contact,
he's starving of warmth. And pleasure is the most important
thing, because pleasure is nourishment.

    I've got an incredibly tight headache. And when I look
at you all, I feel you people are in less stress and pain
than me. You're very distant from me. I feel really dry.
Oh god, the more I talk, the more I get a sense of 'falling
backwards' and getting old. I feel like a jittery old man.
I've made a mess of everything and I'm suffering. I'm not
being allowed to grow up, they've not given me women - I'm
being punished by having to be alone, by having to struggle
and not having pleasure. It's my karma. I've been thrown
back and you people have come forward and responsibility
has fallen on you because I didn't do my job. And you have
been given pleasure. I've been put right back off the scene
altogether and I'm not allowed back again for a long time.

    But there must be a man that is going to be the Man
of the world, and there's going to be a boy born that is
going to be like Jesus. And he's not to make the same mistake
again: Jesus didn't have women, and that's a mistake. He
didn't have women to teach him the proper way. And not having

women meant there was an End: he came to an end and that
was it. He died and there wasn't anyone left to take over.
And that was a very stupid idea. They put him on the cross
and he didn't leave a pregnant woman behind to carry on the
job. He dropped dead, and that was a lot of good! He didn't
put himself to the full use he should have.

Jenny: He was probably an Irish Catholic, still living with
his mother. A bit of a disappointment to you altogether?

Becky: Yes. FRED! Wake up! Stop sitting there with your hands
together. What are you praying for? There's nothing to pray
for and no-one to pray to.

Jenny: This young fellow that will be born, what is his task?

Becky: He's got the chance to carry out a very big task.
In this reading, I keep feeling that I've been thrown back,
a feeling of time passing, of me going backwards and time
rushing forwards, and I've got all that way to go again. I'm
going to have to catch up. Meanwhile, there has to be someone
doing the job. The mother of this young man has to be very
careful how he is brought up. She has to make sure that he
has women. It's essential. When he is born, he will be like
no other male on earth. He is going to be free and he's not
going to have anything to do with the staleness of Earth.
He mustn't. Otherwise it will destroy him. I don't even think
he will learn to read and write because that will confuse him
and take him away from his path in life. It will distract
him. He has to stay with the earth completely, to learn from
the beginning. If he learns to read and write and drive a
car and to go around with machines and to wire things up
and learns all the things men learn, he will get confused,
he'll be completely messed up and muddled up and he'll go
backwards. It's no good. Machines are no good. They don't
last forever. A stone will last forever. It might get ground
up, but then it will go back into the earth; it will never
disappear. I am saying that this young man is to go towards
things that will last forever and he is not to go near things
that will disintegrate in front of him and confuse him. It's
completely vital, a matter of life and death. He is going to

have to deal with the badness of the world and he isn't going
to be protected, except that it won't be injected into him.
But he will have to deal with badness. And he will be the
first and the only one at the time; he will have to take
on to himself the task. He will grow from it and become very
strong. He will have to take on to himself the job that all
the other men who were born special, who were born princes
but who misused it, didn't do. This new boy will have to
be taught to enjoy sorting the world out. It is a privilege,
because Earth is heaven really. It's a big place and if it
was cleaned up, it's a good place; it's got everything you
need to survive. When this boy grows up, it's going to be
more like a kingdom, it's going to be more like a huge family.
Jenny: Earlier in the reading, you said you didn't want to
be seen by anyone. But how should I 'see' you in the other
sense? How should I look on you?
Becky: Look at me as an energy force. Don't try to touch
me or get hold of me, or hold me down or look at me or try
to manhandle me. Just take me as a lesson. I made a mess.
Just make sure you go in the opposite direction. I was put in
charge in the beginning: I was appointed the main man and
I just said to the kids, "Go ahead, let rip." And they let
rip. And I never said, "Stop!" I never took charge as I ought
to have. I just sat back in my arm-chair like an old lay-
about. And now I have a sense that I've not been allowed
to have the responsibility any more. My punishment is that
I'm not allowed to open my mouth. I'm not allowed to step
forward any longer. I've a feeling that there are a few beings out there, there's not just one. There's someone bigger
than me out there. These people appointed me god long ago
and I could have been a real king. I could have put everything right. I had the power for everyone to listen to me
and it could have been a joy to be the main man, but I didn't
use my strength. Then these people stepped forward and knocked me back. But they are using information from me to learn
from.
Jenny: So what is your conclusion?

Becky: That the most important thing is to be physical and emotional and down-to-earth. We can't survive any other way. You have to be earthy on Planet Earth.

Jenny: So why is it that all the religions of the world are anti-body? What's that all about?

Becky: It's a way of trying to get away from it all, of trying to say there's something better 'up there' than what is down here. It's a way of copping out of doing something about what is going on.

Jenny: Well, is there any hope?

Becky: Yes, definitely. I'm looking at that basket full of tangled wools and it's a complete mess, and I'm seeing that as the world. But all those things could be taken out, sorted out and cleared up. You'd need enthusiasm, care and commitment, but it could be done.

Jenny: My father's favourite saying as he faced some big new job about the house was, "Good God, said God, I've got my work cut out!"

*****

About eighteen months after this reading, we gave it again to Snowy. My hope was that her age, maturity, sophistication and capacity for philosophising would produce something more palatable, yes, more conventional. Unfortunately, my sister is born in the Chinese Year of the Monkey, and psychic phenomena do not come through independent of the nature and mode of expression of the medium, so naturally I let myself in for a bag of tricks.

GOD by Snowy

Right, the first thing in this room that I focus on in this reading is those two microphones over there which I am seeing like missiles waiting for the take-off. I don't know what Cruise missile look like, but I see those microphones as warheads, giant rockets, nuclear rockets. And I

notice that they are pointing directly at me. They are like
two great eyeballs piercing from a robot in the dark saying,
"Exterminate."

I feel that I am semi-collapsed. I have a weight across
my back. I have had no pleasure for a very long time. I have
no humour and therefore would not be a good person to bring
up a child. I'd like someone to put something into me to
make me feel better. The pain is to do with the fact that
I've done an awful lot of carrying and it's time for me to
be carried.

(At this point, for various individual reasons such
as going to the loo, all the audience leave the room at the
same time.) ALL RIGHT YOU LOT JUST GO AWAY AND LEAVE ME HERE
DOING THIS ALL BY MYSELF. Don't imagine you can upset me.
Don't imagine I feel alienated, isolated, left alone, peed
off, no, not at all. I feel wonderful. I feel great. I feel
completely One and All with the whole Being of it all. I
just feel completely integrated, completely ecstatic. So
much so, I'd like to end it all. I'd like to go away and
sleep. I'd like to bury myself and die. I feel drained and
empty. I've used up what I had.

Jenny: What made you feel bad?

Snowy: I took in some bad energy. I opened myself. It was
a destructive force, a very powerful force of negativity,
a death force, a force which had a mission to destroy life.
And I had a naive trust which allowed me to be open in the
presence of a very dynamic force for death. I opened myself
to it and I was swamped by it. I didn't take into account
my own weakness: I considered myself invulnerable.

Jenny: What causes you to think that you are invulnerable?

Snowy: Well, I am strong, and I feel my strength and I do
rejuvenate. I've been through many bad downs and I've come
up again and that gives me the sense of indestructibility.
In fact, through going down, I come up stronger. I let myself
be buffeted by tides and winds and feel the downs and then
float up with the ups.

Jenny: You said earlier on that you felt something on your
back - could you say more about that?

Snowy: Responsibility, oh god. I feel like all I've got to do is switch on a certain tape inside my voice box and out will come a nice speech on responsibility. (She starts speaking in a pompous priestly voice and maintains it for the whole of the next passage.)

    I am the sort of person who goes through life initiating things, organizing. I had to reach out into the world, yea verily I am the sort of person who realizes that without responsibility I would not continue to survive. Life is made up of those who give and those who take, and I am a Giver. In a former life, I was a priest. (I must have spent a lot of time in church in my previous life to acquire this voice, because I have not spent much time in church in this life!) I hope you are listening and taking it all in because you may not be able to hear again this message which I bring to you at this, the onset of a new era. To talk of a new age is to talk of something momentous. I am responsible for you my brethren. And you my sistren. And you my fathren and mothren and cousren and babyren, my goodren and my badren. (We're all collapsing by now.) Yea verily I say unto you, I am responsible for all of you. Don't take this lightly. I give you humour to help you down the pill. But that does not mean that the pill is any the less bitter. I tell you that it is indeed bitter. All my life, I have taken of the bitter pill. And what, you ask, is this bitter pill?

Jenny: (giggling) Yes, I do ask you.

Snowy: Well, the Pope is bitter about the pill (groans all round). But the pill, my brethren, is Life itself. I will pause for you to take this in, brethren, for the bitter pill has to be swallowed by you one and all. Yes, even you Louise (looking at the baby playing on the floor), you too must sup of the bitter pill of Life.

Jenny: And why is life a bitter pill? (We are all helpless with laughter at her pompous tone)

Snowy: My sister seems to think that this is humorous. That is because she has not yet supped of the bitter pill. I have supped and been supped. And it gave me backache, which is where we started.

Jenny: But I still want to know why life is a bitter pill.

Snowy: It is hard for me to convey to you, my child. You have to experience it for yourself in all its full-blooded bitterness. It is bitter from birth to death. It is bitter in the middle and it is bitter on the outside.

Jenny: Why is it bitter for you?

Snowy: I do not enter into this. I am but a messenger from the gods. It is not personal. Do not imagine that anything is personal to me. I come from outside to show you that you have to suffer.

Jenny: Thanks a lot. And why do you want to tell us this?

Snowy: Because I have suffered myself. I have let bad energy come into me and so I have to get it out of me. And the only way I know to do that is to put it into something else or somebody else or somebodies else.

Jenny: Oh, great. Ta. Well, tell us more about the bad energy factor, and your role, purpose or message.

Snowy: Well, here on the left hand, we have Death, and here on the right hand, we have Life. We have been taught, my friends, that Death is negative and Life is positive. One would assume from the simplistic logic of this statement that we should try to eradicate Death and have Life on both sides. Let me tell you that this is not only not possible but not desirable. Life and Death are in dynamic opposition to one another. Life and Death are like day and night and other cliches. Life and Death are essential to one another. So when Death came and pushed itself into my Life, what did I have to do? First of all, I had to die. And after I had died, I had to rise again like the Phoenix from the flame, and other cliches. Having risen, I had the memory of my previous life blotted out by my previous death. But I marched forward nobly, knowing that life and death were inside of me, outside of me, all around me, forces to be contended with, to be lived with, to be died with. I no longer feared the Enemy. I no longer feared Death. I no longer feared Life. I just strode forth with these two equal forces in me, one on my left and one on my right.

Fred: And what lesson should we take home?

Snowy: That you too must die. But do not push death away: if you do, you will not live to your ultimate, or even your penultimate. You must, as Don Juan says, live with death on your shoulder. And when you learn to live with Death on your shoulder, then and only then will you truly know the meaning of Life. These simple cliches, these simple short words, Death and Life, they seem not to be very much, four and five letter words, but they are everything. And now I am bored. (Audience in general hysterics.)

Jenny: What would your children be like?

Snowy: When you said 'children', that quite put me off my idea of being an extra-terrestrial creature, and I liked that image. I like the idea of being a messenger from the gods. I have become a messenger of the gods because I'm peed off with the lot of you and I want to get you back. I want to bring you some Bad Tidings of Great Misery. (Starts singing to the old hymn tune) "Bad tidings of misery and sin.." Let's say that I'd died, alright? And I've come to that Council they seem to have up there and they're all discussing what I should do next, and they say, "Well, you could go back into another life." And I say, "WHAT? Boring. I've had enough lives." And they say, "Well, you're not good enough to go up yet to the other school." And so I say, "Well, are there any options? Are there any other choices apart from Life or Graduation?" And they say, "Well, actually we have got a vacancy in the Messenger section." And I say, "Oh, that sounds like my ticket. As long as I can ride a motorbike and go around annoying people." And they say, "Well, I suppose so, yes, we could give you a few tasks that we want sorted out." And I say, "Well, my motivation is entirely malignant." And they say, "It doesn't matter actually because all we really want you to do is take a message from A to B and what malignancy you get out of it on the way doesn't really matter to us particularly. And anyway, you'll only be working some of your karma out. We have our ultimate faith

in what you lot are up to. It seems to work out in the end.
It takes a bit of time and a few nuclear wars here and there
but it doesn't really matter to us up here what you get up
to. If you want to be malignant, go ahead and be malignant,
quite honestly." And I say, "Oh, goody goody, jolly D, when
do I start?" And they say, "Well, come in nine o'clock on
Monday morning."

So I go home and get geared up with me leathers and
things because it's quite cold up there on motorbikes. And
I go in on Monday morning and they say, "Righto, George,
now just pop along there to Venus and go and see Bert and
knock on his door. It's No. 10, it's got a red door-knob
and say you've come to get the message to take down to the
Terrestrials, and take it off and deliver it." And I say,
"Jolly D," and off I go (makes horrible motorbike noises)
off to Venus. Fire and brimstone and all that stuff. See
quite a lot of interesting sights on the way, but anyway
I get to the old door and get the old message and they say,
"Just deliver this. There's a professor chappie working on
one of those nuclear submarines. You'll find him up in Scot-
land. Here's the address, just pop down. The method you use
to present this message isn't important - it's up to you
entirely. You can pop it into a dream of his, or into a letter through the post anonymously, or appear before him in
shining armour. You do whatever you like; all those artistic
aspects are entirely up to you." And I say, "Oh, jolly D.
That'll give me something to think about on the long drive."
And off I go on the motorbike. I put my crash-helmet on in
case I crash into any of those little planets flying around
the place and I pass all the angels flitting around and
all the bloody cherubs - they bore me stiff. (Makes more
horrible noises on the motorbike) Aha! That'll get the lot
of them. Malignancy rules OK? So I leap on to my motorbike
making sure to get lots of black fumes out of the exhaust
just to mess up the old Cosmos. (Laughs maniacally) Silly
old god, said he didn't mind about my malignancy - they'll
see, I'll get malignancy on his porridge. (More ghastly motor-

bike noises)

Anyway, I land at Professor Hobnob's Scottish mansion
and knock on his door. "Och the noo," he says, "Who's there?"
And I think, "Oh damn, I forgot to work out my lines." So I
shout, "It's OK. Nobody." And I go off and stay in a motel
for a couple of days, just to get my head straight. How can
I get the most malignancy out of this situation? I've already
boggled his brain a bit by knocking on his door and then
saying I'm not there. (That's the sort of malignancy I'm
into: knocking on doors and running away, really evil stuff.
And getting fumes on god's porridge!) Now I want to do something really glorificacious for myself. That bit about shining and suddenly appearing from a gorse-bush, that appeals
to me, especially when he's on his Sunday afternoon jaunt
with his dogs and his guns.

So I dive into a gorse-bush one Sunday afternoon all
dressed up in shining robes and all that, and he comes along
going "Och the noo," and I go, "HAIL AND BEHOLD." And then,
"BEHOLD AND BEHAIL! I bring you malignant tidings." And he
goes, "Och the noo, I must have drunk too much whiskey."
And I go, "No, it's not the whiskey. Great tidings of malignancy I bring to thee and all brethren on this Sunday afternoon. I bring you tidings of nuclear submarines." Oh no,
I've got that voice again (she has changed from a working-
class bike boy accent to something like the Loch Ness Monster
blowing bubbles and hissing under water). Well, one of the
aspects of myself is that I change into very many different
beings within One. And here I am now. I have changed from
a witch in shining whatsits into an unseen creature which
is assailing your earholes as you walk along on a Sunday
afternoon. There is this strange voice which is penetrating
your being and saying, "Submarina going to blowa uppa. Submarina going to blowa uppa when you go to worka ona Monday morning." And he goes, "Och the noo, I must have indigestion."
And I go, "No, you haven't gotta indigestion, you've gotta
submarina aboutta blowa uppa in your face-a." And he goes,
"Och the effing noo, I don't want to know anything about
submarines blowing up. I've done my sums and I know where

it's at."

Anyway, that's about it. I've come to bring a message, that it's all going to blow up. Boring isn't it? We've had that message before, haven't we? It seems to be an overriding theme these days.

Jenny: I'd like to know more about you in it all.

Snowy: Alright, well I'll take myself back up to the Council. I return and they say, "Did you take the message?" and I say, "Yes, I took the message, but I'm BORED." And they say, "Well, you've only been in this job one day. Give it a chance can't you?" And I say, "NO. I'm bored. Taking messages is not my scene, man. I want a better paid job." And they say, "Look, there aren't that many choices. You've either got Graduation, Life or Messenger Boy." And I say, "Well, dammit, I'll have to go back into Life." And they say, "Well, there's a good chap. Because really and truly that is what everyone has got to do. Until you're ready to graduate, it's just a cop-out to be a messenger boy really. We hoped you would realize this. We actually just gave you that job to teach you. That chap could have got that message any old how; we didn't really need you driving around on motorbikes and diving out of gorse-bushes. It was just a test for you to discover that in fact not to be involved in life is boring. So now, we're glad you're ready, so here's a choice: you can either be Fred Bloggs or Mrs. Smith." And I say, "Ah, fuck it, just give me any of them. Just give me a number and I'll go."

Jenny: And what's going to be the general purpose of this life-time?

Snowy: It's to do with grounding. I've got malignancy out of my system and now there's actually a softer feeling. I've turned away from the Hell's Angels - I was Heaven's Hell's Angel. Well, anyway, I got that bit out of my system and now I'm going to go back to Earth and I'm feeling that the only thing to do is to work with the earth, with the plants, with the animals, to improve and bring back the life and goodness into the Earth. My task is to purify the water,

the animal-life within the water, and the land around; to
bring back the land and the pasture and the birdlife and
the animals, to bring it all back to full richness.

Jenny: Could you give a clearer picture of your position in
the general hierarchy?

Snowy: Well, it's funny because although I was acting the
idiot around the Council up there, I was still fairly high
up. Somehow I was acting out some last shred of my learning.
I'm coming back now as quite a pure being, a learned one.

I have felt my own sickness throughout the reading.
My own death force, my own stupidity, my own limitations,
my own blocks. And so for me to say that I am a highly evolved being seems strange. And yet that is what I want to say.

Jenny: For most of the reading, you didn't come across like
a human being at all. You said you were a MESSENGER FROM
THE GODS. Did you have any feelings throughout the reading
about who you were?

Snowy: No.

Peter: She sounded like the Devil.

Jenny: What are you like?

Snowy: A tough character, without a lot of give. I feel you
wouldn't be able to get inside me or very near to me. I'm
without softness really. Anything you get from me, you would
not get given. You would 'get' from me like you would from
a good teacher at school: it would be up to you to go out
and take and allow yourself to open, but it would be harsh.

Jenny: So what are you for?

Snowy: I am for teaching. It seems like there is only one
lesson in the world really, to do with life and death, destruction and regeneration, to do with replenishing the earth
after catastrophe. It's to do with accepting cycles and spi-
rals. I am here to teach you to accept the whole life process
even though of course the destructive bits of it, the coming
down from the high plateaux, feel very bad. I want to say
to you that you have to accept those too as part of the whole
creative process, that you couldn't have the nourishment and
the softness, the good bit, unless you had the whole churning

inferno. It's a package deal. And my message is to say: don't
be resisting death, because if you resist it, you stagnate.
And that Garden of Eden image, quite honestly, wasn't very
interesting, was it? It was flat.

Jenny: So you're a teacher. Right: could you explain the
concept of the Devil?

Snowy: How you should view the Devil is as a mythological
representation of destructive force, but which brings with
it challenge and fight. Your reaction to the Devil is to
bring up your own standards. To be in the presence of something malignant and destructive ups your own goals, it makes
you recognize the dangers, it makes you see the fight that
you need to go into, it challenges you. It is very very essential. If it was all just sunshine and grapes and fruits falling off the trees, you would just sink into luxury and flab
and you would disintegrate.

Jenny: You started off this whole reading by saying that
you were fed up with the burden you were bearing, the responsibility you had, and that you wanted energy put into you.
Would you like to say anything about that at this end of
the reading?

Snowy: That that's just a resentful position really, because
it's impossible for anybody to do too much work. You might
think in your life you are doing more than your fair share
but you will only be given what you can do.

Jenny: Not everybody sees life as a spiral and a growth process and not everybody believes in the concept of a continu-
ing hierarchy. Some people think there's just God Up There
and Us Down Here. What would you say about the idea of a
finite hierarchy?

Snowy: Well, I can already see that God has got his limitations. And if he's the limit, well, I'd like to get off and
catch the next bus...

*****

GOD'S SONG

Cain slew Abel, Seth knew not why
For if the children of Israel were meant to multiply
Why should any of her children die?
So he asked the Lord. And the Lord said:

Man means nothing. He means less to me
Than the lowliest cactus flower on the yucca tree
He chases round this desert 'cos he thinks that's where I'll
That's why I love mankind.   [be

I recoiled in horror from the foulness of thee
From the squalor and the fear and the misery
How we laugh up here in heaven at the praise you offer me
That's why I love mankind.

The christians and the jews were having a jamboree
The buddhists and the hindus joined on satellite TV
Picked their four greatest priests and they began to speak
Saying, Lord a plague is on the world,

Lord, no man is free. The temples that we've built to you
Have tumbled into the sea.
If you won't take care of us, won't you please just let us be
So they asked the Lord, and the Lord said:

I burn down your cities. How blind you must be!
I take from you your children; you say, How blessed are we!
You all must be crazy to put your faith in me
That's why I love mankind: You really need me.

GOD'S SONG
by Randy Newman
(on his album "Sail Away")

*****

Well, if that's God — or one of the gods —
who's this character The Devil then? We gave
poor Becky a piece of paper on which was written:
"Is the Devil a person, a concept, an energy
force? What _is_ the Devil?"

THE DEVIL by Becky

As soon as I picked up this paper, my headache got
much worse. It's the kind of headache that makes me very
sharp and alert; I wouldn't have any patience with any nonsense. I feel ready for anything coming at me, ready for any
insult. I've got a tense, strained expression on my face;
my fists are clenched tight. My attitude is: "There's something going on here which I don't like."

I imagine myself as an old colonel from the war, out
of my mind, still thinking I'm commanding a hundred men
and that we're carrying guns around, and yet I might be
in a room full of kittens. I'd kick them around and say,
"Pull yourselves together." Very rigid energy. Stuck. I
would drive people mad. There's no feeling of communication
with anybody. I'm really hard-headed. I'd say, "Right chaps,
we're going this way. It doesn't matter what's in the way,
just knock it over and keep charging ahead." And I might
be at the edge of the world and about to fall off, but I
wouldn't think about that. My head feels as if it's banging
against something and I feel as if I'm struggling for no
reason at all. I'm very strong and I've got lots of hard,
masculine, Yang energy. I feel like a tractor or a steamroller, just ploughing through something, ploughing till I
get to the other side. Then I'd start again with a new project and plough through that. And then I'm exhausted at
night, and I sleep all tensed up and in the morning, I start
again, and I wake up like Frankenstein. I destroy everything
in front of me. I've got pains in my stomach and my teeth
are falling out because I clench them so tight. All the
door-handles are broken off because I grab them so hard,
and all the china is broken because I charge around ready to

explode. I'm completely manic. And I'm so powerful. I've got masses and masses of energy that I don't use; it's physical power, unexpressed. I feel like I did in a reading I did once on Frankenstein: I've got that kind of energy in my hand and I want to put it round someone's neck and strangle. Yet I'm the sort of person who gives reasonable little excuses: "I got out of the wrong side of the bed," after strangling somebody. My attitude is, "We'll get it done, no matter what," like Hitler. Just kill them.

Jenny: How did you get like that? Did you have a bad childhood?!

Becky: My mother was a nice woman, very reasonable. We had a lot of nice cups of tea together. Two-faced. I had to be extra nice to cover over. Have another cup of tea, mother dear. You have to paint smiles on to your face because it's so hard to make a real one. (Pulls horrible faces in an effort to smile) Then you sit down and try and look relaxed (makes horrible tense expressions).

Jeremy: What about your brothers and sisters?

Becky: All lovely, all done it properly. Got certificates, every single one of them. They all did it well. I'm the only one that didn't do quite so well. Actually, I overdid it.

Jeremy: Do you believe in god?

Becky: I'll answer that in a minute. I must just brush my hair. OK, now I can answer it. Well, I don't feel very holy. I couldn't keep it up. I might have been at one time, but nowadays I can't keep it up. I feel best when I'm going mad (she has a frenzied fit around the room, making loads of noise). I'm completely mad. Normally, I would keep all this in; there's an awful lot of it in there. I have loads and loads of energy and want to bring everybody into everything I do. I'm manic about everything. My back is stiff, and my heart is weak.

Jenny: What have we to learn from you?

Becky: That I have to be coped with. Once I start going mad, I'm an awful lot to deal with. I have an image of being

tied down to a bed so that I can freak out.
Jenny: If you weren't coped with, what would happen?
Becky: I would crush everyone. I have a feeling of crawling into everyone, getting into everyone.
Jenny: What part of them are you getting into? What is the hole in them that allows you in?
Becky: Their uncentredness. People waiting for something, people that want to be amused or people that want to believe in something, or that have nothing to do.
Jenny: And what do you do to people?
Becky: I just take them in and consume them.
Jenny: How?
Becky: Well, I have the feeling that I am much bigger than a single individual. The feeling is I could just kick you over and your energy would add to my own. I am a monster that would go through the world, yet all I'd be saying is "Have a cup of tea" and trying to be playful. I would just take people over and everyone will lose their individuality and they won't have any creativity left. They'll forget who they are and I'll take over completely.

I'm like a car revved up ready to zoom ahead, or a TV with picture after picture flashing on, changing from one thing to another all the time. I'm not a person, so what am I? Am I society?
Jenny: How do other people view you?
Becky: God, I've a feeling that people would try and humour me; they'd step aside and say, "Yes," with a smile and get out of my way.
Jenny: So what are you made of then?
Becky: A load of unexpressed energy, madness, too much of something - too much confusion. Perhaps it's too much consumerism. Too much taking in and not enough outlet. But I can't think of anything to let it out into. I feel as big as the world, so where would I let it out into? If I let off energy it'll hit off all those other planets up there.
Jenny: What exactly is it like, your energy?
Becky: Destructive, flattening, my energy is for knocking

things down, barging into things, knocking people over and
squashing them.

Jenny: Why is it like that?

Becky: The image I have is of having taken in an overdose
of things that are unreal, things that are made to fill
people up; and the only way I can get out of it is to explode. I feel like a kid who's gone to the wrong shop and
bought the wrong sort of toy and I didn't quite know what
I was doing, mum. And then I talked to a strange man on
the street and he told me this toy was harmless, and I played with it, and he came out of the sky, so he did. And I
didn't know what I was doing, honest. And anyway, I played
with this toy, and it multiplied and turned into things
like houses and shops and machines, and then all these little things started coming out of the machines and they moved
around and started turning into other little things that
looked like my toy. And I was watching and I didn't know
what was going on.

Jenny: Hmm, I'm not very convinced by your story. Where
were you in it?

Becky: I was reading my comics. Honest, I didn't know what
I was doing. And well, when I was reading the comic, Frank
came in and blew it all up. He lit the matches and I didn't
realize it would set on fire and the flames got bigger and
bigger and I couldn't put the fire out, mum. And everything
went, it all blew up. Please don't hit me.

Jenny: My head's vibrating. The energy of this reading is
very jagged. I feel strange and concussed and spinning.
Has anyone else got that feeling?

Becky: That's how I felt earlier on in the reading. That's
what I do to everyone. I don't normally kill them straight
off.

Jenny: Well, tell me what you're doing to me and why. The
whole room has started to move now.

Becky: I take everyone over. And I turn everyone into me.
I'm evil. I'm taking everything over.

Jenny: Why do you need to do that?

Becky: I bottled all my feelings up and then let them out on to everybody else. And the feeling I didn't express was insecurity. I was insecure so I wanted to hold on to everybody. So now I want to take everybody over and make everybody like me. I try to consume and grab on to everything and everybody and turn them all into me. I'm full of grabby aggressive need.

Jenny: So you are the insecurity in people gone mad?

Becky: Yes, people want to hang on to me. I had phantasies of the Pied Piper.

Jenny: And if I follow you, where will you take me?

Becky: Nowhere. Plop, off the edge of the world. Because I don't know where I'm going.

Jenny: I don't feel like pushing you any more. It's all so heady. My head's gone very strange on it anyway, like a steamroller's been wheeled backwards and forwards over me.

Becky: That's how I felt, like a steamroller. (Unfolds the paper) The Devil!

Jenny: Yes, you certainly looked and sounded like the very Devil most of the time!

*****

Well, I found that reading somewhat mysterious. But there are times when it can be rather frustrating to receive a reading which is absurdly 'precise' and 'straightforward', as happened the day we handed my sister a reading on:

UFOs by Snowy

I feel really jittery, fizzy, scurrying around. (She starts talking in humorous, higgledy-piggeldy language, half-singing) I feel silly, scatty in my brain. I might get lost, go in the wrong direction.

Jenny: I'd like to give you some advice in this reading, which is just to concentrate on the energy of it.

Snowy: Right-o. (Starts speaking quick-fire high-speed high-pitch garbage)

Jenny: And I'm supposed to write that down?

Snowy: I'm a butterfly, a hurdy-gurdy, anything that goes very fast and very skittish and quite superficial. (She is speaking all the time in a high-pitched speedy twitty voice) I'm any colour, red stripes and spots. The title of this reading is "skeddadle-di-doo-doo." (She starts whistling and moving her head in a circular motion)

Jenny: Have I really got to write this down?

Peter: And have I got to publish it?

Snowy: I feel different from the last reading I did.

Jenny: Thank you. That is what you call information in a low key. She is different from Thor Heyerdahl folks. Not the same as. Now you know.

Snowy: I like that (pointing to the big round hollow white lampshade). I could go inside it if you like. And if you didn't like, I'd still do it. I like circles. I like those things on the ceiling. I bet you never knew there were flowers up there. (We look up and notice for the first time that the ceiling has slightly raised circular star-like patterns all over it. Snowy continues buzzing and whizzing.) I'm very interested in Up There. I feel non-verbal. I'd like to dress up, with fairy-lights in the hair. The hair would have to have lots of frizzes in it, with bits of tinsel poked in, and earrings with little bells on the end going pinggg (makes tinkling noises) and false eyelashes that went dingggg (more tinny sounds), and I'd spray on lots of sparkle at the end of them so that they not only went brrrr, but tssssshh as well.

Jenny: OK, I surrender. There is a god.

Snowy: And I'd have a fruff around my neck [whatever one of those is - JJ, harrassed ed.], not a stiff one. It would be made out of candyfloss with electric lights inside so that you could turn it on. It would be green and pink or orange and it would go whee wheee - oh, and if I had hands (she puts her hands in such a position that they come direct-

ly out of her neck), I'd have nails about nine inches long
and they'd all be painted different colours and they'd definitely have a facility for turning them on, and they'd have
different coloured lights on, and each one would have a
different tune (makes a series of musical notes which one
person in the room, David, later told us was the musical
sequence used in the film Close Encounters of the Third
Kind).
Jenny: Well, I did say concentrate on the energy, and you
did that very nicely thank you, but could we now concentrate
on the intellect? Do you find it easy to obey orders?
Snowy: (robotlike) Yes.
Jenny: (Pause, while I am completely stumped)
Snowy: What's the matter?
Jenny: I'm trying to think of questions and I'm finding
it hard. Do you know who you are, or what you are, or any-
thing about yourself?
Snowy: I just get green flashing lights and things swirling
around in the sky.
Jenny: (with exaggerated patience) Yes, I know.
Peter: (laughing) Now, this is serious scientific study.
Jenny: But how am I going to write down beep beep shee whee?
Peter: And in justified type too!
Jenny: Snowy, are you saying you don't know what it is?
Snowy: UFOs?
Jenny: Huh. I am totally dissatisfied because I wanted infor-
mation, not a bleedin' UFO flying around in here. You freak-
ed me out so much, I lost all my normal ability to formulate
questions. Oh, I suppose (turning to Peter the Cynic) that
she got all that from my mind?
Peter: Yes.
Everyone: Oh, come on....
Peter: Our minds collectively; our ideas of what UFOs are.
It's a funny thing going round with lights!
Jenny: But if it was coming from my mind, I'd want her to
be serious and sober. I really want to know if these things
exist.

David: If it was telepathy, you'd think you'd get three people's ideas.

Jenny: Yes, we did: red lights, green lights and blinking orange lights!

David: At what stage did you get a sense that it was UFOs you were reading?

Snowy: Only at the end.

David: Even when you were talking about green flashing lights?

Snowy: I didn't stop to analyse what I was saying.

Jenny: Well, one thing's for sure. That couldn't have been a reading on the neighbour's tom cat...

*****

None of us at Atlantis had ever witnessed a UFO, though our prejudices were inclined very much towards believing the thousands of people who have, rather than the US Air Force who claim they haven't. And then it happened. Becky writes:

In early spring 1981, Snowy and I were coming home from England hitching. We had reached Fintown, a village about fifteen miles from Burtonport, County Donegal, where we live. There were no cars and so we walked about seven miles to the next village. The road between the two villages is winding and lonely.

It was about eleven o'clock at night and the sky was clear; there were no clouds at all, and also no moon. When you looked up, you could see all the stars very clearly above.

Snowy and I were in high spirits chatting away to keep ourselves going. At one point, we rested for a while and looked up at the stars. I said to Snowy, "I wouldn't like to see a UFO tonight." I had always been dying to see one, but tonight it felt spooky and there was only us around and I definitely did not want to see one. But Snowy said

she'd love to and she also said it was just the kind of
night you would be likely to see one.

We carried on walking and chatting and forgot about
our brief conversation. Although the sky was clear, it was
a dark night. We got to a part of the road that is quite
high up. Far in the distance, we could see the lights of
Aranmore Island, off the coast at Burtonport.

Suddenly, looking at the road as I walked along, I
saw the whole road light up in front of me as if it were
daylight. I looked at Snowy and could see her long red hair
and the colour of her clothes. I turned round to look behind
me because I felt that was where the light was coming from.
The light in the sky was a kind of crisp-looking bluey
colour. Snowy and I looked up into the sky because a huge
ball of light the size of a full moon shot up from the horizon into the sky. At first it looked like a rocket firework
with sparkle coming off it. But it was silent and far too
big. When it first appeared, it was as if the moon was suddenly cracking out of the sky. As it shot across the sky,
me and Snowy actually ducked our heads because there was
a feeling of it travelling low and it was coming straight
towards us. When it passed over us, it was an orangey-yellow
ball travelling faster than anything I had seen before,
and just behind it were four little balls following close
behind in formation. There was a blue trail of light behind
the orange ball. It was completely silent except I noticed
a slight crackly electric sound that went with it as it
travelled. There was a feeling that it was definitely coming
from somewhere and knew exactly where it was going! It went
in the direction of the open Atlantic. Seconds after the
bright light disappeared, there was a huge bang, like the
kind of explosion you would get from a quarry; the bang
came from the direction where the light had disappeared.
Snowy and I reckoned it must be the noise of the UFO breaking the sound barrier.

This whole happening took less than a minute. It was
enough to stop me and Snowy completely in our tracks. When

it had disappeared in the distance, Snowy and me held on
to one another and had to confirm that we had both seen
it and how bright it had been and how fast it had travelled. It didn't feel at all malicious, just on its own business, and in a hurry!

Shortly after this, we got a lift in a slow-travelling
car with an old man. We asked him had he seen anything
recently in the sky and all he said was, "Well, a few minutes ago, the whole road lit up before me." He hadn't thought anything of it. The next day after we got home, we
heard that the old men who live on our island had also
seen the bright light and many other locals had heard the
huge bang.

*****

I asked Snowy to write up her account of
this same experience, without seeing what Becky
had written:

Last year myself and Becky were returning from a trip
to England and were on the last leg of our hitch-hike through the country lanes of County Donegal on our way to Burtonport. It was about 10 p.m. on a clear warm starlit evening.
There was practically no traffic on the road and we settled
our pace into a comfortable stride, enjoying the fresh
Donegal air, each other's company and talk, and prepared
for a long walk home. We were not prepared for what actually happened.

We were about a mile to the East of Doochary when
an extremely bright light from behind us lit up the entire
scene. It was a greenish light and was so bright that I
could see every detail of Becky's clothes and surprised
face, the gorse bushes and every pebble on the road in
front of me.

I swung round to see what was causing the light and
saw a very large greenish yellow spherical light, accompanied by several smaller ones travelling at great speed from

East to West across the sky. The lights did not follow the
curve of the Earth but travelled in a straight line; but
at the point where they came closest to the earth, they came
very close indeed. The lights were accompanied by no noise
whatsoever.

Returned to darkness, Becky and I stood stock still
staring at each other and had a hilarious conversation which
went as follows:

"That was a light, wasn't it?"

"Yes, it was bright, wasn't it?"

"Yes, it was big, wasn't it?"

"Yes, it disappeared in the sky, didn't it?"

"Yes, it went quickly, didn't it?"

"Yes, there were little ones with it, weren't there?"

"Yes, but it didn't make any noise, did it?"

"No, and I've never seen anything like it before have
you?"

At that moment, I was extremely glad to have Becky there
to confirm my strange observations. During this conversation,
there was a very loud BANG from the North.

We carried on walking and talking in awed and questioning voices and soon got a lift from a farmer in a van. We
asked him if he'd seen anything unusual and he said that
a few minutes before, the whole road had lit up before him
like daylight but he hadn't seen where the light came from
because he was concentrating on driving and as he had a closed back to his van, he couldn't see the sky behind him. We
dropped off at the pub in Doochary and went in to see if
anyone was driving to Burtonport that night. While we were
waiting, we told the landlady about our strange sighting
and she was very excited and said she'd tell a friend of
hers who was studying UFOs.

*****

I myself had been on Inishfree Island that
night in our cottage. I heard a resounding explosion and said to the others, "The buggers! They

have started mining for uranium in the night
without telling anyone!" Ned who had gone out
for a pee saw the whole sky lit up just before
the bang. The old men, native inhabitants of
the island, had seen the flying object itself
and cursed it firmly: "Rockets from Russia!"
they informed us.

*****

CHAPTER FOURTEEN:
THE MOON, THE SUN, MARS, VENUS, EARTH
STONEHENGE

Well, wouldn't a ridiculous chapter-heading
like that make you wonder who on earth would
allow this kind of stuff to get into print?
What kind of a publisher would stick his neck
out like that?
Well, here he is himself,

MR. PETER RAZZELL'S STORY

My first experience of psychic readings was when I was
staying on Inishfree Island about two years ago. I remember
the ending of a long session with Jenny which had started
with a fight between us. She had done a psychological 'reading' of what was going on inside of me, showing through a
kind of re-enacted psychodrama in front of the commune audience the strangulated feelings of rage that I had been unable
to openly and clearly express. It was as if she had been
able to see directly inside of me, to a central and crucial
part of my personality, and I was shaken to the core by this
very powerful lady.

During my first two-week stay on the island, readings
took place practically every day. Throughout, I was concerned
to work out for myself just what was accurate and convincing
and what was vague and nebulous. This was partly my way of
dealing with what I experienced as a puzzling and a little
bit frightening, something threatening to shake my strongly
held 'scientific' world view. But whatever the perceived
accuracy of the readings, I enjoyed the energy, conversation
and fun that everyone seemed to have when readings took place
- it was like a re-discovery of my own childhood, when I
and my brothers, sisters, cousins, friends (and occasionally
adults) sat around playing games. It seemed like a marvellous
excuse to really let go and say just anything that came into

your head - in other words, to play.

And what then comes to mind was my own experience of
"Atlantis Magic." A year or so after my first visit to Atlantis, I was sitting in the kitchen of their mainland house
with ten or so other Atlanteans, and it was one of the most
enjoyable times I have had there. I myself said very little,
but the sense of fun and enjoyment was enormous: jokes, little bits of immediately improvised philosophy and above all
ENERGY. I went to bed that night with my head spinning with
that energy, energy which felt beautiful, almost like being
on acid. And that night I had one of the most pleasurable
dreams that I had had for a long time: in the dream, I was
with a particularly down-to-earth friend, who is even more
scornful of the immaterial than I am, and I decided to demon-
strate to him my magical powers by moving a cigarette end
into the air - I made it fly about and above the church steps
on which we were standing. It was a totally delightful feeling. I woke up so completely immersed in this feeling, that I
had to try out my new magical powers - but of course, sadly,
the mundane world stayed very much as it always was, and
the candle by the side of the bed firmly refused to move
into the air as I willed it to move with my stare. This illus-
trated for me our dual nature: the magical world of the unconscious, childlike, emotional and 'illogical' on the one hand;
and the rational, scientific, sceptical mind of consciousness
on the other. It is as if there are two worlds, both existing, but having to be reconciled because of their very often
contradictory natures.

My next recollection of readings was when I was staying
with Snowy at the Brixton branch of the commune: it was a
social evening when one or two outsiders had been brought
back to the house and a reading was done by Snowy on one
of them, a young Jewish lad of a likeable but opaque character. I was struck by the way Snowy came into the room and
so clearly 'knew' that the reading she was about to do was
completely right; there was going to be no arguing about
the matter - it was a straightforward matter-of-fact fact

that she knew all that was going on inside this young lad.
The young fellow, when told that the reading was of him,
was disconcerted and denied that it had anything really to
do with him in any significant way. Everyone else in the
room, including me, could see that it was a totally convincing and accurate portrait. Who was right? The hard-headed
natural scientist would clearly reject the 'intuitive hypo-
thesis,' along with most of the other evidence to come out
of the readings - but that is a loss to natural science,
and shows that there are other (and more important) ways
of discovering the truth than through 'objective' scientific
analysis.

So my image of readings now was of an intuitive, emotional way of seeing the truth, a way which was 'soft' and feminine rather than 'rational' and masculine. Although I had
seen the men of Atlantis do readings, I had never found them
as convincing as when done by the women. I don't think that
this was anything factual, but the male readings didn't seem
to have the right feel to them. Then one day, I did a reading
myself. My friend Jeremy Ward had suggested the idea, in
one of the cottages on Inishfree Island, and I did a reading
on what turned out to be a business partner of his. Afterwards he told me he thought the reading had been very accurate and of great interest to him. I had enjoyed doing the
reading, but this was more a feeling of being given licence
to play-act, to muck around with words and act out gestures
and impulses in front of an audience; I didn't have any sense
of 'connecting' with the person of the reading and therefore
it made little or no impact on me.

My next experience of readings was when I went back
to my home town, Ramsgate, for a weekend, spending an evening
with my brother and sister and their families. I offered
to do a reading, and was given one. Almost immediately I
knew that it was of my sister-in-law (who was sitting in
the room) and greatly enjoyed coming out with more and more
details of her attitudes and inner feelings - and the more
I came out with, the more disconcerted she was, which added

greatly to my enjoyment. Then to my disappointment, they
stopped me, telling me who it was and covering their embarrassment and anxiety with some confused questioning about not
understanding the procedures of readings. But later my brother admitted that they had been shaken by what I had revealed,
and had stopped me because I might say too much about his
wife. So I could do readings - and it wasn't a prerogative
of the women. Somewhere in the back of my mind, I had assumed
that I wasn't open enough to do them, and it was an important
step to be able to break through that assumption.

I have witnessed a number of other readings since that
time, and they have had for me the same mix: humour, play-
acting, insight and emotional contact. But the recent experience that affected me most was the evening that David Boadella came round to discuss a proposed book with me, and at
the end of the evening sat in on three readings done by Snowy
and Jenny. There was nothing 'special' about the evening
- no dramatic, emotional atmosphere in the room - yet there
was a feeling of total naturalness and relaxation about what
was going on. It seemed as if there was an undercurrent of
assumed contact and understanding, particularly between Jenny
and Snowy on the one hand, and David on the other.

And so my conclusion is that readings work through a
kind of emotional contact, communication through an intuitive
unconscious transmission of feelings, energy, images and
ideas - in other words, telepathy. I find the idea of telepathy totally plausible and easily reconcilable with a modern
world scientific view. (If a simple electronic structure
like a radio set can transmit messages across space, it is
obvious to me that something as complex as the brain can
do much more.)

But more important than this interpretation of readings
is what the readings directly represent: a simple, enjoyable
and sometimes profound way of discovering the nature of the
emotional world we live in.

PETER RAZZELL

And so back to the business of this chapter. Having launched into the realm of UFOs,
the sky no longer seemed the limit. So we decided
to test out what would happen if we tried to
do readings on whole planets. Would the medium
pick up the same 'vibrations' and attributes
as have been associated with the various heavenly
bodies throughout the ages in astrology? This
area of exploration definitely brought us up
against our limits. It was the least successful
of all - our mediums had a bad time and mostly
felt like dead, cold, 'spaced-out' beings ready
to crack up. I think we were being told very
firmly to get back to Earth where we belong.
The reading on the Earth, in comparison, felt
warm and friendly.

Here, nonetheless, are one or two excerpts.
Firstly, our poor neighbour:

THE MOON by Becky

Whatever I am, I feel completely immersed in my own
tiredness, in my own deadness. I've got a superficial feeling
- I'm all on the surface. My mind's away in the clouds. I'm
not in a state of feeling anything. I feel very up in the
sky, up in the clouds, up in the air. I feel really stagnant.
Once my life was jumbly and messy, but now it is perfect,
but perfect in a sterile way. All my diseases have gone,
my wounds are healing up; I've done all the cleaning, everything is perfect, but I would prefer that messy feeling:
I'm missing it now, the emotion, the ripping apart, the having to fight for my life. I want stress. I want a mess to
sort out. I go dead when everything is 'good.' Everything
is chugging along, but there is something missing in my life.
I have plenty of space, I've cleared everything away, and
now I'm ready for more.

I feel very neat and tidy. I have a feeling of being
very maternal, of being a mother [in astrology, the Moon is

always associated with motherhood.] The pictures on the wall
I focus on are all of fairy tales. I feel graceful and very
proper. I feel that I have been much more emotional. I was
much richer than I am now. If I didn't force myself to talk,
I'd be sitting here quite silent and blank. Once I had serv-
ants and slaves; I was completely queenly. I feel very feminine and have lots of pride in myself. I used to be on stage
dressed up, an entertainer, lots of lights and fun. But now
I have been brought down. I have aged very quickly and got
old and stagnant. I am aware that things can be magical and
exciting, but the sensation in my body at present is like
sitting around for hours and hours and doing just one thing
and going to sleep at night-time and thinking, "Huh, another
day passed, nothing's better, nothing's worse."

*****

A year later, I tried the same reading via
Snowy. Entirely the same energy emerged:

THE MOON by Snowy

I feel uncentred and not particularly happy. I don't
feel very nice at all in this environment. I have absolutely
no what I would call physical buzz off the reading whatsoever. In fact, the opposite - I feel less alive than when I
started. I feel heavier and more sullen. I feel as if my
eyes are sort of half-closed and my lips are down in a cynical sneer. I'm slumped in my energy. I'm freezing cold since I
started this reading. I was hot before.

I've just been doing some writing for Jen's book and
I was about to deal with the subject of readings on phenomena
like rocks, inanimate objects, and it just came to my mind
that this could be a reading of something inanimate.
Jenny: What is your essential nature?
Snowy: Broken, I would say, but sort of pinned together!
Jenny: What would be your influence?
Snowy: I would provide a challenge to people. They would
want to open me up and might feel kindly towards me; but

I wouldn't accept it as kindly at all; I would take it as
aggressive.

Jenny: Where do you come from?

Snowy: Hard and cold, a place where there's not much give.
Distrust, a scroogy place. Whatever has happened to me in
the past has made me bitter. And I feel I've dug myself deep
into a rut: I don't think the future will be anything different from the present. I feel very monochrome.

Jenny: If you had lots of power, what would your effects
be?

Snowy: Oh, I'd shut everything down. I'd just close all the
shops. I wouldn't have anything happen any more, I'd just
stop everything.

Jenny: What are your attributes?

Snowy: Rock-like strength. I would probably be one of the
rocks that stood out on the horizon after a nuclear war,
one of those that didn't get atomized for some reason. But
I wouldn't offer much nourishment or shelter...

*****

At first when I gave Becky a reading to do
on the SUN, I was convinced that there wasn't
any sense in it at all, because she said she
felt cold. But I listened on, just in case ...

THE SUN by Becky

I'm cold. I'm frozen right inside. I've gone stagnant
deep down inside of myself. I'm old and withered up. My soul
is cold. But it doesn't mean I'm a cold person; it just means
that something incredibly huge inside me is dying. It's something I have to extract from myself. All my oldness and deadness is coming up to the surface, something is withering
up inside me. It's like an animal getting a new coat for
the winter, getting rid of the old coat. Something's tight
in me and I'm trying to pull it out and crack it; it's like
a sickness I've got and it has to come out before I can feel
good and warm and happy again. I don't feel at all settled.
I feel jittery, jagged and sharp and incredibly alone; alien

and alienated. I got to a peak in my life, and from that peak, I've gone whoosh! downwards.

Jenny: Can you say what your influence on people would be?

Becky: Something about me brings people's energies out, makes them want to come out and react to me. I wake people up. People that are open like me; but people who feel they have something to hide, they don't like me at all. I make people suddenly start doing things that they don't normally do. They are quite surprised at themselves even. I bring back people's youthfulness, and their daring. And I make them start getting at one another. I bring up their stagnation and deadness and they start seeing it in other people. I make a chain reaction occur in people. I start off pecking orders. People like me for bringing movement into their lives, but they hate me for the fact that it's not comfortable.

Jenny: Can you say what sort of energy you have?

Becky: My energy isn't flowing, it's jerky. There's lots going on inside that hasn't come to the surface yet. There are going to be upheavals in me - some kind of challenging situation where I'll just crack.

The general effect I have is good. Movement. My own movement moves everything. The upheavals inside myself warm up everything: it would be a cleansing thing. There is real happiness and richness. I have a big effect on everything and everyone, things become juicier and warmer and genuinely happier. I am like a light put on to everything.

*****

We gave the same reading a year later to my sister.

THE SUN by Snowy

I am going to look at the tape-recorder and 'scry' off it - tell you the things that occur to me. The first thing that attracts me is the little dial that says 'signal.' I am like a signal; I point the way and tell you when you can stop and when you can go.

I am the sort of entity that goes zooming around the cosmos. I feel completely and utterly focussed on one thing - I have become absolutely specialized. I am just here to carry out my purpose, which is to take signals round; that takes up all the time and energy I've got. I'm very very responsible in an extremely limited sphere, but I've got the impression that it's a very big sphere, covering a lot of space. Mine is a long but very narrow path, that's how I see it, just putting all my energy into one thing. I'm an entity that doesn't want to change anything; I'm very conservative. What I'm doing is important but don't expect me to look outside my sphere to either side. Here I am and that's it. You just let me be myself and trust me with the job I'm doing and I'll do extremely well with great care and precision and you will get what you want from me. You can rely on me.

Jenny: What is your essence, your core?

Snowy: I don't like it at all; I feel horrible and dead and hard and stiff and tight. If only I could find something to crack myself. What would crack me is banging into something really hard, and then the truth would dissolve outward.

Jenny: What part of your life are you in?

Snowy: Well, if I had to think, was I a foetus or a dead spirit, I'd say I was dead. I've finished rather than just beginning. I get a very airy feeling doing this reading.

Jenny: What is your effect on people?

Snowy: I imagine my effect is sharp. I can see things really clearly. My attributes are attention to detail, singlemindedness, dedication, centredness in what I'm doing - all of that is very strong in me. And survival: a very strong survival instinct. I just keep going and you couldn't pull me off centre.

*****

The planet Mars has always been associated in astrology with energy, activity, aggression: it is a male planet. Venus is associated with the softer side of nature, with love and sympathy and under-

standing: it is 'female.' I was intrigued to
find that these two ancient sets of characteristics were reflected in the readings Becky did
of these planets.

MARS by Becky

The first things I've got is a feeling of determination.
I feel strong and sturdy, but stiff and cold and out-of-touch.
I feel old and ever so spaced-out. I don't feel at all at
home in this room. I want to talk LOUDLY. I've got a feeling
that my energy is all over the place: if I did what my energy
is telling me to do, I'd be skipping up and down on the spot
all day long or blundering all over the place.
Jenny: How would you affect anyone under your influence?
Becky: My influence would be to keep things going in some
way. "Come on, everybody, don't space out please. Not just now
- it's not the right time of year." I keep everyone hopping
up and down; I give encouragement. I would say, "Look, everything's in a terrible state, why not let's all fight together.
Come on, let's all do something about it." I would try and
wake people up. But I feel a resistance around me. I don't
actually feel that I get a lot of people to listen to me.

I'm some kind of life-force if you can find a way of
using me and dealing with me. But whatever or whoever I am,
most people would ignore me and turn away from me and get
on with their lives. But then their lives wouldn't change.
I'm a person or something to be used, as I must constantly
unload, and what I unload can be used.

*****

VENUS by Becky

The minute I started this reading, I thought, "Oh dear,
my energy doesn't move very easily. I feel cold, my blood
has stopped in my body. I feel worried, as if I'm going to
crack up. (Becky starts crying) I constantly feel cold.
Jenny: What made you cry?

Becky: I cried as I broke into myself, I feel relief at being told what to do. I need somebody to be firm with me. My nature is that I need to be shown the way. It's easy after that. The difficult way is being defended.

Jenny: How do you think people would respond to you - what would be your influence?

Becky: I immediately think that people would look to me for guidance. I think that I try and give people comfort. I would say, "Get yourself a nice husband or wife and settle down. Get yourself a friend to talk to and you'll be alright." I can imagine being a social worker or a marriage guidance counsellor. I would give people comfort and reassurance, tell them the best thing to do. People would feel safe under my influence, comfortable, looked-after and cared-for. That other fellow [Mars] would mean insecurity; I'm security. I'd say, "Have a good cry dear." People could come to me and I'd have an answer for their little problems, whereas that last chap would come blasting through your house and shake your guts up.

*****

There's certainly no place like home. After all the tortured vibrations that were brought into the room from all those far off planets, it was a relief to hear Becky put on her 'British sporty' accent as she depicted:

PLANET EARTH by Becky

The minute I picked this reading up, I felt like a sporty type of person, sprightly and hoppy. I feel game for anything. My whole body feels bubbly, everything is fizzy inside me and I'm ready to rush off at ten miles an hour down the road. I'd never get puffed out. I keep going. I'm always on the move, working. I've got lots of energy. Look at me, seventy years old and off I go, trotting along, been doing this every day of my life and I still keep doing them. It's good for my health. I use every bit of my energy; I couldn't bear to sit still for one minute and do nothing.

Jenny: How do you handle bad things being done to you?

Becky: I think if someone did something bad to me, I'd first of all stare them in the face and try to stare them out of existence as if to say, "Excuse me, old chap, what do you think you're doing? This is my property, do you mind getting your dirty little body off it? Thank you very much. If you behave in such a disgraceful way, I'll have to ask you to leave." If this doesn't work, I'll have to get violent. I don't like to get violent, but if you push me far enough, I'll have to use a bit of fist. I'm a pretty strong, firm sort of chap. I've always been building my body up, and I never did build it up for hurting people, but then again I don't want to be hurt myself. I don't like aggression, you know, but I will use it where I have to for my own protection, because I'd like to stay on this Earth for a bit longer. I decided when I go, not you, so shove off.

I've got this image of myself as someone who teaches people and I like people to listen to me. I like to make myself heard and I like you all to respond to me. I like Law and Order. Now, we'll have you all lined up, the best man in front and the useless ones at the bottom. You all know what to do, and when I say, 'do something,' you'll all do it. I'll make sure you are all in tune.

I feel like a captain-y sort of person, sharp, alert and awake, and I want everyone to be in harmony. I'll say, "One, two, three, one, two, three," and everyone must dance in time. You'll get the flow of it if you try hard enough.

I'm quite warm-hearted. I get my satisfaction out of doing things with other people, though I don't feel that I have anyone very personally close to me. I'm good at organizing very big groups of people and happenings.

I'm very much into beauty in a very pure sense: I can imagine being up at the top of a hill looking at a landscape. And if I saw a house stuck in the middle of it, something that didn't fit in, it would drive me bonkers.

Jenny: Do you have any fears?

Becky: I think my biggest fear is about my own physical body.

I spend so much of my time using my body and moving my body
that I'm scared of collapsing or of something suddenly coming
on me and me being put out of use. That scares me more than
anything.

Jenny: What do you hate most in people?

Becky: I hate untogetherness. I hate unnecessary things,
and that even includes doing unnecessary things, like going
to shops and buying unnecessary things and going to theatres
and cinemas in unnecessary cars, and having unnecessary bits
and pieces in the home, and people putting themselves through
unnecessary pains and worries. I like things to be very clear
and simple. There's a picture on that wall of people living in
tents, and there are no bits and pieces around the place
- what there is, is what they need to survive, and I agree
with that. I'm very conscious of what's natural and what's
not natural; of what's man-made and what's not man-made.
I feel that in my past, I got very involved in the material
world, the world of unnecessary things. I've gone the other
way now. Now I'm very conscious of Nature and I'm leaning more
towards wanting to live in nature. The pictures on the wall
that stick out are one of a small cottage and water and green
surrounding it; and one of trees and a huge river. I like
that. And mountains with snow on them and people walking
through the mountains. That's what I'm striving towards;
I'm moving away from houses and cars and all the ridiculous-
ness. My future is in the open, with warmth from the sun,
plenty of movement, air and wind and a feeling of being healed
and cleaned out by being out in a natural environment.

*****

There are all kinds of theories about the
origin and function of STONEHENGE. I have twice
given this subject to Becky to 'read.' There
were two years in between the two readings, and
yet they were so homogeneous that I have amalgama-
ted them into one:

STONEHENGE by Becky

The minute I picked up the reading and started breathing deeply, I began to sway back and forwards. I feel slightly dreamy. My eyes are misty, like they want to close up, and the minute I picked up the reading, I felt much slower. I just feel like sitting here and not doing very much. I haven't got a mind at all, nor any strong sensations. I can't get the feeling of what it would be like to relate to people or talk or walk around. But I feel completely in tune with Nature - with natural things that move, birds, and children, and animals. I would not be able to stand speed or noisy machines. I am in tune with the flies buzzing around and the birds singing. I would be completely satisfied lying here saying nothing, just watching the grass and the sky and the animals. I feel heavy and tired. I would like to live out here, sleep out here all summer and breathe the fresh air.

It's not hard to get into me, it's not hard to reach me; what I am, who I am, is on the surface; there's not much hidden in me. I'm completely in my own little world and I'm not very conscious of things outside. I am very relaxed and slowed-down. I feel like I'm rocking back and forwards; there is a real flow inside me. I feel like I'm falling, falling to my side. My head feels very heavy and I feel best when I allow myself not to try to lift my head up. I can imagine meditating all day long on my own and not feeling lonely. I don't change very much. I'm very content. I'm like a very old person who has lived on their own for years. I've lived my life, and here I am, looking after myself now. I feel exhausted as if I've done masses of work.

Jenny: How old are you?

Becky: The first number that came to my mind was 'ten.'

Jenny: Ten what?

Becky: Ten hundred. It felt like 'ten hundred years,' but if I'm a person it seems ridiculous. I feel like a mineral, a substance of some sort. A heavy something.

Jenny: What is your function?

Becky: I feel like I am a kind of radar or thing that energy

is fed into. I notice energy and I pick it up easily. Even
if a bird is flying from behind me, I know that it is coming.
If something is moving, I notice it. I am a measurer. I measure how much it is and what it is. I am here to show people
something. I might just be here to show people that now and
again it's alright not to be zooting around; it's OK sometimes
to relax and to breathe deeply and not to get uptight and
not to get worried; to tell people to give themselves time
and space to themselves and to look more into themselves
rather than doing millions of jobs and always being distracted
by what is outside of themselves. I'm like a guru: I'm here to
show people a way of being, an energy that you can have.
You can take me or leave me. I'm here doing my own thing,
being all cosmic with yellow lights in my head. If you want
to, you can follow me - well, you can't really, because I'm
not going anywhere. But you can follow me in the way I go
about things. I just am what I am and that's the way it is.

Jenny: Do you know anything about your parents?

Becky: Parents? What parents? I haven't got any. Or if I
have, they must be a long long way from me in time and space.
For some reason, I feel that whatever I've come from, I've
become much bigger than them, that I'm massive in size, huge.
I don't feel human, so that means that my parents can't have
been human. It's strange, I don't feel "mum and dad": I feel
more like just "my mum." I was part of my mother, and I was
cut from her and made into something else; and somehow, I've
got bigger. And I feel like something's living on me, growing
on me, a fungus or something.

Jenny: OK, what sort of people created you?

Becky: The first feeling I have is that very sensitive people
created me. Very loving, caring, concerned people. Big people.

Jenny: What do you mean, big?

Becky: Physically. I imagine what Atlantean people must have
been like, really strong, enormous. I think people now are
kind of small and weak, gone to seed. The people that created
me were big and strong and healthy.

Jenny: Why were you made?

Becky: I was made for people, to serve them in some way; for

people to live from me. But something went wrong; I went
out of use and I can't be used now for what I was made. I've
got really old and been forgotten about. I feel that I am
a thing mainly for people to look at and learn from. I feel
like a base, that I am something for other things to happen
around. I am strong, solid, steady. My purpose is like the
floor of a room or the grounds of a house. I am very grand,
very very old, like a painting painted hundreds of years
ago, or a big statue. In my mind, I see big, heavily-built
people. I am really huge and solid and very beautiful. Not
everyone would think I am beautiful though. Some people would
not appreciate me at all; they'd look at me and throw me
away. But other people would appreciate me like they would
an old thatched cottage.

I've known earlier on what it is like to move a lot and
have a lot going on in me and around me. And I've been a
lot happier in the past. Now I'm basically dying, though
I'm still very conscious. I picture myself as being something
really naked and bare and barren and cold and colourless,
with no other life around me. I'm dying because I'm not being
used; I'm not in relation to anything else. I'm on my own,
and if you live on your own for a long time, you just fizzle
out.

I've had a hard time, and the reason for it is to do with
things from now, modern man-made things like buildings and
cars and roads. I feel like there is something almost supernatural about me, and things like noise and cars have destroyed me. I keep thinking that I am Atlantis, the old Atlantis,
and that I should be left in peace. I should have been respec-
ted more, taken more care of. I was pushed in the wrong direction, away from natural sources and towards hard cold noisy
smelly things that I just can't cope with.

<u>Jenny</u>: Could you be brought back to life?

<u>Becky</u>: Yes, I think I could be. The moment you said that, I
got the picture of myself as a little planet all on my own
going round in circles and this little space-ship coming
and landing on me and me feeling really cared-for - someone
coming and seeing me. All I really need is for people to

notice me and care about me and to want to bring me back
to life. There's something really big about me, something
wide, a big space in me for people to live on. There aren't
any sides to me. If I were brought back to life, there'd
be something in me which would open up and I would enjoy
people appreciating me.

Jenny: Have you any special knowledge?

Becky: Only self-knowledge, what has happened to myself,
which is quite a lot. When you say knowledge, I imagine scientific knowledge, things learnt out of books. But my knowledge
is the sort that can show people how to learn from mistakes.
My main importance is to teach cleanliness. I hate to see
plastic things or any unnatural colours around me. I look
at the land and it looks very barren to me. There shouldn't
be any ground with nothing growing on it. You can learn plenty
from me, but it will take an awful long time to put things
right again.

Jenny: What special properties have you?

Becky: The first thing is, I can keep on going for an incredibly long time. I feel indestructible. And there is something
good-natured about me: I care for people, especially for
children, for young new clean life. I take them away from
things that they are not going to grow from, and I put them
on a straighter path. I just had a flash then of wanting
to take children away from grownups, to put children with
children.

Jenny: Are you religious at all?

Becky: I feel religious in my own way, very religious in
fact. The religion of nature and life and openness - I mean
literally outside, in the open. But I don't feel very happy,
because I feel very alone. I am standing on my own. I still
have loads and loads to give. I have already given a lot,
but I have never got renewed. There is no new life going
into me any more. There isn't enough goodness, not enough
air or trees or animals left. I feel that I feed off grass
and air, and there's not enough for me, so I am slowing
down.

Jenny: Can you see what the future holds for you?

Becky: Oh, I feel despair when I think of it. I've got a feeling that I am never actually going to die, I'm not actually going to finish, but I am winding down. I still feel completely warm and solid as I talk, there is something very alive about me, but I am slowing down.

Jenny: How have you been treated?

Becky: Badly. I've been abused and misused. I get an image of a theatre, something like that, really lovely-looking, and a load of skinheads coming in and ripping me to bits with penknives and broken bottles, coming in with boots and kicking me around and me being left bare. My mistake was being too open, being a place that lets the public in, when I should be something that is more closed-up. I feel appreciative of really old and beautiful things. I don't like modern things at all.

Jenny: What was your best time?

Becky: I just had a flash that when I was lying in the garden at the beginning and looking at the trees and grass and the animals and the sky, that I have been everything, that I have experienced being a bird and a goat, and when that was all that I saw and experienced, that was when I was most awake and alive. Once, sitting up on that rock up there, I knew how the world began and what it was. Being a human being is not my element; it's really uncomfortable, the wrong size and shape; being in my body now isn't big enough for this reading. I am much bigger and stronger and more powerful. If I was a part of that ground and grass out there, I would feel comfortable and at home and I would be moving at my own pace. I'm not meant to move as fast as a human body. I feel really uncomfortable. I feel messed around with. I have been experimented with and mixed with a substance that is wrong for me, and now I feel miserable.

Jenny: What would you like most in the world to happen?

Becky: To be brought back to life, to the extent that I was alive before. I've still got this image of being like a theatre, an old opera sort of theatre place; and I imagine people coming in that really care about me and putting me back together again, really using me and having all the things that

happened there before. I want people to really use me in
a good way rather than to be used as a playground for a load
of yobbos.

Jenny: What is the worst thing that happened to you?

Becky: Actually being left and forgotten about. Being torn
apart and destroyed, and then people not even caring, just
saying, "Oh well, that's the end of that." I'm thinking of
beautiful old buildings, how they're torn down and people
prefer to go and live in little boxes that will only last a
few years.

Jenny: Can you remember anything at all about your birth?

Becky: The first image I have is of breaking away from my
mother. I imagine not being quite the right shape. My first
days were taken up with getting me into shape. I was quite
chaotic. I wasn't whole. I wasn't one. There were little
bits sticking out of me.

    When I was first born, people wanted me because I was
energetic and lively and colourful and to do with self-expression. But people didn't know how to cope with me and they
all went a bit wild. I was extremely energetic and I gave
a lot of space for people to let go and express themselves.
People did use me well, but it all got a bit out of control.
I get an image of a whole school of young kids given a room
where they can go completely wild. I imagine them rushing
in and picking up things. All these kids had been closed
in and kept quiet and not really allowed to move about, and
something about me, whatever I was, gave them space to really
let rip as much as they wanted, and they became completely
destructive, violent. I can imagine them actually starting
to kill each other. They'd be screeching and yelling and
running about and anyone that was a bit too weak got left
at the bottom of the pile. Somebody needed to organize what
was going on. I get a feeling of no proper teaching going
on.

Jenny: If you came completely to life, what would you be
like? What would the energy be like?

Becky: Magical. Fun. Playful. Acting and self-expression.
Colour. I have an image of the play we did here - that really

attracts me; really outrageous costumes, really extreme.
I'd like that. I would very much appreciate our life here
at Atlantis at its peak, when everybody is here and it's
packed and millions is going on and all the lights are on
and all the fires are going and it's warm, with laughter
and music and very high spirits.

But that's all very much in my head now. That's how
I've known it. I don't feel it in my body any more.

*****

SIMON'S STORY

So if it was an uneducated eighteen-year-old girl who
did that reading, without knowing the first thing about
what it was about, where on earth did she get all that information from and why is it entirely relevant to the name written
on that piece of paper which she is holding in her hand and
yet has never seen? What subtle vibrations are at work? Did
she sneak a look? Where did she pick up that gesture, that
mannerism? Why is she walking differently from usual? Why
has her mood changed so suddenly? Is it all for real?

If you stay in this place for long, let me warn you,
you quickly lose grip of your normal standards of perception
and judgements, then they'll try anything on you and expect
you to believe it. Quite honestly, I think you're better
off in the city away from the pernicious influence of this
commune.

It is a strange phenomenon altogether this ability to
be able to feel someone else from the inside. It is one thing
to observe and deduce and question and thus gain insight
into another human being, but to actually feel how they feel
in their own body, to actually experience their perceptions,
sensations, even emotions, briefly to experience the world in
all the uniqueness of someone else, now isn't that going
a bit too far? Is it really likely?

And yet I can remember feeling particularly annoyed
towards a friend of mine after having done a psychic reading
of him, having discovered how good he feels inside his body,

inside his world - certainly he felt a lot happier than I
usually do and I can only admit I resented him for it. Generally I experience the world as a somewhat bleaker place than
he does. I can say that with all the confidence of having
experienced his world, which was like having a very mild
and pleasant acid trip. I mentioned so many features that
were identifiably and recognisably him that he himself was
amazed.

So what does this prove? That strange experiences are
in the reach of us all with just a little confidence and
encouragement. The power to suss people out from the inside,
to find the denial of their facade - is anyone safe?! Will
secrets be revealed, the hidden discovered? I have been suspicious for a long time that the women of Atlantis have uncanny
powers of knowing and finding out what I'm thinking and feeling, and, worse still, what I'm wanting. In fact, they know
too much altogether and I'm beginning to wonder if a govern-
ment investigation mightn't be a good idea with the intention
of banning forever with severe punishment for all these witches who contravene the law. I for one would happily abandon the
talent and find for myself a cosy niche to hide myself away
from prying probing eyes and people who know what you're
up to even when you think you don't know yourself.

I have heard and seen many readings done and I have
to admit I have always enjoyed and invariably been fascinated
by them. To see people with whom you are very familiar taken
over by the energy and impulses of another person, to engage
with them and find they react differently from their usual
selves, is certainly something out of the ordinary. I can
particularly remember a time when Jenny was doing a reading
of a communard's girlfriend to whom I was immediately attracted and started to have a very enjoyable interaction with,
in a completely different way from my usual way with Jenny.
There was definitely a stranger in the room that night.

Before I ever came to Atlantis, I had no experience
of the psychic. I was always very derisive as regards such
things, but with a secret hope that maybe there was something
in it. Now, having been impressed, entertained and enlightened

and sometimes even excited by numerous psychic readings,
I can only say, what's the fuss about? It can be done, there
is no room for doubt. Psychic readings work.

I know that if someone starts to confidently tell me
what I am feeling, the more accurate they are, the more annoyed I become, and the more likely I am to want to deny it
utterly. And what if they're telling me pleasant things about
myself? Well, I can sit back and act modest and pretend it's
not me. And what still, if they go down deeper than I've
ever been myself and start wrenching something out that I
had good reason to bury? Hold on, I say, did I want to know
that? Where's the door? Yes, they can be annoying, and also
therapeutic. It is interesting to get someone else's perspective on the feelings and states of being which you take for
normal. Once Snowy told me during a reading of myself that
she was experiencing extreme tension in her body, worse than
ever she had in her whole life. She was talking in horror
about something I took totally for granted and barely noticed.

Psychic readings are very much a part of my experience
of Atlantis, but what their implications are in terms of
human consciousness, I have not begun to think about. That
you can tune into another human being and pick up their energy
patterns merely by giving yourself permission with a piece
of paper with a name on it? Or is there some telepathy involved amongst the people in the room? And anyway, person to
person is one thing; but what about person to city, person
to planet, person to thing, person to non-person? So anything
that is anything anywhere has an energy pattern which can
be tuned into and expressed by anyone who allows themselves
to do so. The possibilities start to sound a bit endless
to me. I'm spaced-out enough without thinking about that.

What if we could just get the name of some extra-terrestrial being and find out how he thinks and feels, and what
his attitude is to human beings.....?

SIMON D. ROOK

*****

CHAPTER FIFTEEN:
BECKY'S DEAD TWIN and
THE ATLANTIS READINGS

But in the end, as in the beginning, readings are for finding out about yourself and those close to you; for focussing on your own path in life and where you stand on it; for shining a light on areas of darkness that trouble you, or areas of mystery that intrigue you.

A lot of the readings recorded in this book were on spectacular subjects chosen especially for experimentation, and reproduced here because they are entities that everyone knows in some way. But the real work of our readings – and yours if you try them – is in personal matters, because it's only the personal that really matters. How you live your life is who you are.

My own separation from the left-wing politics of my earlier days is based on this one issue: the poverty of the lives of those who claim to be concerned about the poverty of other people's lives. This is why our commune is choosing to uproot entirely from Europe and plant ourselves anew in the 'Third World'. We are putting our feet where our mouths are. In a way, we are saying we don't believe all this poverty and deprivation talk. I make the prediction that one day, if there's any Europe left, I'll be sending a manuscript 'home' to my longsuffering publisher about the comparative richness of life amongst so-called 'poor' peoples.

Any area of life we can reclaim from the programming fixed up for us before we are born helps to bring back some of that richness which is our natural right. Doing readings instead of watching telly is a good start.

In the five readings that follow, Becky and Snowy are, of course, simply allowing to flow out of them thoughts about issues that are preoccupying them at the time. It so happens that when you do this, a strangely large percentage of what comes out fits the subject chosen; and yet it is still only us exploring ourselves. What matter if Becky's fantasy of re-meeting her twin is just the hope that every soul has of finding a mate; of if the Old Atlantis didn't really exist as stones and mortar but simply as the representation of something so important within man that he has needed to invent – and maintain – such a legend. I know the effect these readings had on us: it was exciting, sobering, cleansing; and it consolidated us in our determination to go and find out more about ourselves in the mountains of South America, where there is no corner shop, and no local hospital.

That's just our way. There are mediums doing psychic readings in the middle of Piccadilly Circus. I hope, anyway, that this strange book helps you find out more about your way.

*****

When I was pregnant for the first time, at the age of twenty, my husband who was a mental nurse, talked with me about what we would do if by any chance we produced a deformed child. We had no doubts about it. Our belief was firm that it should not be allowed to live; we both agreed that it was cruel to let defective children suffer.

It wasn't until 1981, eighteen years after that first pregnancy, that I heard they now have an early detection method for hydrocephalus and

spina bifida, the deformities that Becky's twin
sister, Nicole, was born with. Now you can get
an abortion, no bother, if these diseases show
up in the foetus. I would definitely have wanted
a termination if I had known I was carrying a
deformed baby. However, the fact that I was expecting twins was not diagnosed. And so I would
have lost my Becky too.

Now, with all this psychic business and
all this outrageous stuff about reincarnation
and souls, I feel a little less single-minded
about my previously positive attitude towards
abortion. And, eighteen years too late, I wonder
uneasily about the way I so calmly left my deformed baby Nicole to cry for three weeks in a hospital before she managed to die, never being held
or fed by me. And yet I had so much milk they
used to take it off me for the incubator babies.
They told me Nicole was heavily sedated the whole
time, "else she would have screamed the ward
down."

I know now how the right energy passing
from one body to another works more miracles
than all the medicines modern science can offer.
And I know for sure that the bad, difficult energy
passing between me and Becky's father created
that deformed baby. She was no accident, and
had I held her in my arms, thereby for sure leng-
thening her life, I would have been forced to
look into her face and look at her inadequate
body, and know myself ten years earlier than
I did. I wasted her, and I wasted a whole part
of my own life as a result. With two babies,
I would never have been able to chase the ugly
moonbeams of university, top office jobs and
goal-less travel. I would have been forced to
do the thing I most feared (long before Women's
Lib. came along to 'politicize' the fear): stay

at home, be a mother, be domestic and dependent
and female and 'conventional', all of which I
thought then spelt death. I now know they could
have spelt life, the emotional, difficult, crazy
side of life that I, by letting my baby - the
baby in me - die, avoided for another decade.

When Becky was about four years old, we
moved to a new town (Croydon). She was sitting
on my lap in my boyfriend's car and suddenly,
out of the blue, she said in a matter-of-fact
voice, "Perhaps we'll find my sister in this
town." I stared at her. As far as I knew, the
fact that she'd been born a twin had never been
mentioned to her.

When I gave Becky a reading to do on Nicole,
I wrote on the paper: "NICOLE - What was the
point of her brief life and her early death?
Is she still with us or a part of us in any way?"

NICOLE by Becky

I look at my hands and my arms and I look really thin.
My skin looks like it is dying. I'm moving in a really weird
way. I am connected to Jenny and Becky and this room and
I know I'm connected. I haven't just popped in from nowhere.
I'm still connected. I'm very flowy in my body, like water
or jelly moving up and down. I've got a feeling of wanting
to take my clothes off to see my body, to see who I am and
what I look like. I am completely intrigued by myself, fascinated by my own body, by how I move and react to things.

Ever since I started this reading, I have had a feeling
of everything twinkling and being magical, as if things in
this room are moving. Nothing is solid, everything is moving
together and everything is connected with everything else.
It's a very magical feeling, a lovely feeling. I treasure
who I am as important, but much as I might try and make myself
ordinary, I'm not. I already feel I know who I am; I knew
from the minute I picked the paper up. I feel that I'm Nicole.

Jenny: What made you feel that?
Becky: Just the moment I picked it up, I felt so sure that
I was connected to you and me and to this room. I could feel
there was no split at all - it wasn't like jumping into doing
a reading and getting a headache or something, or a new feeling. It was just natural; it was just a continuation of how
Becky is feeling now. I had a feeling of just accepting who
I am, accepting the unusualness of me. Shall I just carry
on with the reading?

I feel I look really pale and thin and ill, but inside I
feel healthy. I have the feeling that from the outside I
look really starving, yet I'm full up inside.

I keep thinking something strange is going to happen
- that something is going to come alive in this room, but
it's not going to scare me. It's going to be something that's
never happened before, a wall or something is going to start
moving or the floor is suddenly going to open up, which for
most people would be the most unexpected and horrific thing
on earth, but I would just be able to sit back and say 'Yes.'

I feel quite ill actually. It doesn't hurt, but it could
get bad, it could hurt. It's just starting. I feel really
pale and thin and small. When I started, I wanted to talk,
but now I'm getting blocked somehow, plugged up, stopped. I
keep thinking that I'm going to burst into tears, and I feel
that it would be a complete relief, but that I'm not able
to. I'm looking at everything and I'm not enjoying it to
the extent I could, because I can't cry. I always think of
tears as healing; there is no medicine that is more healing
than tears. It's the most natural medicine, and that's what
would cure me.

I keep getting the feeling of being really short, of
shrinking. I've got a feeling as I sit on this chair that
there's hardly anything between my feet and my shoulders,
there's hardly any body to me. My head feels huge - I don't
know if I am Nicole, but my head feels big and painful. It's
almost as if my brain is full of everything - things I already
know as Becky, and more. My face is really big. I need to
cry but I find it really hard to. I feel sick. I want to

stretch and grow. I'm aching all over. I feel really sick
and ill and faint. I'm about to die. I'm spinning around,
wanting to cry. (She starts crying)

I'm thinking about Nicole and how she had water on the
brain and I think it must have been really simple. It was
just masses of tears. I don't believe it was a disease. If
she had been allowed to cry and cry, she would have healed
herself.

I feel really alive now and I'm breathing well and I
feel energetic. I love the richness of being very affected.

My eyes are wide open. I'm feeling really loving towards
Nicole, really caring about her and sitting here thinking
of sessions I've had when I've said that I had to go through
all the pain she went through, and that I am going to have
to go through that for her. And I feel willing, even if I
have to sit here and cry for hours and hours, I would do
it. I keep feeling that she is still really alive, she is
not just dead, and I am imagining what it would be like to
have her as a sister, that she would be dark and warm. I
do feel really connected to her. (Becky is crying a lot)
I have a feeling of waiting for her and imagining her walking
in the door and imagining what she'd look like, and I've
a feeling that one day I'm going to meet a girl who's going
to look just like her and that she'll be a friend to me -
I'll meet this person and straight away I'll know who she
is, someone I'll be really close to. It'll be someone dark
and energetic.

I'm struggling now; something inside me is pulling me
down, really heavy and tight. It makes me shrink and makes
me short. It's pulling me down and trying to keep me quiet
and shut me up.

There's something very magic about being this person,
and I believe completely in magic. I believe that anything
is possible. I want to move around, walk, but there's something very heavy about me. I'm not in pain but I'm about
to faint or go to sleep - something's about to happen to
me and I know that it's going to happen. I have a swirling,
fainty, dreamy feeling. I am completely conscious, aware

of everything. I know that I'm going to die, that I'm going to
suddenly drop and go unconscious. I know it's going to happen
and I'm completely accepting it and completely relaxed. I
feel like I'm having my death alive - that instead of dying
and going through all sorts of horrors, I'm having all the
feelings now. I'm swimming around, almost as if I'm at my
own funeral. I'm floating over my own grave and looking and
saying, 'In a while, I'm going to lie down there.' I'm sitting
around with the people that in a minute I'm going to say
goodbye to and I'm having it all out now. And even when I
die, I'm not going to be there for very long. I'm going to
come back again very quickly. There won't be a gap between
dying and being reincarnated; I will just die and flip back
straight into life again. I'm experiencing my death being
alive, being conscious in it, and still being on earth.

I'm very old. I imagine that although Nicole died when
she was a baby, she was completely there, she was already
very old; she was already completely developed. She knew
everything when she died. She was completely conscious, she
wasn't just a little baby. I keep wanting to cry. I keep
getting feelings that I know her, and that although she died
all that time ago, somehow I've still grown up next to her.
It's like a story, a phantasy...

Once upon a time, there were two twins, and when they
were born, one of them died because she wasn't strong enough.
But when she died, she reincarnated almost immediately, which
means that she is about three weeks younger than her sister.
And her sister grew up and now and again remembered her and
kept feeling she was going to meet her.

Meanwhile, the sister that was reincarnated grew up
right on the other side of the world and led her own life
amongst much more natural things; she lived a much more natural, free life and she was much wilder. They often thought
about one another, but neither of them knew where the other
one was.

They grew up, and when they were both about twenty,
it's like they had gone in a big, wide circle, and they met.
They came together again and they carried on their lives

together after that. And although they had been so far away
from one another, they had both taken the same kind of path
that led them to meet. They had both gone through just as
much teaching, just as much learning, and they fitted together
perfectly. They didn't take time to get to know each other,
they just knew when they looked at each other that they'd
met before, and they knew each other well, and they fell
into each other's arms and were completely relieved, and
they both cried. They couldn't speak the same language when
they met, but they just knew, and they never really did talk
to each other. Their lives just carried on together, and
all they had to do was to look at each other and they just
knew what they meant. They knew what life was about and they
knew what they were doing and why they were there. They were
on the same path and they were doing the same thing. They
got together and were very strong and they helped put right
what was happening to the world and they were very powerful.

*****

THE ATLANTIS READINGS

When I chose the name ATLANTIS for our new
commune in Ireland back in 1974, I did so because
I thought it sounded nice. Our house was a few
hundred yards from the Atlantic, and I had some
vague notion of a legendary civilization that
was supposed to rise from the sea again one day.
It sounded romantic and felt right, so it became
our name. In those days, I knew as little about
occult matters as I still do about mathematics
– that is, that they exist.

As a result of choosing that name, I have
learnt so much. People have come up to me and
told me about the old Atlantis, putting me in
touch with the existence of a vast subculture
for whom the word 'legend' does not mean 'unreal.'
There are so many theories and notions about

Atlantis, and pending further enlightenment,
I must declare myself a convert to mainstream
'Atlantology' which considers the version of
History doled out to schoolkids very 'now-ist'
that is, so twentieth-century-ocentric that the
idea of vast highly-developed previous civiliza-
tions having existed in other times of the world
is just unthinkable. But lots of people are thinking about it, and very seriously. My favourite
angle on the old Atlantis is that they developed
just beyond where we're at now, though naturally
with very different colours, tastes and attitudes,
and then popped. Whether they blew themselves
up or the earth heaved up under them, I don't
know. But I do know that a personal life is a
series of repeated lessons, and that a whole
civilization is but a mass of personal lives
joined together to make massive mistakes and
learn massive lessons.

What our little Atlantis over there in Ireland is doing is concentrating attention on what
happens in people and between people, and having
gone as far as we feel we can at the moment in
the cushy society of Western Europe, we're going
to upheave ourselves as a living, walking, talking
experiment to see what parts of what we've learnt
hold firm in an entirely new wild foreign environment. If we survive, we'll let you know what
we discover.

Meanwhile, here are excerpts from readings
we did on ATLANTIS - our one, and the ancient
one.

ATLANTIS (IRELAND) by Becky

I feel like a dancer, someone who uses their body a
lot and is completely in tune. I use all my body and all
my power. I feel firm and contained. I'm struggling but I'm

very sober. I feel like putting my hands together as if I'm
walking through a monastery: I'd have a smooth walk, and
I wouldn't trip over. I'd be calm and gracious.

I've got a really spooky feeling. I'm not concerned
with shops or solid things, they don't matter to me really.
What gets to me is the net curtains blowing in the wind,
and the sound of the wind coming through the window, and
the incense sticks burning, and the smoke from the peat fire.
I love the peacefulness of the room and the sound of the
galey wind. I have phantasies of spooky old films. But I
don't feel that I'm someone who lives in a phantasy world.
I do know what's going on, and I'm not really mad. I feel
like a witch, someone with lots of power.

I look out of that window and I hate what I see: red
bricks and chimney pots and houses, and I don't like it at
all. And I know there are shops further down the street,
and I don't like that.

In my mind are memories of films I've seen of witchcraft
and witches and people in long black robes and the ritual
of witchery. I'm not like everybody else. I still have the
everyday problems of life, but that isn't the main thing
in my life. There's something more meaningful.

I'm really worried about getting myself across. I'm
worried that I'll go flat and lose these magical feelings.
I'm not tense in my body, but I feel that my soul inside
is clammed up. I don't want to try guessing who this is,
but I'm going to use the fact that it reminds me of Jen,
of how she's sometimes scared of letting herself have phantasies, scared that she's mad, that if she goes into something,
she won't come out of it. I feel a complete split in me between what's out of the window, what everybody else does,
and what happens in this room. I can hardly believe that
there's a man out there chopping his grass and only about
a hundred yards from him in this room, there's magic going
on. There's something special and magical about this room
and the people in it, but because feelings aren't something
concrete - they're not practical or boxed-off or squared-
off, I'm scared of losing the sensations. I'm not completely

convinced myself. I'm still 'out there' quite a lot. I think, "Well, maybe that is the right way really. Perhaps I should be married, living in a bungalow, and driving a car." Perhaps this is just a phantasy; maybe if the people out there look up here, they don't even see this window. Maybe this house isn't really here at all.

I look out there and I remember what it feels like to live a conventional life. I'm scared of being the same, of slipping backwards. It's so easy; so many people have fallen into it.

Everything that's good is dying, and I am someone who is completely concerned about the state of everything. I'm concerned about how things look and feel. There seems so much wrong I can't cope. I'm seeing too much. I know too much. It drives me mad that hardly anyone else sees what I see. In a way, I'm being tortured by having to live with my eyes wide open, having to experience everything that other people are refusing to experience. I can't bear it, but I'm not willing to turn away. I am in the snake pit with everyone else and I have to experience being bitten by all the snakes, and I have a lot of snakiness about myself; you have to be a bit of a snake to deal with them. I don't like it, but that's the way it is.

So what conclusion have I come to? That I'm the sort of person who can go right into something, swim and dive right into it, but I need to know when to get out, because it's not very good for me. There is something I am searching for in order to get deeper and deeper and sometimes I get deep into the wrong things. It's because it takes so long to achieve enlightenment, that when I actually get there, I think it's going to last for ages, whereas in fact it might only last for five minutes, or an hour or a day, and yet the work of it, the struggle, is in getting there, in making the decisions; that's the work.

So the conclusion of the reading is to pull out of society really; the only hold-back is being scared of people's reactions. Every time we pull a plug out, every time we cut a thread to the outside world, it annoys people. But it's what we need to do.

Everything is coming together really quickly, everything is clicking and slotting into its right place; the picture is going to be completed, and it's the end of a stage. Then another big stage is going to start, and it's all just speeding up and the pictures are coming out quicker, and .. it's good. Whatever is happening up there in the sky is affecting everything quite well. All the hard times were really worth it. We've been struggling for a long time, and all those shitty times when you think you're never going to come out are really worth it; blundering and tripping over and having the mess, being in the mess, just constantly speaking out and splurting out all the mess because the world is in an awful mess. And then when you're not thinking about it, suddenly everything is perfect. It's only when you give up the hope and the struggle that things slip into place. It's only when you're not really thinking about it that it happens. Whoever I am, I have a good head on me, and my eyes are wide open and I'm very sane and very together and I'm going quite well.

Jenny: Anything about the future?

Becky: Well, I've got a constant sickness feeling in my stomach, that I want to be sick or cry or something. I don't know what it is, but one thing I keep thinking about is that I don't want to stay round here. I want to move on. I really feel the urgency in me for a move. We're all moving inside ourselves and we're going to carry on moving no matter where we are, we're not going to stop. But we have to make sure we're in the right place. Here, there are still too many things to distract us. I mean I know we're on earth and we have to face what's around us, but it's like saying, well London is there, so we've got to live in the middle of it. You don't have to have things you don't want. You make things the way you want them. I have the feeling we're only staying here out of duty, out of being attached as if to say, "We've put our foot in and now we've got to carry on putting our foot in it." But we've got to know when to say stop. It's no good saying, "Oh, we have a beautiful garden here." We've

got to be more radical; we've got to take our foot out completely and just carry on travelling and moving on.

*****

ATLANTIS (IRELAND) by Snowy

I've got a feeling to do this reading with my eyes closed
and to create a world of my own, a sort of cocoon which is
dark and warm and juicy and sexual and a place which because
I'm cutting out things from it, is richer. That's something
I often feel myself, that when I cut down on the sillinesses,
things become richer. When there's a lot going on, a lot of
people, I get thinner and thinner, my energy spreads over
a bigger area and so things become less intense and more
speedy. But when I cut down and cut down, things get richer
and thicker and juicier altogether, by narrowing my focus
and just finding more and more in each small thing.

I like the deepening and the enriching, bringing things
down, dividing and dividing, cutting away, paring away, getting to the core, bringing everything down to the core. I
know that you could see this as bad and narrow and small-
minded and all sorts of negative things, but I don't. I see
it as really good and rich, intense, real learning. So if
this is a reading of a person, which I question anyway, it
would be a person who is like what I am describing or who
has an appreciation of it. This is the intensity of the mind,
intensity of stillness and focus.

I'm tuning in to an energy which is maturity and the
sort of wiseness that comes through suffering and pain and
acceptance of pain. I'm reminded of recently when I was working in the greenhouse and I dropped something on my foot
and it really hurt and I was on my own, and I lay down on
the sofa and I let the pain build up and as I let it be,
I just experienced it as intense energy rushing upward from
my foot right up my body, and it was enjoyable, it was actually enjoyable, which is completely ridiculous, isn't it? But it
was. So this is a person who is sort of Zen in a way, a Zen

person who has been able to take experience in as teaching direct.

All the way through this reading, I keep thinking of an incident that happened between me and Tim the other night when we were in bed together and I was teaching him something, and I was really loving him in my teaching. Sometimes I hate him when I'm trying to teach him things, but this time I was really loving him, and he has an amazing facility for letting me take him over completely, as long as he understands what I'm doing. All I've got to do is to engage his brain so that he understands, and then he relaxes completely. I didn't know what I was going to do when I took him over, but I did it, and it worked completely, and it was sexual; it was a step on the road towards having sex, and all I did was weave a cocoon with words.

This reading reminds me of that a lot: creating a complete atmosphere, a complete world, which is really just taking one single aspect and making it the whole, making it everything, just having that one aspect and shutting everything else out and making it really rich. When I was doing this with Tim, I never worried that he might be saying, "Oh, but there's other things," and I overrode any thoughts I might have myself that you can't be so single-minded. I just allowed myself to be it, and it was amazing. I don't know why I'm saying all this, what the connection is with this reading. Jenny: We do though. It's Atlantis, this Atlantis.

*****

At another time, we wrote down for Becky: "ATLANTIS - the old one. What was it like? What meaning has it for the world now?"

ATLANTIS by Becky

I feel strong and good and I look good. I love the feeling of this reading. I am alert and ready, cleansed and clean. I'm ready for adventure. I am proud of myself. I am strong and I can fight the cold. I am impatient with people who play

safe and with people who don't like me. In my own terms,
I'm conventional, though other people wouldn't see me like
that. I am never satisfied with myself, or with anyone else.
I never think, "Well, that's enough, we'll sit back now,"
or "Well, that's an end of that, we won't bother moving on
any more." I am always ready for more. I want more experience.
I don't feel scared of anything. The only thing that would
disappoint me is if I met my death, because I don't feel
that I am ready for it. I'm not scared of it, but I would be
disappointed. I'm geared up; my mind is really expanded.
I feel 'well-cooked'; there's nothing bland or pasty about
me. I've been through thick and thin, from one extreme to
the other. I'm filled up now with knowledge and it's never
going to leave me. I've grown a lot physically and I'm strong.
I wasn't years ago, I wasn't big enough for the work. But
now I feel ready. I'm well-prepared. I'm ready to burn my
boats as so often before and to set off and travel. I may
get hurt on my travels, but I've got a luck about me, I've
got luck with me. I'll be able to rise above it somehow.
Lots of little predictions I've had in the past really matter
to me now: that I am like a luck-charm, I have a strength
about me. I like that image of myself. Even if there's danger
and badness and evil around, there's good about me that en-
ables me to carry through. I'm not about to lie back and
be trampled. I'm too solid and determined for that. There
are things I have to be scared of, but they don't cripple
me. I'm really into image, big images. I have a big image
of myself. I have the image of being witch-like and of having
magical powers. I like that. I keep thinking of blackness
- I want to have magical powers, but black. I like the fact
that there's an element of evil about me, because I know
it's not really evil. I like the fact that I'm willing to
use my badness and my blackness. I appreciate my blackness.
I don't want to try to be white, I want to be as black as
black, to be extravagant. I want to let loose and show off.
    I feel stuffy in here now. And I've developed pains
in my stomach. I think of 'growing pains.' I feel that I'm not
really up to my full height. I've got my own rigidities.

I've got my wild side alright, but I've also got my middle
that's tight. It's making me cave in on myself, it's stopping
me from growing. It's the tightness of trying to fit in,
of not being the full size I should be. And I don't fit.
It's ever so painful trying to fit in to place you don't
fit. There's lots wrong with me. I have images of how I am,
but I don't really be them fully. I dress acceptably, I tense
myself up to be conventional, I don't step out of place and
do the wrong thing; I keep to the line. I don't expand nearly
as much as I need to. I don't do what I want to do for fear
of looking different. My sickness is trying to fit in. It
wouldn't take much really to fit in completely except for
my name. People know who I am, and where I'm from and that
makes a big difference. I can't ever really pretend. I'm
a different nationality, a different shape and colour. [One
occult theory has it that the Old Atlanteans came down here
from somewhere else!]

I feel bogged down. I've eaten the wrong things and
lived in the wrong climate. I've worn the wrong clothes and
done the wrong things with my body. And I feel sick.

I need to completely break away. I sense how big I am
and how important I am, yet I've done nothing yet really.
I am broken away compared to what I was like in the past,
but compared to what I want to be, I must do more. I've fitted
in through fear, fear I'd be losing something I think I've
had or could have. Always there is that little hook, the
Hook of Hope that you can get what you want by hanging on,
trying to fit in. I want to get rid of it completely. I want
to end cleanly whatever I'm doing now, so that whatever I'm
going into, I will experience it more freshly than I have
ever experienced anything before. And then I'll never want
to look back. It feels like death to look back.

I started this reading by being excited, but then all
my little attachments started coming to the surface. Like the
other day I gave away a big pile of possessions, but there
are still millions of things which I just keep. And when
I think of giving up my whole room, it makes me want to destroy it. I want to smash everything. I haven't the patience

to take things apart slowly, to slowly clean up. I would
have to be extreme, I would hate to wipe it all out.

Materialism makes me unhappy. All it does is make me
ill and rotten and destroys me. I'd like to set light to
what I own. I'd make a big bonfire in the middle of it and
just <u>burn</u>. And I'd enjoy it. And funnily enough, my image
of burning, say, my own room up, is that it brings me closer
to people. I would then always have to live with someone
else. I hate having a huge space and living there on my own.
I love the thought of living in a cave with everybody else.
I want to destroy my own room so that I will have the excuse
to be in contact with people, the excuse to sleep in a bed
with somebody else, the excuse to be completely communal.
I hate the split of everything being all over the place.
I hate the feeling of everything splitting to neutrons of
things being broken up and broken up until they explode.

After I have destroyed everything I own, things can
only improve really. I can only become more in communication
with other people. I'll be more open, more fulfilled, warmer.
I can only be happier then.

*****

We gave the same reading - the Old Atlantis
- to Snowy on a different occasion.

ATLANTIS by Snowy

Immediately I was handed this paper, I had the impulse
to open it. I'll try and find out what that means. It wasn't
like a desperate curiosity to know who I was, it was just
incredibly natural - somebody handed me a piece of folded
paper, and I naturally went to open it and read it. It was
just what you do with folded paper. And yet how many hundreds
of readings have I done and never ever considered doing that.

Well, I'm a person who doesn't want secrets. There aren't
any weird things in the world; there aren't any extraordinary
unknowns. There's just naturalness and ease and simplicity and

straightforwardness, and why not? Why have any bother or
hoo-ha? Let us de-hoo-ha the world!
Jenny: Ehm, would you like to enlarge on this 'hoo-ha,' just
for the sake of the audience?
Snowy: Certainly. 'Hoo-ha' is something that people who have
nothing put in. Hoo-ha is unnecessary. Hoo-ha is all the
extraneous material, and hoo-ha is a bit like bally-hoo!
Well, if you were a simple, straightforward chap like me,
you'd see it straight away and I wouldn't have to explain
it. It's obvious. The world is basically the sky and the
sea and the earth and shelters and food and people and that's
it. All these other bits and pieces are the hoo-ha. What
I am leaning on [luxurious cushions] is hoo-ha. Most of what's
in your head is hoo-ha - I'm sorry about this, I'm sure it's
very meaningful hoo-ha to you, but it is hoo-ha. And this
- and this (picks up various objects in the room)! Trees
aren't hoo-ha and plants aren't hoo-ha. Mind you, that plant
up there is bordering on the hoo-ha (points to a fluffy exotic
indoor pot-plant). Yes, a borderline case that! And those
baskets... Bally-hoo! Joss-sticks are hoo-ha made to cover
up other hoo-ha! I think we have laboured this point enough.
(The audience has collapsed laughing)
     Ah yes, but when you look at it on another level, it
isn't funny. I just saw, "New soft hankies luxury 3-ply white"
written over there and I read it as 'nuclear power', and
that's what it's like really: behind all this hoo-ha is all
that nuclear shit and all that chemical shit and all that
going-out-to-work and all that money shit and all that office
and transport shit and all that road-building and jet-plane
shit. So we may be able to laugh at it in one way, but how
much hoo-ha do you think is involved in making that for example? (She holds up some entirely useless object) All the
typists and telephones and cars and petrol and aeroplanes.
If you were to see all the connections leading from that
little piece of trash outwards, you would go everywhere,
right up to nuclear war.
     So that brings me back to being the sort of person who,
when handed a piece of folded paper, opens it up to read it,

because they don't like things that are hidden or not understood. I hate obscurity. I'm here for openness and clarity,
and therefore understanding. In fact, the reason I'm here
today is for clarification; that's why I came. I seem to
be pretty tuned in to the old cosmos. Things work pretty
well for me. I keep feeling all along that I'm not doing
a reading of a person exactly.

It's blowing up outside, isn't it? We'll have to move
the boat later on.

Well, I was in a little world of my own just then. I
was just noticing that I've got the reading right next to
my ear and I was trying to hear it, trying to get it to talk
to me and trying to hear its voice, which I haven't ever
done with a reading before. I didn't hear anything by the
way! It didn't speak to me, but my mind was wandering and
I was thinking about Don Juan - didn't he have little creatures, lizards or something, and he got them to talk to him?
Anyway, it reminded me of such magical things.

Well, I'll put this next to my ear and I'll tell you
what it says. It's a quiet little voice, it's squeaking and
grunting. It's having trouble getting through to me. It's
either coming from another world, or coming through another
language, or maybe coming from an animal. There's some difficulty of communication anyway. But it's going to break through
those barriers and get through eventually. There's a little
voice, a quiet voice. It's saying, "I hope the reception's
clear and that you can get everything that I'm saying, because
I've come to talk to you specially. I want to start off by
saying things that will help you to relax and trust me, just
normal things, mundane things. I'll just start off by saying
anything that would relax you completely, so that you trust
me. I don't want you to think that there's anything strange
going on. Though in fact there is. I'd like you to trust
that the strangeness of the situation is quite normal. I'd
like you to link your own normality to the strangeness so
that I can be a bridge between the two worlds for you, and
so that I can take you from one world into the next world
with smoothness and ease and gentleness and naturalness,

because I don't want you to be freaked out at all. I don't
want you to put up any barriers or blocks that will interfere
with what I have to say. What I have to say is quite important
to you. It's very simple, so you may not see the importance
of it now, but it will come to you at a later date. There's
some blood. It looks like blood. And there's some trouble
coming, but you just keep calm, that's the main thing. The
main thing is just to know yourself and know your qualities
and stay with them. Stay within your self. Don't flip out
and try to become something you're not. Never ever try to
be something you're not. Just be yourself completely, that's
all you need. You don't have to have talents that you don't
have, and you don't have to have knowledge that you don't
have. You're quite enough as you are, you're perfect and
great as you are. Just relax in the peace and the knowledge
of your own centre. Like last night on the island when we
were dancing.

Jenny: On the island? What were you using for music?

Snowy: Oh, jars of pegs, anything. We had one song that lasted
for four hours. There were moments in the dance when I knew
that I was perfect. I knew that I could integrate everything
that I had in my body and my thoughts and my consciousness
and in my world - for instance, I was making cheese at the
same time as I was dancing - just bringing it all in.

I don't know what this has to do with the reading, but
just taking the message and remembering last night - there
were moments (I'm not saying it was like this all evening)
when I just knew for complete certain sure that to simply
express everything works. Simplicity is the message of this
reading really, to accept everything in the most natural
way and the most straightforward immediate way. When I do
that, everything around me just falls and slots into its
right place. And it was like that. It was amazing. Beautiful.

So what is this reading? Basically, this is crisis talk.
This is preparation for crisis. The voice is saying, "Now
is a time of ease and rest and learning and harmony and richness and nourishment. Now is a time of great understanding and
great preparation for the times of barrenness and difficulty

and cold and the winds and the trouble and the starvation
to come. Just be ready, keep yourself intact and still and
calm. Get ready, but don't flip out: you mustn't get extravagant and you mustn't cheapen yourself. You mustn't get spoilt
on it all, on the richness of the present time, the luxury
and opulence of the present time. It's important not to get
flabby; don't let it make you unconscious or over-easy or
middle-class or comfy in any way. Just take it as nourishment,
take it directly, and say thank you and be grateful and know
that it is passing, know that it's only preparation. I don't
mean that you should live in the future, but just to know
that there is something else coming. Let it strengthen you,
not weaken you. Don't get slovenly and unready. Always be
ready at any moment, to die basically, so that your death can
always be clean and bright.

Fred: Any more little messages?

Snowy: No, I've finished I think.

*****

So now let us bring this space-ship gently
down to earth with Ned's story. Ned is one of
our many Tauruses in the commune, and Taurus
is the sign of solid earth!

NED'S STORY

My first experience of psychometry or of anything psychic
for that matter happened on my first night in Atlantis. We
had spent the day working in the garden and were sitting
around the peat fire. It was after dinner and we were in
a stone cottage on Inishfree Island.

Looking back, I find it amazing how casually I took
that incredible evening. I think it was the casual way the
readings were presented, the matter-of-fact, everyday, humorous way that Snowy slipped into each perfectly accurate reading. Somehow, if there had been plenty of build-up and ritual
involved, more artificial reverence, I think I might have
been more impressed, or rather allowed myself to feel, and

show, the huge impression that the readings did in fact make
on me.

The longest reading that Snowy did that night was my
own. She spoke for about half an hour and left me dumbfounded.
It was an experience I shall never forget. She gave details
of my inner longings, of how my insecurity felt from inside,
as well as practical things such as my love of the land, of
working it and building up solid things. I moved from incredulous, stunned, amused, to extremely grateful. Snowy had given
me a present, a very personal picture of myself. There were
moments when she expressed parts or aspects of myself that
I felt and knew but hadn't really become conscious of. Certainly I couldn't have expressed them in words like she did.
As she came out with these things, I felt like weights taken
off me.

I'm afraid that I didn't give any of this feedback to
Snowy at the time. Why, this woman knew enough in her off-
hand way without me admitting what felt like such a huge
debt to her. I remember when someone asked me for feedback
afterwards grudgingly saying only, "Very accurate." Actually
I felt far too embarrassed to admit just how accurate the
more personal parts had been.

I tried doing readings myself after a few months of
living in Atlantis. At first, I couldn't do it at all. I
would try too hard and not be able to think of things to
say, or just say things that I'd think I should say. When
I finally did do a good reading after a few tries, it was
completely effortless. Although I couldn't really believe
that I was doing a reading, I felt completely confident about
all the stuff I was saying; it was just what I felt, without
me pushing anything.

I discovered that I have to be reasonably clear and
worked-out in myself before I can do a reading. If I'm in
a bad state at all, stuffed up with feelings, and not straight
about what I'm wanting in myself, then I certainly can't
do a reading on someone else, because then what comes out
is just me. In fact I would say that the clearer and more
evolved a person is in themselves, the better they are able to

use their psychic powers.

I love the feeling when I do a strong reading, of letting a new kind of energy into my body. Often I can't stop yawning at the beginning of a reading when this happens, and I have noticed the same thing happening to other people. I might feel taller, smaller, sharper, stronger, softer, fierier, creepier or more stupid, or I might go through all those feelings as I elaborate and get insights into different aspects of the person.

Doing psychic work has opened my mind up to the wide possibilities of perception constantly available to us all. I used to believe in grand ideas about 'man's huge potential' and stuff like that. Now I begin to know it to be true in the flesh. It's just a matter of becoming more aware of myself, more sure of the ground I stand on, more centred, - instead of transcending and rising above myself as I tried to do in my religious trips. I just need to find out more about my normal self.

From there, I can tap the powers which are everyone's right.

*****

Becky wrote to a boyfriend of hers in the United States telling him of our proposed emigration to South America. He sent her a travel-guide called 'The South-American Handbook', the sort of thing I'd never dream of looking at. But I have a habit of taking everything that comes to me through the post or through the door as being 'magically meant' in some way. It's fun, it's a nice way of looking at the world, and it pays dividends.

But this book really did look boring - hotels and tourist sights, I didn't want to know about that. However, I was impressed by the fact that it had fallen open at the 'Peru' section. Peru was at that time the country we thought we might

end up in. So my glance lingered for a second, and
fell upon a footnote written in tiny writing,
which said something about, "Tristan Jones, the
first man to cross the continent of South America
in an ocean-going vessel."

This immediately fascinated me. In the whole
of Atlantis commune at the time there was not
a single person who knew the first thing about
sailing, or even about the sea, except that it
is wet and you have to be careful not to fall
in it when travelling in our little rowing-boat
between the mainland and Inishfree. Nonetheless,
we had become sickened with being power-tripped
by those in-the-know to whom we applied for non-
fuel-powered transportation for the commune across
the Atlantic and had decided to take the plunge
(oh dear) into the boating world. We bought ourselves a lovely old wooden sailing boat and were
working hard learning its ins and outs and ups
and downs. I grandly say 'we.' Actually, my sister
and others were doing that bit. I myself was
sitting at home being pregnant and worrying.
About routes and whens and wheres and winds and
hows and whos and governments and how to forge
vaccination certificates.

And in my better moments, I had intuitions
and visions. One of them was to sail into South
America. I scanned our pathetically-inadequate
map of the continent pinned to my bedroom door
and got excited about river-systems, but couldn't
see any that joined up exactly. So, back to
the footnote in the travel-guide, how did this
geezer I'd never heard of called Tristan Jones
CROSS South America in a sailing boat? If you
want to know the answer to that one, you'll have
to go to your local library. Which is eventually
what we did. But FIRST I wrote to said South
American Handbook people asking who was this

Tristan Jones, did they know him, where could
I find him, was he alive or dead, and had he
written anything about his journey?

In reply I was told they knew nothing about
him, and that they doubted whether I'd ever be
able to track him down. In other words, give
up.

Giving up not being one of my habits, I
got a friend in England to go to a library. My
faith was rewarded by the beautiful sight of
a fat paper-back book arriving through the post:
The Incredible Voyage by Tristan Jones.

He did it!

The next thing, after reading the book,
which I did whilst breast-feeding my new tiny
baby on Inishfree, was to discover: is this man
alive or dead? Because reading that book told
me one thing: this man had exactly the right
mix of practical madness to fill a big gaping
hole in our plans.

We needed a captain.

I've had experiences of writing to the auth-
ors of books I've loved before. They don't answer
you. But this one did. I wrote telling him of
our crazy plans. He answered saying the nearest
thing to 'Yes' that it was possible to say without
looking at our boat to see if it leaked and looking at us to see if our brains leaked.

But there was something Bigger, Huger, More
Mindblowing in Tristan's envelope than his near-
as-dammit 'Yes.' His letter came from New York
- he's Welsh - and contained a leaflet headed
THE ATLANTIS SOCIETY. In it, Tristan explained
in simple, beautiful, inspired and practical
terms his next project: he intends, with the
help of many interested parties, to seek the
lost Atlantis. Physically. In boats, with divers.

*****

We have offered Tristan our boat for use on his project after he has delivered us to the heart of South America via the vast river systems that lead up into Paraguay. And he has offered us permanent places on that boat to share in his search for Atlantis.

One of the reasons that Tristan wants to find physical evidence of the existence of the old Atlantis is because he believes it may hold signs of what they did to themselves.

He, like us, has this hope that if those signs are found, he may be able to pin them up on the world's notice board to say, "DANGER. NOT THIS WAY."

There is another way.

*****